T0306087

Interest Rates, Prices and Liquidity

Many of the assumptions that underpin mainstream macroeconomic models have been challenged as a result of the traumatic events of the recent financial crisis. Until recently, it was widely agreed that short-term interest rates were a sufficient instrument of monetary policy. However, early on in the financial crisis interest rates effectively hit zero per cent and so central banks had to resort to a set of largely untested instruments, the purchase of financial assets under quantitative easing (QE). This book brings together contributions from economists working in academia, financial markets and central banks to assess the effectiveness of these policy instruments and to explore what lessons have so far been learned.

JAGJIT S. CHADHA is Professor of Economics at the University of Kent, Canterbury.

SEAN HOLLY is Professional Fellow at Fitzwilliam College and Director of Research at the Faculty of Economics, University of Cambridge.

Macroeconomic Policy Making

Series editors

Professor JAGJIT S. CHADHA *University of Kent, Canterbury*

Professor SEAN HOLLY *University of Cambridge*

The 2007–2010 financial crisis has asked some very hard questions of modern macroeconomics. The consensus that grew up during 'the Great Moderation' has proved to be an incomplete explanation for how to conduct monetary policy in the face of financial shocks. This series brings together leading macroeconomic researchers and central bank economists to analyse the tools and methods necessary to meet the challenges of the post- financial crisis world.

Interest Rates, Prices and Liquidity

Lessons from the Financial Crisis

Edited by

Jagjit S. Chadha and Sean Holly

CAMBRIDGE UNIVERSITY PRESS

CAMBRIDGE
UNIVERSITY PRESS

University Printing House, Cambridge CB2 8BS, United Kingdom

One Liberty Plaza, 20th Floor, New York, NY 10006, USA

477 Williamstown Road, Port Melbourne, VIC 3207, Australia

314-321, 3rd Floor, Plot 3, Splendor Forum, Jasola District Centre, New Delhi - 110025, India

79 Anson Road, #06-04/06, Singapore 079906

Cambridge University Press is part of the University of Cambridge.

It furthers the University's mission by disseminating knowledge in the pursuit of education, learning and research at the highest international levels of excellence.

www.cambridge.org
Information on this title: www.cambridge.org/9781107014732

© Cambridge University Press 2012

First published 2012
First paperback edition 2015

A catalogue record for this publication is available from the British Library

Library of Congress Cataloging in Publication data
Interest rates, prices and liquidity : lessons from the financial crisis / edited by Jagjit S. Chadha, Sean Holly.
   p.   cm. – (Macroeconomic policy making)
Papers presented at a conference held in Cambridge, England in Mar. 2010.
ISBN 978-1-107-01473-2 (hardback)
1. Interest rates.   2. Monetary policy.   3. Global Financial Crisis, 2008–2009.
I. Chadha, Jagjit.   II. Holly, Sean.   III. Title.
IIG1621.I588   2012
339.5′–dc23

                                                    2011030680

ISBN 978-1-107-01473-2 Hardback
ISBN 978-1-107-48003-2 Paperback

Contents

Figures

Tables

Contributors

EVREN CAGLAR University of Kent, Canterbury

JAGJIT S. CHADHA University of Kent, Canterbury and CIMF, Cambridge

SPENCER DALE Bank of England

JOHN DRIFFILL Birkbeck College, University of London

DOUGLAS GALE New York University

HANS GERSBACH Center of Economic Research at ETH Zurich and CEPR

DOMENICO GIANNONE European Center for Advanced Research in Economics and Statistics (ECARES)

RICHARD HARRISON Bank of England

SEAN HOLLY University of Cambridge and CIMF, Cambridge

SHARON KOZICKI Bank of Canada

MICHELE LENZA European Central Bank

JACK MEANING University of Kent, Canterbury

MARCUS MILLER University of Warwick

HUW PILL European Central Bank

LUCREZIA REICHLIN London Business School

ERIC SANTOR Bank of Canada

LENA SUCHANEK Bank of Canada

STEFANIA VILLA Birkbeck College, University of London

JAMES WARREN University of Kent, Canterbury

ALEX WATERS University of Kent, Canterbury

JAN WENZELBURGER Keele University

MICHAEL WICKENS University of York and Cardiff Business School

JING YANG Bank for International Settlements, formerly Bank of
    England

1   New instruments of monetary policy

Jagjit S. Chadha and Sean Holly

1   Introduction

The chapters in this volume are the outcome of a conference held in
Cambridge in March 2010. The title of the conference was 'New instruments of monetary policy'. Its purpose was to bring together economists
from academia, financial markets and central banks to discuss some of the
challenges that arose from both the financial crisis itself and the response
to that crisis. Many of the assumptions that underpin mainstream (core)
macroeconomic models have been challenged as a result of the traumatic
events of the past three years. In particular, it became clear that the
modern, micro-founded, form of macroeconomic model failed to allow
adequately for the financial sector.

This failure, in part, reflected the belief that one could safely separate
issues concerned with financial stability from the conduct of macroeconomic policy: macroeconomic policy, and in particular monetary policy,
should be devoted to the stabilisation of inflation and output, and the short-
term nominal interest rate used as the instrument of policy. Although it is
well known that such a policy will be problematic when nominal interest
rates are close to the zero interest rate floor, in practice it seemed that policy
was successful in keeping the economy away from this region. The long
road to price stability in the UK led down a number of cul-de-sacs, from
monetary targets, shadow exchange rate targets, explicit exchange rate
targeting and inflation targeting – without and then with operational central
bank independence – and seemed to have arrived at its destination.

However, the exceptional circumstances of the financial crisis – which
first manifested itself as a liquidity crisis for financial intermediaries[1] – and
the consequent need to loosen monetary policy as much as possible, meant

We thank Francis Breedon, Alec Chrystal, David Cobham, Spencer Dale, Colin Ellis,
Douglas Gale, Richard Harrison, Sharon Kozicki, Marcus Miller, Huw Pill, Jan
Wenzelburger and Mike Wickens for helpful comments and conversations. All remaining
errors are our own. We also thank Jack Meaning for excellent research assistance.
[1] See Chapters 2 and 8 in this volume on this point.

that the zero interest rate floor became the over-riding constraint acting on monetary policy. It had been broadly expected that the economy would operate at the zero lower bound for around only 2 per cent of the time at 2 per cent inflation targets.[2] But the eventual binding of the lower bound constraint meant that *so-called* unconventional or *new* monetary policies had to be adopted. In 2004 Bernanke et al. set out three types of response to the zero interest rate floor. First, a communication strategy must be used to influence expectations as to what interest rates and price levels will be in the future. Second, there must be an expansion in the size of the central bank's balance sheet. Finally, there must be direct use of the composition of the central bank's balance sheet to change relative yields. These three principles essentially encapsulate how central banks around the world responded in different ways to the crisis.

1.1   Macroeconomics and the crisis

The financial crisis has pushed the perennial questions of money and banking back to the fore of macroeconomic analysis. Until recently, it was widely agreed (at least outside of Frankfurt) that although the stock of money had a role to play, in practice it could be ignored as long as we used short-term nominal interest rates as the instrument of policy because money and other credit markets would clear at the given policy rate. Allied to this view was the belief that shocks to financial markets should not especially matter for the conduct of monetary policy when you are using the short interest rate as the main instrument over and above any impact they will have on the forecast output gap.[3]

But it has become increasingly difficult not to agree with the proposition that financial regulation, fiscal policy and even the objectives of overseas policy makers may constrain the actions of monetary policy makers. Indeed, in his June 2010 Mansion House speech, the Governor of the Bank of England welcomed wholeheartedly the Chancellor's plan to recombine monetary and financial policy: 'The Bank (will) take on (responsibilities) in respect of micro prudential regulation and macro prudential control of the balance sheets of the financial system as a whole. I welcome those new responsibilities. Monetary stability and financial stability are two sides of the same coin. During the crisis the former was threatened by the failure to secure the latter.' Indeed, prior to the financial crisis a form of separation principle was in place, whereby

---

[2] Bean (2003), for example, makes this point. Naturally a higher inflation target changes the duration downwards.

[3] We will discuss Poole's (1970) analysis of this question in Section 2.

monetary policy concentrated on inflation and financial or credit policy was treated as essentially a matter of microeconomic regulation.

From the imaginary vantage point of the first few years of the twenty-first century, the collapse of the separation principle would seem rather surprising. The new monetary policy consensus that emerged appeared to have solved many of the technical problems of monetary policy management. A representative view from this era, though written with circumspection, is that of Ben Bernanke (2004), who argued: 'Few disagree that monetary policy has played a large part in stabilizing inflation, and so the fact that output volatility has declined in parallel with inflation volatility, both in the United States and abroad, suggests that monetary policy may have helped moderate the variability of output as well ... my view is that improvements in monetary policy, though certainly not the only factor, have probably been an important source of the Great Moderation.' He suggested several reasons for this: (i) low and stable inflation outcomes promoting a more stable economic structure; (ii) better monetary policy may have reduced the size and distribution from which measured shocks are drawn; and (iii) variable inflation expectations stop becoming an exogenous driver of macroeconomic instability. But the most important was arguably understanding the limitations of monetary policy. Bound by severe information constraints about the correct model and the current state of the economy, monetary policy concentrated on gauging the correct current level and prospective path for short-term interest rates in order to stabilise inflation and aggregate demand over the medium term. There was a general acceptance that a simple rule was likely to dominate a fully blown optimal rule, which was, in any case, always predicated on a particular model and subject to time inconsistency.

From an older perspective, the *Art of Central Banking* predated the *Science of Monetary Policy* and tended to define central banking not so much in terms of a narrow price stability but also in terms of objectives that might now be termed financial policy and involved policies to safeguard the continuing health of the financial system.[4] This art developed as a response to the multiplicity of roles 'grabbed' by a developing central bank but also fundamentally in response to crises. Bagehot (1873) famously outlined the principles of central banking in a crisis: (i) the central bank ought to lend freely at a high rate of interest to borrowers with good collateral; (ii) the value of the assets should be somewhere between panic and pre-panic prices; and (iii) institutions with poor collateral should be allowed to fail. The general understanding of these

---

[4] Compare the work of Hawtrey (1934) and Clarida et al. (2002).

principles has been associated with the avoidance of banking panics in England since the Overend and Gurney crisis of 1866, which was the previous example of a bank run in the UK until Northern Rock in 2007. The relevance of Bagehot's principles for the current crisis has recently been acknowledged by, among others, Mervyn King at the Bank of England (King, 2010) and Brian Madigan at the Federal Reserve Board (Madigan, 2009).

While short-term liquidity support, of varying kinds, was ultimately offered by all major central banks following the August 2007 freeze in interbank markets, another issue emerged shortly thereafter: how to deal with the zero lower bound on interest rates. In each case, the response has been to increase the size of the central bank balance sheet.[5] The basic idea here has borrowed from an older literature in which 'the size, composition and risk profile' (Borio and Disyatat, 2009, p. 5) is used to control financial conditions more generally. Because of imperfect substitutability across financial claims and a degree of market segmentation, a central bank that uses its balance sheet to alter the structure of private-sector balance sheets can influence financial prices (Tobin, 1958) and change the relative yields on assets (Brainard and Tobin, 1968). In this sense, balance sheet operations are really forms of extended open market operations with the objective of altering longer-term interest rates to an enduring extent.

1.2   Non-standard monetary policies

In this volume we outline some tentative views on non-standard policies from macroeconomists. We consider the theoretical case for bolstering the liquidity and capital holdings of financial intermediaries in line with the recently published Basel III recommendations.[6] A new generation of macroeconomic models suggests that financial frictions matter substantially in explaining business cycle fluctuations since they not only amplify the impact of a typical range of shocks but also can contribute directly to fluctuations. We also throw light on the implications of relaxing liquidity premia in a variety of newly developed macroeconomic models. Typically, the size of the central bank balance sheet has to be expanded considerably in order to offset the lower bound interest rate constraint. Chapters 5 and 7 from central

---

[5] This leads to the question of whether balance sheet operations and commercial bank reserve policies are independent of the short-term interest rate or simply complementary to the zero lower bound constraint.

[6] See the pages of the Bank for International Settlements (BIS) at www.bis.org/bcbs/basel3.htm.

bank-based economists show that the impact of balance sheet policies on both long-term bond prices and components of aggregate demand are far from insignificant, if carried out as part of a credible strategy to combat the zero bound. Finally, the UK's policy of quantitative easing is explained and some criticism of the current state of models is offered.

Let us start with a development of the criticism of baseline New Keynesian macroeconomics, that monetary policy with an explicit (or implicit) inflation target could not adequately capture information from money, asset prices and the accumulation of debt about medium-term macroeconomic disequilibria.

2   Directions old and new

The long-run neutrality of money is a central plank of monetary policy making (Lucas, 1996). Although it is quite a simple matter to find long-run non-neutralities in many standard New Keynesian models, it is generally found that long-run non-neutralities should not be exploited as there is no clear enhancement in the welfare of the representative household.[7] Naturally, though, perturbations in the money market will lead to temporary changes in the market clearing level of (overnight or short-term) policy rates and, because of various forms of informational uncertainty or indeed structural rigidity, will lead to temporary deviations in the expected real rate from its natural level and thus act on aggregate demand. The key question, however, is the extent to which shocks emanating from the money market can be stabilised by an interest rate rule, or indeed whether an additional tool may be required.[8]

In a seminal analysis of this question, Poole (1970) took a standard IS–LM framework and analysed the impact on output variance from setting either interest rates or the money supply in the presence of stochastic shocks to either or both of spending or money market equations. When shocks to financial markets dominate relative to shocks in the real part of the economy, the natural assignment is then broadly to use interest rates rather than the stock of money as the main policy instrument. But Poole also showed that, in general, neither instrument would necessarily stabilise the economy better than the other as it depended on the relative magnitude of shocks in these sectors and the sensitivity of output to these respective shocks. An often overlooked implication of his analysis was that in general, some use of both instruments was likely to stabilise the output better than one instrument alone, a point to which we shall return,

---

[7] See Khan et al. (2003) on this point.   [8] See Chadha et al. (2008) on this point.

but one that is perhaps echoed by the experience of policy makers world-wide as they have had to augment interest rate tools with the expansion of the central bank balance sheet.

The Bank for International Settlements, from a disinterested position – as it does not actually have to set monetary policy – regularly expressed concern about what we might call a 'worrying triplet'. This triplet comprises high internal and external debt levels, high asset prices and rapidly growing broad money aggregates. White (2006) added to worries about whether it was sensible to partition monetary and financial issues with a further concern: the horizon over which policy sought to stabilise was also part of the problem. 'Central banks have put too much emphasis on achieving near term price stability' (p. 2) at the expense of considering in detail what the implications may be for longer-run macroeconomic stability coming from the build-up in domestic and international 'imbalances'. Of course, central banks have explored the notion of flexible inflation targeting, whereby financial considerations may operate as an occasionally binding constraint which would, in principle, extend or contract the horizon over which inflation would be brought back to target (see Bean (2003) and Svensson (2009)).

Any direct discussion of a special role for financial intermediation leads to the reconsideration of the relevance of Bernanke and Blinder's 1988 model of credit and demand, a version of which we develop in Section 2.1 below. In comparison with the two-asset world of the LM curve where there is simply a choice between money and bonds, if credit is not a perfect substitute for bonds then the quantity of loans and the external finance premium matters. In other words, spending will be affected by interest rates in the broader credit (or loan) markets and so the allocation of funds across narrow and broad money by financial institutions will matter for the level of aggregate demand. In the next sub-section we develop a version of this model to help us understand QE. This important point was mostly neglected in the great dynamic stochastic general equilibrium (DSGE) revolution of monetary policy making that took place over the subsequent two decades, in which the Modigliani–Miller theorem held continual sway, as issues of real economy structure and monetary policy strategy took centre stage, with financial intermediation and monetary quantities having no special role to play over the short-term policy rate.

From the policy perspective the prosaic answer of the Bundesbank and, latterly, of the European central bank (ECB) is that money does indeed matter. And so it is broad money growth that is associated equiproportionally with growth in nominal expenditure and that timely and accurate analysis of monetary dynamics constitutes (arguably) the most important part of the central bank's information set. Indeed, Mervyn King, the

Governor of the Bank of England, in a paper written while he was Deputy Governor, argued that money is important because it is an imperfect substitute for a wide variety of assets and so a change in its quantity will induce some rebalancing of financial portfolios and therefore will have an impact on nominal demand, with both direct effects on real assets and indirect effects, as financial yields will change and so the yields from many financial assets may enter the broad money demand function (King, 2002). With some prescience he argued that money may matter simply because it relaxes transaction costs and promotes liquidity, a point taken up in several chapters in this volume (for example, see Chapter 4).

Using money, or at least central bank liabilities, as an additional instrument of monetary policy fits well with the need to augment interest rate policy at the zero bound or indeed simply to deal directly with a malfunctioning financial system. Whether the use of central bank liabilities does indeed offset a shift in the supply curve for money and its counterparts too far to the left is one issue, but the development of new instruments fits very well into the game theoretic armoury available to central bankers. This is because complementary instruments may well augment the signalling impact of both the current level of interest rates and their expected path.[9] Note that one popular solution to the problem of controlling a forward-looking system of rational agents is to make it easier for those agents to forecast future policy and so condition their plans in line with the policy maker's objectives.[10] And so any strategy that is consistent with signalling a long period of low interest policy rates may help reduce real rates over a longer horizon and so raise price level expectations.

2.1   A framework for QE

If we leave to one side the signalling effect through a communications strategy, we can think about the (fiscal and) portfolio channels within the context of simple equilibria for money and spending equations in the economy. The discussion of a special role for financial intermediation leads us to reconsider the relevance of credit in determining demand. In comparison with the two-asset world of the LM curve where there is simply a choice between money and bonds, if credit is not a perfect substitute for bonds then the quantity of loans will matter for the

---

[9] Work by Gürkaynak et al. (2005) suggests that the empirical impact of monetary policy on asset prices reflects both the level of rates and the likely future path, or stance of policy.

[10] See Woodford (2003) on the timeless commitment technology of monetary policy makers.

determination of macroeconomic equilibrium. And so we can consider a simple model with money, bonds and loans:

$$L_t^d = y_t - \eta_1(\rho_t - i_t), \tag{1}$$

where loan demand, L_t^d, is a function of the interest rate on bonds, i_t, the interest rate on loans, ρ_t, and the level of transactions, y_t, and η_1 is an elasticity. The commercial bank balance sheet comprises: reserves, R_t, loans, L_t^s, and bonds, B_t, as assets, and deposits, D_t, as liabilities. Without any loss of generality, let us assume that reserves equal τD_t, a fraction, τ, of deposits, so that the bank balance sheet is as follows:

$$B_t + L_t^s + R_t = D_t \tag{2}$$
$$B_t + L_t^s = D_t(1 - \tau), \tag{3}$$

and loans supply has the following form:

$$L_t^s = \eta_2(\rho_t - i_t) + D_t(1 - \tau), \tag{4}$$

which is increasing in the premium of loans over bonds and deposits and decreasing in reserves. As before η_2 is an elasticity. Solving for clearing in the loans market:

$$y_t - \eta_1(\rho_t - i_t) = \eta_2(\rho_t - i_t) + D_t(1 - \tau)$$
$$y_t = (\eta_1 + \eta_2)(\rho_t - i_t) + D_t(1 - \tau) \tag{5}$$

$$\rho_t = \frac{y_t - D_t(1 - \tau)}{(\eta_1 + \eta_2)} + i_t, \tag{6}$$

which tells us that the excess of interest rates on loans over bonds increases in output and reserves and decreases in deposits and the elasticity of loans demand and supply. Now let us consider the deposit market. Supply is given as follows:

$$D_t^s = \frac{1}{\tau}R_t,$$

and the demand for deposits is given by:

$$D_t^d = y_t - \eta_3 i_t, \tag{7}$$

which clears for:

$$y_t = \eta_3 i_t + \frac{1}{\tau}R_t \tag{8}$$

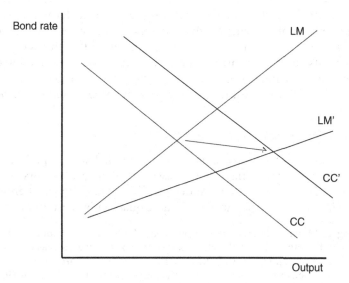

Figure 1.1 QE in a CC/LM framework

and gives the standard LM curve, but one in which increases in reserves push out the curve. The spending curve responds to both interest rates on bonds and to loans:

$$y_t = -\eta_4(i_t + \rho_t), \tag{9}$$

which can be rewritten as:

$$
\begin{aligned}
y_t &= -\eta_4 i_t - \eta_4 \left(\frac{y_t - D_t(1 - \tau)}{(\eta_1 + \eta_2)} + i_t \right) \\
&= \frac{\eta_4}{\eta_1 + \eta_2 + \eta_4} \left[R_t \left(\frac{1}{\tau} - 1 \right) - 2(\eta_1 + \eta_2)i_t \right]
\end{aligned}
\tag{10}
$$

so the spending equation will be negative in bond rates and shifted out by increases in reserves. Following Bernanke and Blinder (1988), we term this the CC curve. Figure 1.1 shows the impact of a quantitative easing in this setup. The swap of bonds outstanding for reserves increases reserves and so pushes out the CC curve and the increase in reserves also acts to push out the LM curve. Although output will rise, the actual impact on bond rates will be ambiguous as it will depend on the impact of reserves on the money supply and the extent to which any easing in the external finance premium increases aggregate demand. If the former dominates the latter, interest rates will fall. If, however, spending effects dominate then the latter would dominate. The early empirical results on the announcement effects of QE suggest that there has been more of a downward interest rate effect. It might very well be therefore that financial market participants have not transmitted the possible impact on spending down the asset price channel, but it is still early days and the lagged effects of QE may imply higher interest rates as the economy is expected to recover.

2.2   There is little new under the sun

The recent focus on quantitative easing has led to comparisons with events in the past. Initially it was assumed that QE was first used in Japan in 2001.[11] However, Anderson (2010) has drawn attention to events in the 1930s when in all but name quantitative easing was used.[12]

During 1932, with congressional support, the Fed purchased approximately $1 billion in Treasury securities (half, however, was offset by a decrease in Treasury bills discounted at the Reserve Banks). At the end of 1932, short-term market rates hovered at 50 basis points or less. Quantitative easing continued during 1933–36. In early April 1933, Congress sought to prod the Fed into further action by passing legislation that (i) permitted the Fed to purchase up to $3 billion in securities directly from the Treasury (direct purchases were not typically permitted) and, if the Fed did not, (ii) also authorized President Roosevelt to issue up to $3 billion in currency. (Anderson, 2010, p. 1)

In the post-war period, there was also an attempt to use changes in the composition of the central bank's balance sheet in order to tilt the yield curve. 'Operation Twist' was a policy adopted by the Federal Reserve Board in February 1961. This represented a change in the policy that had been in place since 1953. The New York Fed, as the operating arm of the Federal Open Markets Committee (FOMC), was restricted to purchasing and selling short-term bills as part of its open market operations. The new policy allowed it to buy also long-term government bonds of up to ten years' duration. The intention of this policy was to try to stimulate domestic economic activity and at the same time to help improve the US balance of payments position which had been in deficit for many years. The hope was that the reduction in long-term interest rates as a result of the purchase of bonds would stimulate domestic demand, while higher short-term interest rates would attract foreign capital. The New York Fed as the implementer of the policy, was required to buy no more than $500 million before the next meeting of the FOMC. In total, some $8.8 billion of bonds and bills over one-year maturity were purchased. This is equivalent, at

[11] For a detailed dissection of QE in Japan, see Werner (2002).
[12] For a more detailed discussion, see Meltzer (2003).

today's prices and proportion of national income, to almost $225 billion –
well short of the $1.7 trillion that was purchased under the QEI policy and
$600 billion under QEII.[13]

There was also a short period in UK monetary history, when a policy of
'overfunding' was used as a way of doing the inverse of QE and constrain-
ing monetary growth by issuing government bonds in excess of needs to
finance government expenditure and selling them to the non-bank private
sector. Nigel Lawson (1992), then the Chancellor of the Exchequer,
admitted that the use of overfunding was a way of massaging the money
supply to make it look as if monetary policy was tighter than it actually was.
Overfunding averaged £3.4 billion a year over the four years 1981–2 to
1984–5. On average M3 grew by nearly 4 per cent a year less than if there
had been no overfunding. By selling more gilts than was necessary to fund
the budget deficit the Bank of England bought Treasury bills or commercial bills from the market. This led to complications in the longer run as
the Bank of England accumulated a vast and growing mountain of bills
which in practice made the day-to-day conduct of monetary policy
increasingly difficult. It slightly tilted the yield curve lowering short-term
interest rates and raising long-term interest rates. The policy was eventually abandoned at the end of 1985.[14]

2.3   Quantitative easing

QE came into the general lexicon of economics as the zero bound on
policy rates began to bite outside of Japan. Figure 1.2 illustrates the scale
of the recent problem for the UK. Broadly speaking, policy rates lie close
to the rate of growth in nominal gross domestic product, (GDP), as this
comprises real economic growth and inflation, and corresponds to the
rate implied by an active interest rate rule. What we can immediately
observe from the 2008–9 recession is that bank rate just looked too high
against this metric and so another tool seemed to be required. Figure 1.3
reminds us that at the time of writing most major economies were at levels
of policy rates close to those chosen by the Bank of Japan since the
beginning of 2009.

The term quantitative easing was first coined in Japan to describe the
adoption of a 'novel' approach to the conduct of monetary policy when
interest rates are close to zero. Following the collapse of asset prices in
December 1989, Japan began to experience deflation by early 1995.
Forecasters   and   policy   makers   consistently   underestimated   the

---

[13] For a critical evaluation of Operation Twist, see Ross (1966).
[14] Lawson (1992) describes this result as an 'own goal', p. 459.

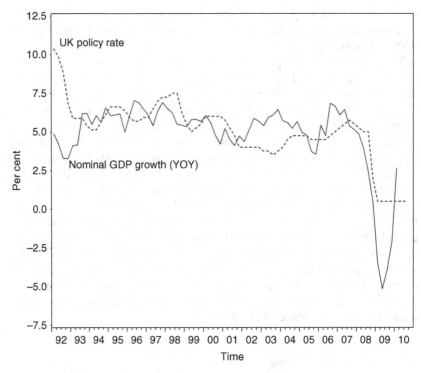

Figure 1.2 UK policy rate and nominal GDP growth

seriousness of Japan's economic problems. After conventional monetary action proved ineffectual, the Bank of Japan began quantitative easing on 19 March 2001 and continued the policy until 9 March 2006 (see Figure 1.4).

Under this policy, the Bank shifted its day-to-day operating target from the overnight, call money rate to the level of reserves (current account balance) held by banks at the central bank. Over the five years the Bank of Japan raised the reserves target nine times by purchasing Japanese government bonds from the banks and 'printing money' to pay for it. The objective was to flood banks with excess reserves in order to encourage them to lend. At the same time the Bank committed itself to maintain QE until the core consumer price index (CPI) (excluding energy and food) either reached zero or rose on a year-over-year basis for several months. Figure 1.5 shows the path of Japanese CPI inflation over this period.

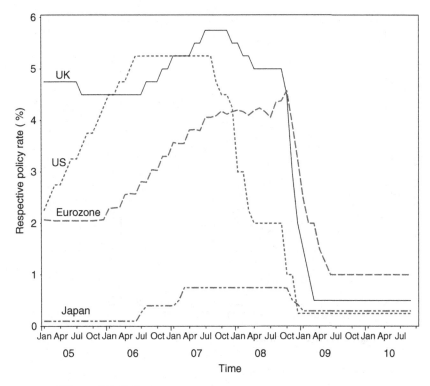

Figure 1.3 Policy rates

The question is, did it work in Japan? This raises the usual problem of the counterfactual. The headline inflation rate did turn positive at the time of the exit from QE and remained positive for much of the period until 2009, although the core inflation rate remained negative for much of the same period. Underlying output growth fared better, with an average growth rate of 2.7 per cent for 2006–7, before the onset of the financial crisis, compared with an average of 1.19 per cent from 1990 to 2005. Ugai (2007), in an empirical analysis of QE, identified that the channel that worked on the expected future path of short-term interest rates was the most important. Baba et al. (2006) considered how QE affected the economy in Japan. They focus on a neglected effect of QE on the credit risk premia financial institutions pay. They found that QE lowered risk premia to extremely low levels, especially in money markets. As a result, not just the levels but also the dispersion of money market interest rates among banks has been reduced to near zero.

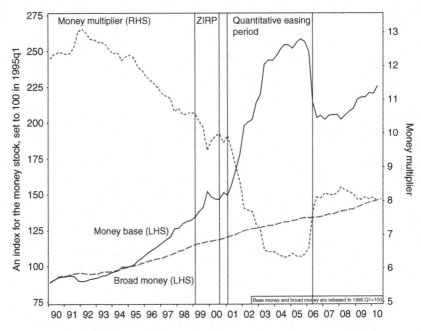

Figure 1.4   Money multiplier

Wieland (2009) provides some further empirical evidence for the Japanese experience. During this period the Bank of Japan was able to expand the monetary base and this translated into a greater and more lasting expansion of M1 relative to nominal GDP. As base money grew with QE, so did M1, increasing by more than 30 per cent of nominal income between 2001 and 2005. This expansion of base money encouraged additional deposit creation by banks, but came to a halt in 2006 with the ending of QE. However, Figure 1.4 shows that there was no strong link between excess reserves and bank lending. So despite expansions in excess reserve balances, and the associated increase in base money, during the zero-interest rate policy, lending in the Japanese banking system did not increase and the money multiplier shrank.

Although the financial crisis was regarded as a once-in-a-century experience for many western countries, from the Japanese point of view it was actually the second crisis in twenty years. One difference for Japan, and which marks it out from what happened in the 1990s, is that this time the cause lay with an exogenous shock from the rest of the world, rather than – as was the case in the 1990s – an endogenous banking crisis arising from

Note: Core inflation excludes food and energy prices

Figure 1.5 CPI and core inflation in Japan

the banking system's involvement in the commercial property market in Japan. The contraction in world trade that followed the financial crisis hit Japan particularly badly. Although the Japanese financial system had some exposure to complex securitised assets, it was much smaller than in Europe and the US. Japan adopted a number of policies which differed in many ways from what happened elsewhere. In order to protect the operation of the financial system, Japanese regulators moved quickly to carry out stress tests on financial institutions. To ensure the proper functioning of financial markets, steps were also taken to discourage short selling of shares. The Bank of Japan also sought to provide liquidity to financial markets. With the onset of the crisis Japan returned in 2008 to various forms of easing, in particular the purchase of asset-backed commercial paper and corporate bonds. However, Japan's return to QE was nothing like the scale of 2001–6, nor as large as that taking place in North America and Europe. This therefore put upward pressure on the yen; Brazil also felt this. Japan did not return to QE until 2010, faced with falling prices and an appreciating yen. Despite prompting from the

Japanese government at the end of 2009, the Bank of Japan declined to do so, arguing that the policy would not be effective.

The Federal Reserve Board, along with other central banks, responded to the financial crisis in 2007 in the conventional way by lowering short-term interest rates dramatically. The Fed also used open market operations to inject liquidity into the banking system. However, because of a reluctance on the part of banks to be seen borrowing at the discount window, in December 2007 a new method for providing liquidity to the financial system was adopted: the Term Auction Facility (TAF). This facility was part of a coordinated strategy among the major central banks around the world. In response to the continuing financial crisis, the Federal Reserve extended the range of its unconventional instruments.

The US Federal Reserve began a policy of quantitative easing in December 2008. Bernanke (2009) was quick to argue that it should perhaps be described as 'credit easing', to distinguish it from Japanese QE. The Fed finally announced the introduction of quantitative easing in March 2009, a little time after the Bank of England's introduction of QE. Initially, $1.2 trillion was used to purchase government bonds and also mortgage-related securities. A further $500 billion was then added. By the autumn of 2010 there was further discussion about the possibility of launching QE2, an extra tranche of quantitative easing. Figure 1.6 simply shows the stock of bond purchases in the UK and in the US under the first bout of QE and there seems to be little direct impact over time, but any relationship is likely to be highly complex.

The way in which the ECB responded to the financial crisis differed in many ways from how other central banks responded. These differences, it is argued, reflected the different economic and financial structures in the euro area compared with, in particular, the US. With the onset of the interbank crisis in the summer of 2007 the ECB immediately increased the availability of liquidity to the banking system. It provided €95 billion within a few hours of the crisis emerging. A year later, in September 2008, with the virtual paralysis of the interbank lending market, the ECB introduced a facility whereby banks had access to virtually unlimited liquidity at maturities of up to six months. The ECB also expanded the range of assets that it would accept as collateral. Because of the central role that the banking system performs in the euro area, the focus of ECB policy has been on the preservation of the banking system.

The ECB at first did not use quantitative or credit easing by purchasing government bonds in the euro area because it did not believe that this was the appropriate instrument in conducting monetary policy for the euro area. The non-conventional measures focused on the provision of liquidity to the banking system. More recently, in May 2010, in response to the

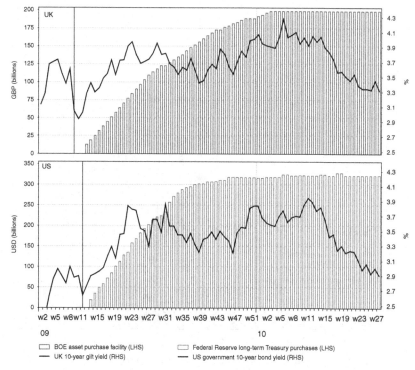

Figure 1.6 Bank of England and Federal Reserve purchases of assets

sovereign debt crisis, the ECB introduced the Securities Market Programme, whereby the ECB can intervene in particular financial markets to ensure depth and liquidity where those markets have become dysfunctional, with the possibility of 'disorderly deleveraging' and the associated disruption of the transmission mechanism of monetary policy. These interventions would be in both public and private markets.

The Bank of England launched its programme of quantitative easing in March 2009. The purchase of nearly £200 billion of UK government gilts since then by the Bank's Asset Purchase Facility (APF) has increased the size of the Bank's balance sheet to three times its normal size: to levels not seen since the end of the Second World War or the aftermath of the Napoleonic wars. These purchases amount to some 14 per cent of GDP or well over 20 per cent of outstanding UK public net debt. The APF has operated with full indemnity from the Treasury, which receives all profits and will bear any losses. Figures 1.7 and 1.8 show the impact of these measures and others on the size of the central bank balance sheet.

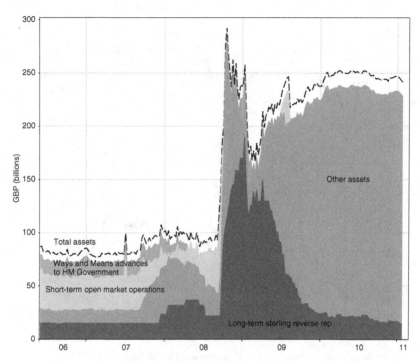

Figure 1.7 Bank of England's balance sheet – assets

The APF has three functions: to borrow at Bank rate from the Bank of England; to use that cheap funding to buy government bonds from the non-bank financial sector; and to stand ready, on the instructions of the Monetary Policy Committee (MPC), to sell those bonds back to the same sector in some more stable state of the world. In response, the rest of the financial system has taken the following steps: the Bank of England has financed its loans to the APF by issuing reserves to the banking sector, the non-bank financial sector (other financial corporations, OFC) has gone short £200 billion bonds in exchange for bank deposits, commercial banks have ended up with higher deposits and matching reserves and, concurrently, the government has issued a further £135 billion of net debt over the same period.

A rough back-of-the-envelope calculation would suggest that if the average coupon on purchased gilts (absent the small quantity of corporate bonds bought) is 5 per cent, £200 billion of bonds pays the Treasury £10 billion a year, while the interest paid on the increased reserves at the Bank of England is only 0.5 per cent. It looks as though the Treasury is making a

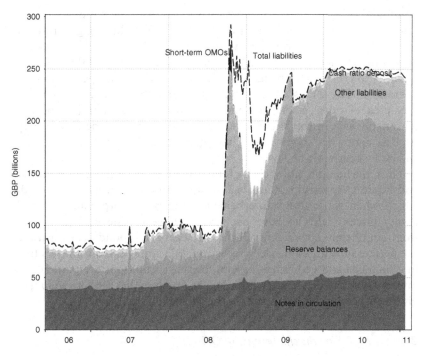

Figure 1.8 Bank of England's balance sheet – liabilities

tidy profit of more than £9 billion, or at least subsidising its own payment of interest by that amount. This, of course, has to be set against possible capital losses as the APF sells bonds in the future back into the bond markets. But if easing lasts the five years that the Bank of Japan maintained QE, it would require a very large rise in yields on debt to wipe out the profit.

There has been some concern from financial market participants about the way in which the total quantity of purchases was explained and arrived at, but given the scale of the crisis, some lack of transparency and ongoing discretion in plans is forgivable. At, or near, the zero lower bound, bonds and cash become very close substitutes and even in normal times UK government bonds seem very nearly as liquid as cash. This means that there is little scope for APF purchases to have much traction on portfolios and wealth holdings, and yet each auction of government bonds was very well covered, with OFCs more than willing to exchange large fractions of their holdings of government debt for cash.

One answer is that the scale of the purchases and their duration were able to magnify any small degree of imperfect substitutability between bonds and cash, which may in any case become that little more different in times of great stress. An alternative possibility is that buying government bonds allowed OFCs to absorb more easily the increase in government debt without prices having to fall too much. Either way, the APF sells pure liquidity to OFCs in exchange for an annual return of 4.5 per cent on its operations. The OFCs, flush with this liquidity, then can have its temporary pick of other assets, including newly issued government bonds, reasonably safe in the knowledge that it will eventually be able to buy back its debt when interest rates have gone up and the price of that debt will almost certainly be lower.

Thus, the liquidity now held by OFCs ought to move along the maturity and liquidity spectrum of assets and bump up prices across the board, which when we examine interbank lending rates, corporate debt and equity prices seems to have happened. However, the evidence is far from completely convincing. But if we accept that bonds and cash are not perfect substitutes in a deep recession, QE simply exploits the fact that in a financial and economic log-jam, private institutions are particularly interested in having access to liquidity, so much so that they are willing to give up several times Bank rate for the privilege.

2.4   Modelling the effectiveness of QE

The New Keynesian framework used to underscore so much of monetary policy analysis in the past decade has considerable difficulty with incorporating open market operations, such as QE, and assigning them a role. In a classic statement, Eggertsson and Woodford (2003) show that the existence of a rational expectations equilibrium is independent of the quantity of base money, the composition of the central bank balance sheet and the composition of the government's non-monetary liabilities. This is because any changes in these 'do not change the state-contingent consumption of the representative household, (which) depends on equilibrium output' (p. 160). Therefore, in order for open market operations to matter directly, we need to establish some link between portfolios and equilibrium output, which we will consider shortly.

The alternative, and that is the heart of the New Keynesian case, is simply to argue that all types of monetary policy announcements, such as QE, are simply devices supporting the commitment of the monetary authorities to hit any given inflation target. (Or preferably, the price level trend implied by the inflation target over the long run.) By ensuring that monetary policy commits to a course of action that will keep the economy growing at its flex-price optimal rate, forward-looking agents will expect the price level to conform to that consistent with the attainment of the inflation target. And so, if credible, even in the midst of deflation or disinflation, agents will still expect a positive rate of inflation in order to hit the long-run price level target, which will imply a negative real rate at near zero nominal rates. This kind of channel implies a very important role for forward-looking expectations and implies a commitment to a level of central bank money expansion that would occur if rates could move sufficiently negative.

The problem with a purely signalling effect of QE is that if it does not have any effects within the maintained model, it is difficult to understand why using it would matter for the determination of quantities and prices. That is not to argue that signalling does not matter, as there is a substantial literature on the importance of communication and explanation of the likely path of monetary policy to which new tools of monetary policy might usefully contribute (see Gürkaynak et al., 2005), but if, in the model employed, a particular tool has no role, how can its signal then also matter?

Let us now turn to an alternative possible channel. The fiscal channel suggests that monetary injections may relax the government's budget constraint and allow an excess of expenditure over receipts without necessarily leading to an increase in the private sector's holdings of government debt. Auerbach and Obstfeld (2005) construct a model in which a permanent, or credible, monetary injection can immediately alter the price level because the trade of money for interest rate-bearing government liabilities reduces debt service costs. The impact is considerably attenuated in the case of a temporary monetary injection and the welfare benefits depend on the extent to which future distortionary (labour) taxation is replaced by an inflation tax. The authors interpret the increase in excess reserves in Japan, following the start of QE in 2001, in terms of their model as implying that the monetary base expansion was not treated as permanent and/or that the return to positive interest rates was treated as quite distant and so any increase in broad money was delayed.

The monetary, or portfolio, channel, rather than a simple force driving inflation, is based on the idea that money and other assets are imperfect substitutes. And so an increase in the money supply will induce the private sector to rebalance its portfolio and so raise prices and lower expected returns of non-monetary assets. But if money is treated as an asset, yielding safe returns equal to the negative of the inflation rate, it is possible that money may just be held and so have a limited portfolio rebalancing. Clearly, the central bank might have more impact under these circumstances from purchasing assets that are more rather than less illiquid.

Earlier work (see Bernanke et al. (2004), for instance) examining the Japanese experience with QE found little by way of announcements effects, though there did seem to be significant yield curve consequences from purchases of US Treasuries by overseas institutions, with $1 billion of purchases leading to around 0.6–0.7bp off medium-term yields and from a macro-finance yield curve some evidence to suggest that Japanese yields were 50bp lower than expected during QE. Recently released empirical estimates of the impact of the initial £125 billion of QE and then the full £200 billion (14 per cent of GDP) on UK gilt yields by Meier (2009) and then Joyce et al. (2010) suggests that yields are 40–100bp lower than they would otherwise have been in the absence of QE.[15] For the US, Gagnon et al. (2010) find that the $300 billion of US bond purchases, which amount to 2 per cent of GDP, resulted in falls of 90bp in US ten-year Treasuries. These results do seem to fit the results of Krishnamurthy and Vissing-Jorgensen (2010), who find that a reduction in public debt outstanding of around 20 per cent of GDP in the US will reduce yields by 61–115 bp. The former estimates are mostly based on an events study approach of announcements rather than actual purchases and emphasise the importance of the portfolio rebalancing channel rather than the *pure signalling* effect. Although plausible, the results do not seem especially uniform across the announcement dates and we await more detailed results from estimation of the supply and demand curves for government liabilities, which are complicated by the continuing and large-scale issuance of government debt over this period.

3   Contribution in this volume

Money itself does not enter the objective function of central banks and sits somewhere as part of the information set on which interest rate paths are predicated. To that extent the analyses of Douglas Gale in Chapter 2 of this volume are particularly welcome, as they focus on what economic theory can tell us about the regulation of liquidity in a financial system. The efficient provision of liquidity is analysed in an 'Arrow–Debreu' general equilibrium model of the financial system. This benchmark model allows the causes of market failure to be identified, along with the circumstances in which, to improve welfare, central bank interventions might be necessary. In particular, the incompleteness of markets can lead to inefficient liquidity provision and, in some cases, market crises. In certain circumstances, market failures are relatively benign and can be rectified by requiring banks to hold adequate amounts of liquid assets – which pay the risk-free rate of return – and implies that financial intermediaries hold either or

---

[15] Chapter 11 of this volume briefly surveys these results.

both of reserves and T-bills. In other cases, more extensive interventions by the central bank are required as 'lender of *first* resort to replace frozen markets'.

Gale suggests that these central bank interventions may also require an expansion of wholesale funding and asks whether this will be possible without risking instability. The answer depends on the successful implementation of effective liquidity regulation. Apart from the desire to increase the capacity for lending in the global financial system, a revival of the parallel banking system may offer an opportunity to improve the transparency, stability and efficiency of the financial system by creating a new and well-regulated type of limited-purpose financial company, what he calls a narrow bank, to replace the miscellany of vehicles that blossomed in the boom years before the crisis of 2007–8. The key insight from Gale is that we need to understand the reasons why liquidity dried up in order to avoid a repeat of the sub-prime crisis, and to design a more stable and efficient financial system for the future.

In Chapter 3, Hans Gersbach and Jan Wenzelburger investigate analytically a banking system embedded in an overlapping generations model, which is subject to repeated macroeconomic productivity shocks. They show how a series of negative shocks may cause a systemic default of the banking system. By lowering interest rates, the central bank can increase intermediation margins, which promotes bank recapitalisation. They go on to present a positive analysis of how interest rate policies may resolve a banking crisis and also provide reasons why banking crises may cause long-lasting economic downturns. They suggest that when interest rate policies are aimed only at avoiding a systemic default, the economy may converge to a consumption trap. In the consumption trap, entire bank savings are needed to cover the banks' obligations and GDP growth is minimal. The key policy conclusion in this model is that central banks must act to ensure that banks are adequately capitalised and this can be, of course, brought about by a number of policy initiatives, running from large-scale liquidity provision to the purchase of badly performing assets through to nationalisation of banks. The need to maintain adequate bank capital to prevent a consumption trap may imply a link between financial and macroeconomic stability, which had been neglected previously.[16]

In Chapter 4, John Driffill and Marcus Miller try to understand recent developments with reference to a macroeconomic model, which includes the effects of quantitative easing in particular. They first sketch how the

---

[16] In other words, what has become known as the Separation Principle, whereby monetary stability and financial stability are pursued separately, may not hold. See Clerc and Bordes (2010).

model of Kiyotaki and Moore (2008) can be used to illustrate the threat posed by the liquidity crunch. Then they report the results of a numerical exercise by the New York Fed, which uses this framework to calibrate the effect of QE in avoiding severe economic contraction in the US. The first question posed is, why should entrepreneurs hold money if other assets – equity in particular – offer higher yields? The answer is simply that these other assets may become illiquid: if limits to equity sales and new equity finance become binding, for example, shares will not provide the purchasing power needed by entrepreneurs who come up with new ideas for investment. Knowing that future investment initiatives may be thwarted in this way generates a precautionary demand for money by forward-looking entrepreneurs. The rate of capital formation is simply determined by Tobin's q, where entrepreneurs will have an incentive to go ahead if the market value of investing exceeds the cost of the resources required, i.e. so long as Tobin's q is greater than one, where Tobin's q represents 'the shadow price in terms of consumption goods of a unit of installed capital'. The margin required between market value and replacement cost is usually explained by the need to cover increased costs of installation: however, the margin may also be due to the presence of credit constraints that bind more heavily as investment increases. These credit constraints on the calibration presented imply a depression of 10 per cent from baseline, which can be ameliorated to a deep recession of 6–7 per cent below baseline. In the model this increase in liquidity is achieved by a swap of illiquid equity for liquid money. Naturally, the effectiveness of the policy depends on the liquidity premium on cash and the quantity of the swaps undertaken, but in general it is only a depression rather than recession that can be avoided.

In Chapter 5, Richard Harrison considers a simple modification of the NK framework by allowing imperfectly substitutable assets. The model posits a financial intermediary that borrows from the government at both long and short maturities and makes one-period loans to households. Portfolio adjustment costs are introduced into the profit functions of financial intermediaries so that the larger their holdings of short-term bonds, the more they value long-term bonds. This assumption is motivated by the notion that agents are more willing to hold less liquid assets if they have ample holdings of liquid assets. The result is that the rate of return faced by households is a weighted average of the market yields on long-term and short-term debt. The market yield on long-term bonds in turn depends on the portfolio mix held by financial intermediaries. This setup creates a wedge between the market rates of return on long and short bonds. This approach is a simple and elegant way to capture the notion that relative asset prices depend on their relative supply and provides a channel through which asset purchases by the policy maker can affect aggregate demand. Because assets are imperfect substitutes, the policy maker can use asset purchases to alter the relative supplies of assets and hence bond returns.

To the extent that central bank asset purchases reduce long-term interest rates (over and above the effect of expected future short rates), aggregate demand can be stimulated, leading to higher inflation through a conventional New Keynesian Phillips curve. But this channel also implies that the operation of traditional monetary policy is constrained because long-term interest rates depend not only on the current and likely stance of policy rates but also on the relative liquidity of financial intermediaries. In principle, a given change in policy rates will have less of an impact on long-term rates because it will induce a change in debt-financing costs and cause the financial intermediary to switch its portfolio of short- and long-term assets in the opposite direction to the change in short-term rates. In the version of the model with perfect substitutability, a 100bp cut in policy rates will lead to a 8bp fall in the five-year spot, but with imperfect substitutability, long-term rates will fall by around only 4–6bp. For this calibration it is implied that liquidity effects reduce the effectiveness of monetary policy in stabilising the economy.

In Chapter 6, Stefania Villa and Jing Yang estimate – using Bayesian estimation techniques – a recently developed model of Gertler and Karadi (2011) that combines financial intermediation and unconventional 'monetary policy', using UK data. To validate the fit of the estimated DSGE model, they provide an evaluation of the model's empirical properties. They then analyse the transmission mechanism of the shocks during a downturn before finally estimating the empirical importance of nominal, real and financial frictions and of different shocks. Their main findings are that the data strongly favour a model with financial frictions for the UK economy; the sharp rise in spreads since the recent crisis can be mainly attributed to credit supply shocks; and so some form of credit policy – over and above Bank rate – might help to make the simulated contraction less severe.

In Chapter 8, Domenico Giannone, Michele Lenza, Huw Pill and Lucrezia Reichlin come to the same conclusion from an almost diametrically opposed position. They show that the behaviour of key financial and monetary aggregates – notably bank loans to non-financial corporations and (albeit to a somewhat lesser extent) households – can be explained on the basis of historical regularities estimated in the pre-crisis sample, once developments are conditioned on the actual path of economic activity. In other words, one does not need to rely on exceptional or aberrant behaviour in the financial sector to explain developments in money and credit following the failure of the global financial services firm, Lehman

Brothers. The ensuing weakness of economic activity is sufficient to account for what was observed. These results can be interpreted as evidence that the non-standard measures introduced by the ECB following Lehman's demise were successful in insulating bank credit provision to households and firms from the breakdown of financial intermediation seen in the interbank money market. By implication, propagation via financial collapse – seen as central to the emergence of the Great Depression in the 1930s – was largely avoided. In this sense, the non-standard monetary policy measures introduced by the ECB in the autumn of 2008 can be seen as successful. This does not imply that there were not macroeconomic consequences but that any extra amplification via the financial collapse may have been avoided, at least in the first round.

In Chapter 7, Sharon Kozicki, Eric Santor and Lena Suchanek consider the impact of quantitative easing on long-term interest rates. They examine the effect of central bank balance sheets on long-term forward rates for a sample of developed countries. The empirical results show that – controlling for expected inflation, projected fiscal indebtedness and other macro variables – an increase in central bank assets is associated with a decline in long-term interest rates. The approximate impact found from an increase in the ratio of central bank holdings of government debt to GDP, or the ratio of central bank assets to GDP, suggests a wide range of responses in ten-year government bond yields from around –0.3 to –0.07 percentage points, which in the UK would imply a fall in yields of no less than around 100bp.

In Chapter 9, Spencer Dale outlines the lessons from quantitative easing on the anniversary of the first operations in March 2009. He addresses three key questions: What is the theoretical foundation for such a policy? What are the key channels of transmission? And what can we say about its impact to date? These questions are naturally critical for both the operation and study of monetary policy. He echoes the observation that the financial crisis posed questions which models most commonly used to analyse monetary policy were not well suited to answer. Although there is an emerging literature that responds to these shortcomings, it is important – for both the theory and practice of monetary policy – that this continues. Dale's estimate of the impact of QE was that the £200 billion of purchases of bonds from non-bank financial intermediaries had reduced medium-term bond yields by 100bp.

Mike Wickens, in Chapter 10, challenges the perception that the financial crisis was due to flawed macroeconomic and finance theory. Much of this is media criticism, he argues, but written by academics. He insists that the fault lies more in the failure of banks, and other financial market participants, to use existing theory correctly, especially the theory of risk. Although most modern macroeconomic models do not include a banking sector, and much of finance theory takes little or no account of the macroeconomic environment, a consequence is that the financial crisis has stimulated a huge amount of research on how best to model the banking sector in DSGE models. Compared with the previous generation of DSGE models this might be thought of as unconventional macroeconomic modelling. Unfortunately, much of this research is misplaced as it involves introducing arbitrary exogenous restrictions and ignores the key issue of default.

For example, as already noted, Harrison (Chapter 5 in this volume) assumes that households have an exogenous target ratio of long- to short-term debt. In a widely cited paper, Kiyotaki and Moore (2008) assume that firms invest with an exogenous probability, only a fraction of new investments can be funded initially, and only a fraction of a firm's financial capital can be used initially to offset this funding restriction. All of this creates a liquidity constraint. Negative shocks to these frictions, such as those that started the financial crisis, make the constraint more binding and the likelihood of a recession more probable. Not surprisingly, once these constraints are alleviated by, for example, a liquidity infusion by the central bank, the crisis and the recession can be checked.

Wickens feels that such explanations do not address the real cause of the crisis, namely, default risk. This was largely ignored by the banks when providing new mortgages, by the credit rating companies when evaluating mortgage-backed securities, and by the financial sector when buying these securities. Default risk also lies behind the liquidity crisis as it deterred interbank lending. What is required is the inclusion of a banking sector in these models in which default risk drives a wedge between lending and borrowing rates. The probability of default should be modelled as endogenous rather than exogenous as it depends on the business cycle, being higher in periods of recession than boom.

The final chapter, by Evren Caglar, Jagjit Chadha, Jack Meaning, James Warren and Alex Waters, assesses the conjunctural impact of QE in the UK and provides some preliminary results of the impact of non-standard policies in DSGE models, which take seriously the role of financial frictions. The authors find that it is possible to generate the correct qualitative effects of a lower zero bound in the DSGE models by (i) offsetting the liquidity premium embedded in long-term bonds, and/or (ii) providing a countercyclical subsidy to bank capital, and/or (iii) creating central bank reserves that ameliorate the costs of loans supply. But the correct quantitative response and the appropriate interaction with standard monetary policy, particularly with respect to the exit strategy, remains an open question.

4   Concluding remarks

In launching this conference and this new Cambridge series on Modern Macroeconomic Policy Making, we hope to improve the dialogue between academics, city-based economists and policy makers. The challenges ahead require not only more work but, to coin a current phrase, a 'coalition' across various methodologies and approaches. One lesson from the financial crisis is that a high degree of belief in one model across many agents does not necessarily lead to aggregate stability. But as well as pooling resources, economists are learning about genuine gaps in their understanding of the causes of aggregate fluctuations. And rather than abandoning progress along a difficult road in matching micro-foundations to macroeconomic theories of fluctuations, the discipline is developing a class of models in which collateral or liquidity constraints and financial intermediaries play a substantive role in determining macroeconomic outcomes and, as a signifi-cant by-product, helping us understand the monetary transmission mechanism.[17]

Much of the focus of the new work has been to develop unconventional monetary policies, such as QE. The question is, then, also whether we ought to treat QE as an extreme measure or something that might, in time, become part of the central bank's regular toolkit. For example, could we use negative QE – or overfunding as we have referred to it earlier – as well as raising interest rates if house prices, debt and money were to expand at a worrying rate? Perhaps also the absence of significant purchases of assets other than gilts ought to make us ask why there is so little corporate debt in the UK financial system compared with the US. Also, we wonder what we learn about the limits to the private-sector supply of liquidity in that it was unwilling to enter in exactly the same trade using cheap money. With the emphasis on the quantity of liquidity as well as its price, central banks seem to be telling us something about the limits of standard interest rate rules and imply a truth from an old economic maxim: that when prices, in this case of money, cannot adjust, quantities must.

As well as reading the runes in emergent theory, policy makers had to deal with the crisis as it unfolded and quickly accepted that the limits to our understanding could not prevent some sort of response being fleshed out. Immediate questions such as whether to bail out individual banks were quickly overtaken by issues of systematic liquidity shortages, as the interbank market froze. Liquidity issues developed into ones of credit risk and it became clear that the unwinding of compressed spreads in financial markets

---

[17] See Caballero (2010) for a more pessimistic view on the ability of mainstream (core) models to successfully adapt in the face of the financial crisis.

compounded the vulnerability of households and firms with considerable debt on their balance sheets. These debts were the counterparty of high and escalating levels of gearing by financial intermediaries. Whatever the instruments used to stabilise the economy at or near the zero bound, the levels of outstanding gross claims across financial institutions and private agents, as well as, latterly, across governments, seem likely to play a role in determining the level of economic activity for some time to come.

Many among the previous generation of macroeconomists were concerned with the trade-off between output and inflation and found that attaining monetary policy credibility was the route to establishing the best, or optimal, trade-off. It would be ironic if the new obligations to ensure both financial and monetary stability that are likely to be handed to central bankers provide another set of trade-offs which threatens hard-won monetary credibility. If two objectives are to be pursued, at least two instruments are likely to have to remain in play. We shall see.

References

Anderson, R. G. (2010) The first U.S. quantitative easing: the 1930s, Economic Synopses, Federal Reserve Bank of St Louis, No. 17.

Auerbach, A. J. and Obstfeld, M. (2005) The case for open-market purchases in a liquidity trap, *American Economic Review*, 95(1), 110–37.

Baba, N., Nakashima, M., Shigemi, Y. and Ueda, K. (2006) The Bank of Japan's monetary policy and bank risk premiums in the money market, *International Journal of Central Banking*, 2(1), 105–35.

Bagehot, W. ([1873] 1897), *Lombard Street: A Description of the Money Market*, New York: Charles Scribner's Sons.

Bean, C. (2009) Quantitative easing: an interim report. Speech to the London Society of Chartered Accountants, 13 October.

(2003) Asset prices, financial imbalances and monetary policy: are inflation targets enough? BIS Working Paper No. 140, Bank for International Settlements.

Bernanke, B. S. (2009) The crisis and the policy response, the Stamp Lecture, London School of Economics, January.

(2004) The Great Moderation, Speech to the Eastern Economic Association, Washington, DC, 20 February, available at www.federalreserve.gov/boarddocs/speeches/2004/20040220/.

Bernanke, B. S. and Blinder, A. S. (1988) Credit, money, and aggregate demand, *American Economic Review*, 78(2), 435–9.

Bernanke, B. S. and Reinhart, V. R. (2004) Conducting monetary policy at very low short-term interest rates, *American Economic Review*, 94(2), 85–90.

Bernanke, B. S., Reinhart, V. R. and Sack, B. L. (2004) Monetary policy alternatives at the zero bound: an empirical assessment, Brookings Papers on Economic Activity, 2, 1–78.

Borio, C. and Disyatat, P. (2009) Unconventional monetary policies: an appraisal, BIS Working Paper No. 292, Bank for International Settlements.

Brainard, W. C. and Tobin, J. (1968) Pitfalls in financial model building, *American Economic Review (Papers and Proceedings)*, 58, May, 99–122.

Caballero, R. J. (2010) Macroeconomics after the crisis: time to deal with thepretence-of-knowledge syndrome, *Journal of Economic Perspectives, 24(4), 85–102.*

Chadha, J. S., Corrado, L. and Holly, S. (2008) Reconnecting money to inflation: the role of the external finance premium, Cambridge Working Paper in Economics 0852, Faculty of Economics, University of Cambridge.

Clarida, R., Gali, J. and Gertler, M. (2002) The science of monetary policy: a New Keynesian perspective. *The Journal of Economic Literature*, 37(4), 1661–707.

Clerc, L. and Bordes, C. (2010) The art of central banking of the ECB and the Separation principle, Documents de Travail 290, Banque de France.

Cottarelli, C., and Viñals, J. (2009) A strategy for renormalizing fiscal and monetary policies in advanced economies, IMF Staff Position Note 09/22, Washington, DC: International Monetary Fund.

Eggertsson, G. B. and Woodford, M. (2003) The zero bound on interest rates and optimal monetary policy, *Brookings Papers on Economic Activity*, 1, 139–211.

Gagnon, J., Raskin, M., Remache, J. and Sack, B. (2010) Large-scale asset purchases by the Federal Reserve: did they work? Federal Reserve Bank of New York, Staff Report No. 441.

Gertler, M. and Karadi, P. (2011) A model of unconventional monetary policy, *Journal of Monetary Economics*, 58, 17–34.

Goodhart, C. A. E. (1989) The conduct of monetary policy, *The Economic Journal*, 99, 293–346.

Gürkaynak, R. S., Sack, B. and Swanson, E. (2005) Do actions speak louder than words? The response of asset prices to monetary policy actions and statements, *International Journal of Central Banking*, 1(1), May, 55–93.

Hawtrey, R. G. (1934) *The Art of Central Banking*, London: Longmans.

Joyce, M., Lasaosa, A., Stevens, I. and Tong, M. (2010) The financial market impact of quantitative easing, Bank of England Working Paper No. 393.

Khan, A., King, R. G. and Wolman, A. L. (2003) Optimal monetary policy, *Review of Economic Studies*, 70(4), 825–60.

King, M. (2010) Banking – from Bagehot to Basel, and back again, Speech at the Second Bagehot Lecture, Buttonwood Gathering, New York, 25 October.

(2002) No money, no inflation – the role of money in the economy, *Bank of England Quarterly Bulletin*, Summer.

Kiyotaki, N. and Moore, J. (2008) Liquidity, business cycles and monetary policy, unpublished.

Klyuev, V., de Imus, P. and Srinivasan, K. (2009) Unconventional choices for unconventional times: credit and quantitative easing in advanced economies, IMF Staff Position Note, SPN/09/27, November.

Krishnamurthy, A. and Vissing-Jorgensen, A. (2010) The aggregate demand for Treasury debt, unpublished.

Lawson, N. (1992) *The View from No. 11*, London: Bantam Press.

Lucas, R. E. Jr (1996) Money neutrality, *The Journal of Political Economy*, 104(4), 661–82.

Madigan, B. F. (2009) Bagehot's dictum in practice: formulating and implementing policies to combat the financial crisis, Federal Reserve Bank of Kansas City's Annual Economic Symposium, Jackson Hole, WY, 21 August.

Meier, A. (2009) Panacea, curse, or nonevent: unconventional monetary policy in the United Kingdom, IMF Working Paper No. 09/163.

Meltzer, A. H. (2003) *A History of the Federal Reserve, Volume 1: 1913–1951*, University of Chicago Press.

Miles, D. (2010) Interpreting monetary policy, Speech at the Imperial College Business School, London, 25 February.

Poole, W. (1970) Optimal choice of monetary policy instruments in a simple stochastic macro model, *The Quarterly Journal of Economics*, 84(2), 197–216.

Ross, M. H. (1966) Operation Twist: a mistaken policy? *The Journal of Political Economy*, 74 (2), 195–9.

Svensson, L. E. O. (2009) Flexible inflation targeting – lessons from the financial crisis, Speech at Netherlands Bank, Amsterdam, 21 September.

Tobin, J. (1958) Liquidity preference as behaviour towards risk, *Review of Economic Studies*, 25(67), 65–86.

Ugai, H. (2007) Effects of the quantitative easing policy: a survey of empirical analyses, *Monetary and Economic Studies*, 25(1), 1–48.

Werner, R. A. (2002) Monetary policy implementation in Japan: what they say vs. what they do, *Asian Economic Journal*, 16(2), 111–51.

White, W. (2006) Procyclicality in the financial system: do we need a new macro-financial stabilisation framework? BIS Working Paper No. 193, Bank for International Settlements.

Wieland, V. (2009) Quantitative easing: a rationale and some evidence from Japan, NBER Working Paper No. 15565, December.

Woodford, M. (2003) *Interest and Prices: Foundations of a Theory of Monetary Policy*, Princeton University Press.

2 Liquidity and monetary policy

Douglas Gale

1 Introduction

In the period leading up to the financial crisis of 2007–8, financial institutions of all sorts increased their leverage in the wholesale markets, relying heavily on collateralised borrowing in the form of repurchase agreements ('repos') and issuance of asset-backed commercial paper (ABCP). As the crisis approached, lenders became nervous and significantly shortened the maturity of the loans they were prepared to make. When the crisis hit, the disappearance of short-term funding created severe problems for many financial institutions. Some large firms failed and further failures were prevented only by the intervention of the central banks.

Although the origin of the crisis may have been the US sub-prime mortgage market, the early stages looked like a crisis of liquidity provision. At the end of July 2007, two Bear Stearns funds filed for bankruptcy and a third suspended redemptions. More bad news followed and then, on 7 August, BNP Paribas halted redemptions from three investment funds because it could not 'fairly' calculate their net asset value (NAV). Potential investors, mainly money market mutual funds (MMF), declined to roll over their purchases of ABCP. Since many of the vehicles that comprised the parallel banking system (PBS) were sponsored by banks and/or had liquidity guarantees from banks, there was a fear that these assets would end up on bank balance sheets. This in turn raised concerns about counterparty risk among the banks and caused LIBOR to shoot upwards.[1] The European central bank was forced to inject €95 billion in overnight lending into the market in order to cope with the demand for liquidity (Acharya et al., 2010).

Two aspects of these events are notable. First, the events that triggered the collapse in the ABCP market were not themselves large. Second, the

---

[1] The London Interbank Offer Rate (LIBOR) is a daily reference rate used in a variety of financial contracts. It is based on the rates at which a panel of London banks is willing to make unsecured loans to other banks.

impact was felt by very different funds and institutions, some of which had nothing to do with sub-prime mortgages. One famous victim of this 'market freeze' was the British bank, Northern Rock (Goldsmith-Pinkham and Yorulmazer, 2010). Originally a mutual organisation known as a building society, it had converted to a bank in 1997. By 2007 it had grown to be the fifth largest mortgage lender in the UK. In order to achieve this market share, it had relied on securitisation and wholesale funding rather than retail deposits. By mid-September the longer-term funding markets were closed for Northern Rock. When Lloyds TSB's offer to purchase the bank fell through, the Bank of England was forced to extend emergency assistance to Northern Rock directly. The announcement of the Bank's support for Northern Rock resulted in a run on the bank, which ended when the government announced it would guarantee all Northern Rock's existing deposits. This was effectively the end of Northern Rock as an independent entity. Although the bank would turn out to have its share of troubled assets, at the time of its near collapse its problems seemed to be mainly liquidity related.

The failure of Bear Stearns in mid-March 2008 is another example of a liquidity freeze.[2] As an intrinsic part of its business, Bear Stearns relied day to day on its ability to obtain short-term finance through secured borrowing. At this time, Bear Stearns was reported to be financing $85 billion of assets on the overnight market (Cohan, 2009). Beginning late Monday 10 March 2008, and increasingly through that week, rumours spread about liquidity problems and eroded investor confidence in the firm. Even though Bear Stearns continued to have high-quality collateral, counterparties became less willing to enter into the normal funding arrangements with the firm.[3] By the end of the week, counterparties were unwilling to make even secured funding available to the firm on customary terms. This unwillingness to fund on a secured basis placed enormous stress on Bear's liquidity. On Tuesday 11 March, the holding company liquidity pool declined from $18.1 billion to $11.5 billion. On Thursday 13 March, Bear Stearns' liquidity pool fell sharply and continued to fall on Friday. In the end, the market rumours about Bear Stearns' liquidity problems became self-fulfilling and led to the near failure of the firm. Bear Stearns was adequately capitalised at all times during the

---

[2] The discussion that follows is based on a letter from Christopher Cox, Chairman of the Securities and Exchange Commission, to the Basel Committee in Support of New Guidance on Liquidity Management, available at: www.sec.gov/news/press/2008/2008-48.htm

[3] This high-quality collateral consisted mainly of highly rated mortgage-backed assets which had low but not inconsequential credit risk by this time in the sub-prime crisis.

period from 10 March to 17 March, up to and including the time of its agreement to be acquired by J. P. Morgan Chase. Even at the time of its sale, Bear Stearns' capital and its broker dealers' capital exceeded supervisory standards. In fact, the capital ratio of Bear Stearns was well in excess of the 10 per cent level used by the Federal Reserve Board in its well-capitalised standard (Acharya et al., 2010).

The financial crisis disrupted large parts of the financial system. The parallel or 'shadow' banking system, consisting of structured investment vehicles (SIVs), conduits, asset-backed securities (ABS), collateralised debt obligations (CDOs), etc., has virtually disappeared. Some estimates put the size of the global PBS in the neighbourhood of $11 trillion in 2007 (Gordian Knot, 2009). Its collapse has sharply reduced the financial system's lending capacity. In spite of the well-known problems with sub-prime ABS, securitisation has proved to be a valuable technique for spreading risk and expanding sources of funding. Restoring the PBS and its demand for ABS is an important step in the reconstruction of the financial system.

Reviving the PBS is also important as a way of getting ABS off the balance sheets of banks and central banks. He et al. (2010) have estimated that around $700 billion of the ABS previously held in the PBS have found their way onto the balance sheets of banks, assisted by the lending facilities extended by the central banks. More ABS are held by the Federal Reserve System (FRS) and government-sponsored enterprises (GSEs). If the central bank's balance sheet is to be restored to its normal size and the banks' credit channel is to be unblocked, these securities will have to find a home somewhere else. This will require an expansion of wholesale funding. Whether this will be possible without risking instability depends on the successful implementation of effective liquidity regulation.

Apart from the desire to increase the capacity for lending in the global financial system, the revival of the PBS offers an opportunity to improve the transparency, stability and efficiency of the financial system by creating a new and well-regulated type of limited-purpose financial company to replace the miscellany of SIVs, CDOs and conduits that flourished in the boom years before the crisis of 2007–8. A proposal along these lines is discussed at the end of the chapter. These 'narrow' banks may provide an alternative to the regulatory and commercial failures of the last ten years.

Understanding the reasons why liquidity dried up is obviously important both to avoid a repeat of the sub-prime crisis and to design a more stable and efficient financial system for the future. This chapter focuses on what economic theory can tell us about the regulation of liquidity in the financial system. In Section 2 we describe a general equilibrium model of the financial system and characterise the efficient provision of liquidity.

This benchmark model allows us to identify some of the causes of market failure and the central bank interventions that might be necessary to improve welfare. In particular, in Section 3 we see how the incompleteness of markets can lead to inefficient liquidity provision and, in some cases, market crises. In certain circumstances, market failures are relatively benign and can be rectified by requiring banks to hold adequate amounts of liquid assets. In other cases, more extensive interventions by the central bank are required. In Section 4 we discuss a variety of policies that might improve the allocation of liquidity in the financial system. Finally, in Section 5, we discuss a proposal to revive the PBS.

2 Optimal liquidity provision

In this section, we describe a general-equilibrium model of the financial system, characterising the conditions under which market provision of liquidity is efficient. This model is a special case of the model developed in Allen and Gale (2004). The Allen–Gale model is itself an extension of the familiar Bryant–Diamond–Dybvig model (Bryant, 1980 and Diamond and Dybvig, 1983). The two main innovations in the Allen–Gale model are the introduction of asset markets and aggregate uncertainty about asset returns and liquidity shocks. Asset markets allow banks to share risks and liquidity. The introduction of aggregate uncertainty about asset returns and liquidity shocks shifts the focus from sunspot phenomena, such as the panics in the Diamond and Dybvig (1983) model, to the analysis of real shocks and their impact on the allocation of risk and liquidity.

For the purpose of studying liquidity regulation, the model has a number of attractive features: (i) it incorporates sophisticated financial institutions in a general-equilibrium theory of markets; (ii) it endogenises the costs of liquidating assets; (iii) it provides a robustness check on results obtained using simpler models; (iv) it allows one to study the relationship between liquidity provision and asset pricing; (v) it provides a foundation for the welfare analysis of financial regulation; and (vi) variants of the model can be used to explore financial fragility, excess sensitivity and sunspot phenomena.

2.1   Model primitives

Time is divided into three dates, indexed by $t = 0, 1, 2$. At each date, there is a single good, which can be used for consumption or investment.

There are two assets, a short-term asset and a long-term asset. The short-term or 'short' asset is represented by a storage technology. One unit of the good invested in the short asset at date t yields one unit of the good at date $t + 1$, for $t = 0, 1$. The long-term or 'long' asset is a constant returns-to-scale technology that takes two periods to mature. One unit invested in the long asset at date 0 yields $R > 1$ units of the good at date 2. The asset structure represents the trade-off between liquidity and returns, a sort of stylised yield curve: the short asset offers an earlier return but has a lower yield; the long asset offers a later return but has a higher yield.

Aggregate uncertainty is represented by two states of nature, indexed by $s = 1, 2$. The state is uncertain at date 0 and publically observed at the beginning of date 1. The initial probability distribution of states is denoted by $\pi = (\pi(1), \pi(2))$, where $\pi(s) > 0$ is the probability of state s at date 0.

At date 0 there are two ex ante types of consumer, indexed by $i = 1, 2$. A consumer's ex ante type is publically observable. We follow Diamond and Dybvig (1983) in representing liquidity preference in terms of uncertainty about the timing of consumption. Initially, consumers are uncertain whether they value consumption at date 1 or date 2. At the beginning of date 1, each consumer learns his ex post type: either he is an early consumer, in which case he only values consumption at date 1, or he is a late consumer, in which case he only values consumption at date 2. The probability of being an early or late consumer depends on the state of nature and the consumer's ex ante type. A consumer of type i has a probability $0 \leq \lambda_i(s) \leq 1$ of being an early consumer in state s. If a consumer of type i has a consumption bundle $\mathbf{x}_i : \{1, 2\} \to \mathbf{R}_+^2$ that promises $x_{it}(s)$ units of the good at date t in state s, then his utility is given by

$$U_i(\mathbf{x}_i) = \sum_{s=1,2} \{\lambda_i(s)u_i(x_{i1}(s)) + (1 - \lambda_{is}(s))u_i(x_{i2}(s))\}.$$

We assume that $u_i(\cdot)$ has the usual properties (continuously differentiable, concave, increasing).

Finally, each consumer is assumed to have an initial endowment consisting of one unit of the good at date 0 and nothing at dates $t = 1, 2$.

An investment plan for this economy is a four-tuple $\mathbf{y} = (y_0, y_1(1), y_1(2), y_2)$, where $y_0 \geq 0$ is the amount invested in the short asset at date 0, $y_1(s) \geq 0$ is the amount invested in the short asset at date 1 in state $s = 1, 2$, and $y_2 \geq 0$ is the amount invested in the long asset at date 0. An allocation consists of an ordered triple $(\mathbf{x}_1, \mathbf{x}_2, \mathbf{y})$, where $\mathbf{x}_i$ is a consumption bundle for $i = 1, 2$ and $\mathbf{y}$ is an investment plan. An allocation $(\mathbf{x}_1, \mathbf{x}_2, \mathbf{y})$ is incentive compatible if

$$x_{i1}(s) \leq x_{i2}(s), \text{ for } s = 1, 2 \text{ and } i = 1, 2. \tag{1}$$

If this inequality were violated, a late consumer would have an incentive to imitate an early consumer, withdraw at date 1 and store the goods for consumption at date 2. The allocation $(\mathbf{x}_1, \mathbf{x}_2, \mathbf{y})$ is attainable if it is incentive compatible and satisfies the conditions

$$y_2 + y_0 = 2, \tag{2}$$

$$\sum_{i=1,2} \lambda_i(s) x_{i1}(s) + y_1(s) = y_0, \text{ for } s = 1, 2, \tag{3}$$

and

$$\sum_{i=1,2} (1 - \lambda_i(s)) x_{i2}(s) = y_1(s) + R y_2, \text{ for } s = 1, 2. \tag{4}$$

The first condition (2) simply says that the total amount invested in the short and long assets at date 0 must equal the total endowment of the two ex ante types. The second condition (3) requires that, in each state s at date 1, the total consumption of early consumers plus the investment in the short asset must equal the returns to the short asset. Similarly, the third condition (4) requires that, in each state s at date 2, the total consumption of late consumers equals the returns of the long and short assets.

An attainable allocation $(\mathbf{x}_1, \mathbf{x}_2, \mathbf{y})$ is incentive efficient if there does not exist an attainable allocation $(\mathbf{x}_1', \mathbf{x}_2', \mathbf{y}')$ such that $U_i(\mathbf{x}_i') \geq U(\mathbf{x}_i)$ for all i and $U_i(\mathbf{x}_i') > U(\mathbf{x}_i)$ for some i.

2.2   Decentralisation

To decentralise an efficient allocation, we use both markets and financial institutions. We assume there is a complete set of contingent commodity markets. Since all uncertainty is resolved at the beginning of date 1 (agents learn their types and the true state of nature is revealed), markets will be complete if there are markets at date 0 for the good at date 0 and for the good in state $s = 1, 2$ at date $t = 1, 2$. In other words, there are five contingent commodities. The assets can be interpreted in the usual way as claims to bundles of contingent commodities and priced accordingly. Let the good at date 0 be the numeraire and let $\mathbf{p} = (\mathbf{p}(1), \mathbf{p}(2))$ denote the contingent price vector, where $\mathbf{p}(s) = (p_1(s), p_2(s))$ is the vector of dated commodities in state s.

Markets for contingent commodities provide insurance against aggregate risk, but we also need intermediaries to provide insurance against idiosyncratic liquidity shocks to consumers. An intermediary takes deposits at date

0 in exchange for a complete contract $\mathbf{x}_i$ that promises $x_{it}(s)$ units of the good to a depositor of ex ante type i who withdraws at date t in state s. Because a depositor's ex post type is private information, we require the complete contract $\mathbf{x}_i$ to be incentive-compatible.

We assume that each intermediary caters to only one ex ante type of consumer. Otherwise, an intermediary could act as a central planner and internalise all gains from trade without needing to use markets. Since we want to investigate the use of markets to facilitate risk sharing and liquidity provision, we assume that transaction costs prevent this kind of super-intermediation. Thus, in equilibrium, there will be two types of intermediaries: those catering to depositors of ex ante type 1 and those catering to depositors of ex ante type 2.

There is assumed to be free entry into the banking sector, so intermediaries earn zero profits in equilibrium. Competition among intermediaries forces them to maximise the expected utility of their depositors in equilibrium.

In addition to the restrictions on intermediaries' ability to intermediate among different types of consumers, we restrict access to markets. In particular, we assume that intermediaries have access to all contingent and forward markets, whereas depositors do not have access to any of these markets. Depositors are allowed to hold the short asset, however; that is, they have access to the storage technology. These restrictions on market participation are needed to motivate the use of intermediaries. In fact, as Cone (1983) and Jacklin (1986) have shown, if depositors have access to forward markets at date 1, they will engage in arbitrage against the intermediaries. In equilibrium, it will be impossible for the intermediaries to generate any welfare gains by providing liquidity insurance.

An intermediary for consumers of type i chooses a complete, incentive-compatible contract $\mathbf{x}_i$ to maximise the consumers' expected utility subject to a budget constraint that requires that the value of the contract be less than or equal to the value of the deposit. Then the optimal contract $\mathbf{x}_i$ solves the decision problem

$$\begin{array}{ll} \max & U_i(\mathbf{x}_i) \\ \text{s.t.} & \mathbf{p} \cdot \mathbf{x}_i \leq 1. \end{array} \tag{5}$$

Although it is natural to think of intermediaries as holding assets, the existence of complete markets makes this unnecessary: whatever contingent commodities are needed to meet the intermediary's commitments can be purchased using the markets that exist at date 0. Someone must hold the assets, however, and in the Arrow–Debreu tradition we can assume that profit-maximising producers play this role. More precisely, a representative producer has access to a production set Y that is defined by

$$Y = \{ \mathbf{z} \in \mathbf{R}^5 : \mathbf{z} = (-y_0 - y_2, y_0 - y_1(1), y_0 - y_1(2), y_1(1)$$
$$+ Ry_2, y_1(2) + Ry_2), \exists \mathbf{y} \in \mathbf{R}_+^5 \}$$

and the producer chooses $\mathbf{z} \in Y$ to maximise $\mathbf{p} \cdot \mathbf{z}$. In equilibrium, the producer earns zero profits and this implies that the no-arbitrage condition

$$\sup \{ \mathbf{p} \cdot \mathbf{z} : \mathbf{z} \in Y \} = 0 \qquad (6)$$

must be satisfied. This in turn implies that any investment plan $\mathbf{y}$ satisfies the no-arbitrage condition

$$\sum_{s=1,2} \{ p_1(s)(y_0 - y_1(s)) + p_2(s)(y_1(s) + Ry_2) \} \leq y_0 + y_2.$$

We do not need to concern ourselves with the portfolio chosen by the bank since the completeness of markets assures us that any investment plan $\mathbf{y}$ satisfying (6), including $\mathbf{y} = \mathbf{0}$, is optimal.

Now we are ready to define an equilibrium of the economy: an equilibrium consists of an attainable allocation $(\mathbf{x}_1, \mathbf{x}_2, \mathbf{y})$ and a price vector $\mathbf{p}$ such that $\mathbf{x}_i$ is optimal, that is, it solves problem (5) and satisfies the no-arbitrage condition (6).

This equilibrium shares the usual properties of the competitive equilibrium in an Arrow–Debreu economy with complete markets.

Proposition 1
Under a mild non-satiability condition, slightly stronger than the usual one because it has to take account of the fact that banks are restricted to incentive-compatible contracts, it can be shown that every equilibrium allocation is incentive efficient.

In fact, in the special case studied here, the possibility of storing goods between date 1 and date 2 implies that the optimal contract must satisfy the first-order condition

$$u_i'(x_{i1}(s)) \geq u_i'(x_{i2}(s)).$$

Otherwise, the intermediary could increase expected utility by reducing consumption at date 1, storing goods until date 2 and increasing consumption at date 2. This implies that the incentive constraint $x_{i1}(s) \leq x_{i2}(s)$ is not binding, so the incentive-efficient allocation is actually a Pareto-efficient allocation. This stronger result depends on the special features of Diamond–Dybvig (1983) preferences and does not hold in general, of course.

2.3   Incomplete contracts and default

In the preceding account of efficient liquidity provision, the intermediaries differ from the banks in the Bryant–Diamond–Dybvig model in one important respect: the intermediaries offer completely contingent contracts instead of the standard deposit contracts we associate with banks. This is important because the contingency of these contracts rules out the need for default. In order to bring our model in line with standard practice in the banking literature, we need to restrict banks to using contracts with debt-like features. Allen and Gale (2004) allow for a general characterisation of incomplete contracts, that is, contracts which are measurable with respect to a partition of states. They also allow for the possibility of default. The possibility of default is important both for realism and because it allows for potential welfare gains by increasing the contingency of the contract over and above what is allowed by the definition of incomplete contracts. For example, in the current environment with only two states, we could require incomplete contracts to satisfy the requirement that payoffs be independent of the state, that is,

$$x_{it}(s) = x_{it}(s'), \forall t = 1, 2, \forall s \neq s.$$

The possibility of default allows for an expansion of this set of contracts to allow for contracts that have the feature that in one state, call it $\bar{s}$, the bank must liquidate its assets and pay them out immediately (i.e. at date 1) to early and late consumers alike, in which case the consumption levels will be

$$x_{i1}(\bar{s}) = x_{i2}(\bar{s}) = y_0 + \frac{p_2(\bar{s})}{p_1(\bar{s})} R y_2.$$

With this change in the model, we have to change the definition of efficiency: an attainable banking allocation is required to be an attainable allocation as previously defined with the additional requirement that the contracts are required to be incomplete. An attainable banking allocation is defined to be constrained efficient if there is no attainable banking allocation that Pareto dominates it. We define a banking equilibrium in an analogous way, adding the requirement that the banks must choose incomplete, incentive-compatible contracts. Then the following proposition shows that, in this sense, there is no market failure in equilibrium.

Proposition 2
Under a mild non-satiability condition, slightly stronger than the usual one because it has to take account of the fact that banks are restricted to incomplete, incentive-compatible contracts, it can be shown that every banking equilibrium allocation is constrained efficient.

The importance of this result is that it shows that liquidity provision is efficient under *laissez faire*, even if incomplete contracts require default in some states of nature, as long as markets are complete. There is no market failure and the incidence of crises is socially optimal. In other words, there is no rationale for government intervention.

Incomplete contracts and the possibility of default introduce non-convexities into the banks' optimisation problem. As is well known, the existence of equilibrium can no longer be taken for granted unless we take advantage of the convexifying effect of large numbers. Since we have assumed a large number of banks, we can allow banks of the same type to offer different contracts. More precisely, we have to allow for mixed allocations in which there is a distribution of contracts chosen by the intermediaries catering to each type i. This kind of equilibrium is interesting because it illustrates that optimality does not require banks of a given type i to do the same thing.

Proposition 3
Under standard conditions, there exists a mixed equilibrium.

The efficiency condition is straightforwardly extended to mixed equilibria.

The assumption of complete markets provides a baseline that helps us understand the requirements for an efficient financial system, but it must be emphasised that it is a very demanding and restrictive assumption. Implicit in the assumption of complete markets are several subsidiary assumptions. First, all contingent commodities are defined in terms of publicly observable states of nature. There is no private information and hence no asymmetry of information in these markets. Second, there are markets for trades contingent on all possible states of nature, where a state has to describe the characteristics and condition of every possible trader. Third, the financial intermediaries that trade in these markets satisfy a budget constraint with probability one, so that they are always in a position to make good on their promises to deliver in any state of nature. There is no possibility of default and no counterparty risk. These assumptions are unlikely to be satisfied in practice, but that does not make them irrelevant. One interpretation of the role of the central bank is that it replaces the missing markets by providing ex post the liquidity that intermediaries were unable to obtain ex ante.

3   Incomplete markets

The existence of a complete set of contingent markets allows intermediaries and banks to arrange at date 0 for the provision of liquidity at dates 1 and 2. This is what we call ex ante provision of liquidity. In practice, markets are incomplete and liquidity must often be obtained ex post, after the state of nature is realised.

3.1   Market provision of liquidity

To illustrate the provision of liquidity with incomplete markets we make
a number of changes in the model. First, we assume that there are no
contingent commodity markets, but that intermediaries can hold assets to
transfer wealth between dates. Second, we assume there is an asset market
that allows the long asset to be traded at date 1 for the current good. As
before, we begin with the case of intermediaries that can offer depositors
complete, incentive-compatible contracts.

In the absence of contingent commodity markets, intermediaries have to
hold assets in order to provide for future liquidity needs. Let $\mathbf{y}_i$ denote the
investment plan chosen by an intermediary of type i. Let $\mathbf{q} = (q(1), q(2))$
denote the asset price vector, where, for each state s, $q(s)$ denotes the price
of the long asset in terms of the current good at date 1. The budget
constraints faced by the intermediary are

$$y_{i0} + y_{i2} = 1,$$

$$\lambda_i(s)x_{i1}(s) + y_{i1}(s) = y_{i0} + q(s)(y_{i2} - z(s))$$

and

$$(1 - \lambda_i(s))x_{i2}(s) = y_{i1}(s) + Rz(s),$$

where $z(s)$ is the amount of the long asset held until the last date.

The asset market allows intermediaries to collapse their sequence of
budget constraints into a single 'present value' budget constraint at date 1.
Using the date-0 budget constraint to write the investment in the long
asset as $1 - y_{i0}$, we can write the date-1 budget constraint in present value
terms as

$$\lambda_i(s)x_{i1}(s) + \frac{q(s)}{R}(1 - \lambda_i(s))x_{i2}(s) = y_{i0} + \frac{q(s)}{R}(1 - y_{i0}), \text{for } s = 1, 2.$$

$$(7)$$

The intermediary of type i chooses a production plan y_{i0} and an incentive-
compatible contract $\mathbf{x}_i$ to maximise $U_i(\mathbf{x}_i)$ subject to the budget
constraints (7).

While this reduced form of the intermediary's decision problem suffices
to determine the maximum utility, we also need the no-arbitrage conditions that come from the complete problem in order to characterise
equilibrium. The return on the short asset is 1 and the return on the
long asset is $\dfrac{R}{q(s)}$. The asset market will not clear unless the return on the

long asset is at least as great as the return on storage (i.e. $q(s) \leq R$). Also, there is no storage unless the return on storage is at least as high as the return on the long asset (i.e. $q(s) = R$). Then the no-arbitrage conditions can be written as

$$q(s) \leq R \text{ and } q(s) < R \text{ implies } y_{i1}(s) = 0, \text{ for } s = 1, 2. \qquad (8)$$

An equilibrium for the economy with incomplete markets consists of an attainable allocation $(\mathbf{x}_1, \mathbf{y}_1, \mathbf{x}_2, \mathbf{y}_2)$ and a price vector $\mathbf{q}$ such that $(\mathbf{x}_i, \mathbf{y}_i)$ satisfies the no-arbitrage conditions (8) and maximises $U_i(\mathbf{x}_i)$ subject to the budget constraints (7) for $i = 1, 2$.

To simplify, we assume the two ex ante types of consumers are mirror images. This requires that the two states are equally probable,

$$\pi(1) = \pi(2) = \frac{1}{2},$$

and the liquidity shocks have the same marginal distribution

$$\lambda_1(s) = \lambda_2(s') = \begin{cases} \lambda_H & \text{if } (s, s') = (1, 2) \\ \lambda_L & \text{if } (s, s') = (2, 1) \end{cases}.$$

Then there is no aggregate uncertainty since

$$\frac{1}{2} \sum_{i=1,2} \lambda_i(s) = \frac{1}{2}(\lambda_H + \lambda_L) = \bar{\lambda}, \text{ for } s = 1, 2.$$

Further, there exists a symmetric equilibrium in which each type of intermediary chooses the same initial portfolio y_0, the deposit contracts $\mathbf{x}_i$ are identical, modulo the permutation of states, and the asset price is independent of the state,

$$q(1) = q(2) = 1.$$

This equilibrium is generically inefficient because markets are incomplete. Moreover, it is constrained inefficient in the sense of Geanakoplos and Polemarchakis (1986).[4] As an illustration, suppose that the two types of agents have the same power utility functions:

---

[4] Geanakoplos and Polemarchakis (1986) consider an equilibrium with incomplete markets to be constrained efficient if it is impossible to make agents better off (or some agents better off and no agents worse off) by changing the allocation at the first date and allowing markets to clear at the subsequent dates. In the present context, this amounts to saying that the investment decisions at date 0 can be manipulated but the usual equililibrium conditions must be satisfied at dates 1 and 2.

$$u_i(c) = \frac{1}{1-\rho} c^{1-\rho}.$$

Pareto efficiency requires that consumption be independent of the state, that is,

$$\mathbf{x}_i(1) = \mathbf{x}_i(2)$$

for each type i. However, if the coefficient of risk aversion ρ is greater than one, we can show that the optimal incentive compatible contract $\mathbf{x}_i$ satisfies

$$x_{i1}(s) > \frac{q(s)}{R} x_{i2}(s),$$

that is, the present value of consumption at date 1 is greater than the present value of consumption at date 2. Intuitively, the higher the coefficient of risk aversion, the more 'insurance' the optimal contract provides to the early consumers. Given this inequality, an increase in the fraction of early consumers will raise the cost of the deposit contract, other things being equal. Since the value of the intermediary's portfolio is constant across states, the budget constraint requires a compensating reduction in consumption at both dates. Thus, $\mathbf{x}_1(1) \ll \mathbf{x}_1(2)$ and $\mathbf{x}_2(1) \gg \mathbf{x}_2(2)$.

The equilibrium allocation is clearly not Pareto efficient, but we can go further and show that it is not even constrained efficient. Constrained inefficiency requires that we can make everyone better off ex ante by changing the choices at date 0 and allowing markets to clear at dates 1 and 2. Allen and Gale (2004) demonstrate that such a Pareto improvement can be achieved by regulating the amount of liquid assets held by both types of intermediary. The effect of increasing the quantity of the short asset (and reducing the price of the short asset) is to increase the price of the long asset at date 1. Changing the price of the long asset (which competitive intermediaries take as given) is the key to improving welfare.

Proposition 4
Asset prices are too high (too low) if relative risk aversion is less than (greater than) one. Welfare can be improved by imposing a maximum (minimum) on holdings of the short asset.

3.2   Arbitrage, fire sales and asset price volatility

The preceding example shows that we do not need aggregate uncertainty to have inefficient provision of liquidity, but aggregate uncertainty makes the sources of the inefficiency clearer. In particular, if we allow for asset price volatility, we can investigate the role of fire sales in raising the costs of obtaining liquidity. Optimal insurance should offer a payment in states where the marginal utility of money is relatively high and demand a premium in states where the marginal utility of money is relatively low. If markets are complete, intermediaries can obtain liquidity in states where they need it (the marginal utility of money is high) and pay for this insurance in other states (where the marginal utility of money is presumably low). When a firm is forced to sell assets in order to obtain liquidity, there is a risk that it will end up selling assets at 'fire sale' prices. In other words, it is paying the insurance premium for liquidity in the very states where its marginal utility of money is highest. This is the opposite of what optimal insurance would require.

Things can be even worse if several banks have to sell assets at the same time. The simultaneous sales may drive down prices, forcing the banks to sell even more assets, causing a vicious circle that results in large reductions in prices and capital losses for the selling banks. Ex post, these losses do not represent a deadweight cost because they are merely transfers of wealth from sellers to buyers; however, they do represent inefficient risk sharing ex ante, as in the previous example, because the seller is paying for liquidity in the state where his marginal utility of money is high rather than in the state where his marginal utility of money is low. The greater the fall in price, the greater the distortion.

This raises the question why arbitrageurs do not anticipate the fall in prices and provide liquidity to the market by buying up the assets. The reason is that providing liquidity is expensive. The opportunity cost of holding the short asset is the forgone return on the long asset. The expected capital gains from buying assets at fire sale prices compensate for the cost of holding the short asset. If arbitrage completely eliminated the fire sale, there would be no incentive to hold the short asset in the first place. Thus, in equilibrium, arbitrage cannot eliminate the risk of fire sales altogether.[5]

We can illustrate the relationship between the cost of liquidity and price volatility using a special case of the model. Suppose that consumers of ex ante type 1 are risk neutral and have no liquidity preference ($\lambda_1 = 0$), whereas consumers of ex ante type 2 have power utility functions with coefficient $\rho > 1$ and random liquidity parameters $\lambda_2(1) < \lambda_2(2)$. Since type-1 consumers only value consumption at the final date, we might expect intermediaries of type 1 to invest exclusively in the long asset.

---

[5] Allen and Gale (1998) studied this phenomenon and noted that, when markets are incomplete, arbitrage cannot eliminate asset price volatility and ex post liquidity provision is necessarily inefficient.

Their customers have no need of liquidity at date 1 and the long asset has a higher return than the short asset. But this ignores the fact that the intermediary can do even better if the price of the long asset is low at date 1. By holding the short asset, the intermediary can buy up the long asset at date 1 and make a profit that compensates for the low return on the short asset.

Consider an equilibrium $(\mathbf{x}_1, \mathbf{y}_1, \mathbf{x}_2, \mathbf{y}_2, \mathbf{q})$ that satisfies the following two conditions:

$$q(s) < R \text{ for } s = 1, 2 \text{ and } 0 < y_{10} < 1.$$

The first of these conditions says that holding the short asset between date 1 and date 2 is dominated by holding the long asset. The second simply says that the type-1 intermediaries hold both assets at date 0. This first condition implies that, in each state, a type-1 intermediary sells the short asset at date 1 and buys the long asset. For each unit of the short asset held at date 0, the intermediary can buy $\frac{1}{q(s)}$ units of the long asset in state s at date 1. This means that, on average, the intermediary ends up with $\frac{\pi(1)}{q(1)} + \frac{\pi(2)}{q(2)}$ units of the long asset at date 2. Alternatively, it can invest one unit in the long asset at date 0 and end up with one unit at date 2. In equilibrium, since it is willing to hold both assets at date 0, the intermediary must be indifferent between these two strategies. In other words, the expected returns must be equal:

$$\frac{\pi(1)}{q(1)} + \frac{\pi(2)}{q(2)} = 1. \tag{9}$$

Since the short asset is not held between dates 1 and 2 in either state, so the market-clearing condition for goods at date 1 becomes

$$\lambda_2(s)x_{21}(s) = y_{10} + y_{20}$$

for $s = 1, 2$. Substituting this equation into the first-order conditions for optimality at date 1 gives us

$$\sum_{s=1,2} \pi(s)\left(\frac{y_{10} + y_{20}}{\lambda(s)}\right)^{\rho}(1 - q(s)) = 0,$$

or

$$\sum_{s=1,2} \pi(s)\lambda(s)^{-\rho}(1 - q(s)) = 0. \tag{10}$$

Thus, we have two equations, (9) and (10), in two unknowns, $q(1)$ and $q(2)$.

Using these equations to solve for the equilibrium prices, we find that asset price volatility is large relative to the size of the liquidity shock when risk aversion is high. To illustrate this relationship, consider the following numerical example. Let $R = 2$, $\lambda(1) = 0.5$, $\lambda(2) = 0.6$, $\pi(1) = 0.5$ and $\rho = 2$. Then the equations above become

$$\frac{0.5}{q(1)} + \frac{0.5}{q(2)} = 1$$

$$0.5(0.5)^{-2}(1 - q(1)) + 0.5(0.6)^{-2}(1 - q(2)) = 0.$$

Solving these equations, we obtain the price vector

$$(q(1), q(2)) = (1.2198, 0.84732).$$

Note that although the liquidity shock is only 20 per cent,

$$\frac{\lambda(2) - \lambda(1)}{\lambda(1)} = \frac{0.6 - 0.5}{0.5} = 0.2,$$

the price change is -44 per cent,

$$\frac{q(1) - q(2)}{q(2)} = \frac{1.2198 - 0.84732}{0.84732} = 0.43960.$$

This turns out to be a general property of equilibrium.

Proposition 5
Consider an economy in which $u_1(c) = c$, $u_2(c) = \frac{1}{1-\rho}c^{1-\rho}$, $\lambda_1(s) = 0$ for $s = 1, 2$ and $0 < \lambda_2(s) < 1$ for $s = 1, 2$. Let $(\mathbf{x}_1, \mathbf{y}_1, \mathbf{x}_2, \mathbf{y}_2, \mathbf{q})$ be an equilibrium and suppose that $q(s) < R$ for $s = 1, 2$ and $0 < y_{10} < 1$. Then

$$\log\left(\frac{q(2)}{q(1)}\right) = \rho \log\left(\frac{\lambda(1)}{\lambda(2)}\right).$$

Intuitively, the total consumption at date 1 is constant (see the market-clearing condition above), so as the liquidity shock goes up, the per capita consumption goes down (and it goes down relative to the future consumption). For this adjustment to be optimal in equilibrium, prices have to go down by more than the change in relative consumption because demand is relatively inelastic ($\rho > 1$).

A fuller investigation of this example is contained in the appendix to this chapter.

3.3   Limited market participation

We have argued that incomplete markets can lead to sub-optimal provision of liquidity because institutions that need liquidity may have to obtain it by selling assets in 'down' markets. Similarly, incomplete participation in markets can lead to sub-optimal provision of liquidity by discouraging investors with high liquidity preference from participating in the markets where their liquidity may be needed. Allen and Gale (2004) show how heterogeneity in attitudes toward risk and liquidity preference can lead to unnecessarily high asset price volatility.

Suppose there are two types of investors, A and B. Type A have low liquidity preference and low risk aversion; type B have high liquidity preference and high risk aversion. Investors have Diamond–Dybvig preferences and the fraction of early consumers is random (i.e. there is real aggregate uncertainty). As usual, there are two assets: a long asset and a short asset. The market for the long asset has a fixed 'entry cost'.

If only type A enter the asset market (this decision must be made at the initial date and cannot be reversed later), the amount of liquidity in the market will be low because type A have low liquidity preference. Then asset prices are volatile because there is little liquidity in the market, so a slight increase in the fraction of early consumers leads to a large fall in price. Under these conditions, type B are rational to stay out of the market. Type B either have to hold a small amount of the long asset, in which case it is not worth paying the entry cost, or they have to face significant uncertainty due to the asset price volatility.

There can also be an equilibrium in which both types enter the market, type B hold a large amount of the short asset and, by providing this liquidity to the market, can dampen the fluctuations in asset prices. In that case, the value of entry can be greater than the cost, so it is rational for both types to enter.

Under certain circumstances, these equilibria can be Pareto-ranked, showing that incomplete participation is associated with excess volatility in both the statistical and the welfare senses.

A key ingredient of this story is the fact that asset prices are determined by the amount of 'cash' in the market, rather than by the usual fundamentals. Another interesting feature of the model is that liquidity and asset volatility depend on the *composition* of the market, i.e. who participates, not the size or *depth* of the market.

3.4   Policy lessons

We have seen that a regulated increase in liquid assets can lead to a Pareto-improvement under certain circumstances. In our specific example, this requires that the coefficient of relative risk aversion be greater than one. In that case, an increase in liquidity causes an increase in the price of the illiquid asset, which in turn increases ex ante expected utility. More generally, the work of Geanakoplos and Polemarchakis (1986) tells us that equilibria are generically constrained inefficient when markets are incomplete. So it is no surprise that market provision of liquidity is constrained inefficient when markets are incomplete. What makes the welfare analysis tricky is that the Geanakoplos and Polemarchakis result tells us nothing about the policy that will cause a Pareto-improvement. It guarantees only the *existence* of a welfare-increasing intervention. Identifying this policy may not be easy and implementing it may be impractical. For example, in a general-equilibrium system, we cannot assume that there is a benefit from increasing liquidity. A counter-example is provided by Proposition 4: if the rate of relative risk aversion ρ is less than one, there will be too much liquidity in equilibrium and the regulator can increase welfare by forcing intermediaries to reduce their holdings of the short asset at date 0.

Even if we are willing to assume that market liquidity is too low, the examples we have constructed do not imply that minimum liquidity ratios would solve the problem. What our examples show is that requiring banks to hold more of the short asset may raise the future asset price or reduce asset price volatility, *but only if the banks are free to use the short asset to buy the long asset*. More generally, if banks are forced to hold a certain amount of the short asset come what may, this is of no value in providing liquidity for the system as a whole. This is just another example of Goodhart's (2008) taxi (the taxi that could not accept a fare because of the regulation that at least one taxi must be at the railway station at all times). The beneficial effects of having 'cash in the market,' as Allen and Gale (1994) call it, are limited to cash that can be used whenever the opportunity arises, rather than cash that banks are forced to hold as a result of minimum liquidity requirements.

What conclusions can be drawn then? There is a gap between the conclusions that can be drawn from a simple theory model and the complexities of the real world, and any serious proposals for liquidity regulation require a solid empirical base that may not exist yet. At the same time, the regulation of liquidity is nothing new. It used to take the form of reserve requirements, which now seem quaint, but it has always been accepted, in principle, as part of the regulator's toolkit. What has changed is the nature of banking, particularly the sources of funding and liquidity, and this has made the older methods of liquidity regulation obsolete. These changes include (i) greater reliance on wholesale deposits and funding through the repo and CP markets; (ii) less reliance on core deposits; (iii) the growth of the share of loans and illiquid assets such as ABS; and (iv) the growth of off-balance-sheet commitments such as lines of credit, as well as conduits,

ABS, SIVs, etc. These changes were particularly marked in the decade leading up to the financial crisis. The banks that were most vulnerable to liquidity shocks as measured by reliance on wholesale deposits and market funding, and which had the smallest share of core deposits and highest ratios of illiquid assets, tended to be the larger banks, which represent the bulk of the assets in the financial system (cf. Cornett et al., 2010). Although financial innovation and advances in liquidity management may have brought us somewhat closer to the theoretical ideal of complete markets, we are still a long way from that ideal, as the events of 2008 demonstrated all too clearly. In fact, the extreme reliance on short-term debt as experienced by Bear Stearns and Lehman Brothers is the opposite of the complete contingent markets described in Section 2.

Even if we cannot say with theoretical certainty that liquidity is too low, it is true that, when markets are incomplete, there will be a welfare-relevant pecuniary externality that results from any change in one bank's holding of liquid assets. Holding liquid assets entails an opportunity cost – in order to hold liquid assets one has to forgo the higher return that could have been earned on illiquid assets – so there is some reason to think that banks may not hold enough liquid assets or may rely too much on funding sources that are not reliable. Ex post it seems all too plausible that forcing banks to hold larger amounts of liquid assets or to reduce their reliance on wholesale and market funding would have avoided both some bank failures and the disastrous credit crunch that occurred in the fourth quarter of 2008. A simple counter-factual calculation by Cornett et al. (2010) gives prima facie support for the view that a more liquid financial system would have given rise to much greater credit growth and much smaller liquidity hoarding in the post-Lehman period (i.e. Q4 2008).

Assuming, for the sake of argument, that the period leading up to the crisis was characterised by excessive liquidity creation and lending, what can be done to restrain these excesses during the boom? As indicated above, rigid liquidity ratios give rise to their own problems, but there are several alternatives. One is the payment of interest on liquid balances or reserves, essentially a Pigovian subsidy on liquidity. This would encourage the accumulation of liquid balances that can then be run down when profitable opportunities arise. Another is the creation of liquidity facilities by the central bank, essentially an extension of its role as lender of last resort. A third would be the introduction of some sort of liquidity insurance, in effect an attempt to replicate the complete markets of the first model we looked at. A fourth would be to include measures of (il)liquidity in the capital adequacy standards of future versions of the Basel accords. For example, capital ratios might be linked to measures of maturity mismatch, such as the ratio of average maturities of assets to liabilities.

The greater the maturity mismatch between assets and funding liabilities, the greater the amount of capital that would be required. Similar adjustments to capital requirements could be made for relying on core deposits instead of wholesale or market funding. The advantage of this approach is that it imposes a cost to illiquidity that gives the bank an incentive to manage its liquidity prudently, without imposing strict ratios. The capital ratio itself is still a constraint, however. How well these alternatives will work is beyond the scope of this chapter, but they all deserve further study.

4   Liquidity provision in a crisis

We argued above that there may be an inadequate level of liquidity in the financial system when markets are incomplete. This conclusion is consistent with the view of Goodfriend and King (1988) that, *under normal conditions*, financial markets allocate liquidity efficiently. So, under normal conditions, the job of the central bank is to ensure adequate liquidity in the system as a whole. In a crisis, however, providing adequate liquidity in the aggregate may not be enough. When the stability of the entire financial system is threatened, there is a tendency for liquidity to 'dry up' and there may be a 'flight to quality' and an unwillingness to lend at any but the shortest maturities. Banks may hoard liquidity or be unwilling to lend to one another because of fears of counterparty risk. In short, even if there is adequate liquidity in the system as a whole, the markets are frozen.

4.1   Models of liquidity freeze

There is a growing literature on the role of illiquidity in the recent financial crisis. Here I want to mention just a few contributions that deal with market freezes and the drying up of liqudity.

Acharya et al. (2010) have shown that market freezes can occur even when the quality of assets is not in doubt and there is no problem of asymmetric information. They focus on the problem of rollover risk when asset holdings are financed using short-term debt, such as ABCP. The essential assumptions needed for their results are (i) a maturity mismatch between assets and liabilities; (ii) a small liquidation cost if the borrower defaults and the assets used as collateral have to be sold; and (iii) a very high frequency of refinancing. Under these conditions, it can be shown that an information event, signalling a very small change in the fundamental values of the assets, can result in a drastic fall in the debt capacity, that is, the maximum amount that can be borrowed against the collateral value of the assets. According to this theory, what happened following the BNP Paribas announcement in August 2007 and preceding the collapse of Bear Stearns in March 2008 was that relatively small information events caused lenders to fear that the debt could not be rolled over indefinitely and hence that it was unsafe to lend at all.

Geanakoplos (1997, 2009) and Fostel and Geanakoplos (2008) have also emphasised the importance of leverage in creating cycles in asset values. A critical assumption of Geanakoplos (2009) is that investors have heterogeneous valuations of assets because of different beliefs, different attitudes towards risk, etc. Some, the natural owners of the assets, are optimists, and others, the natural lenders, are pessimists. Since pessimists have lower valuations of the underlying asset, the amount that they are willing to lend against the security of the asset is less than the value that the optimist places on the asset. Nonetheless, the ability to leverage the asset allows the optimistic owners to pay more for the assets than they could if they used only their own wealth. Thus, leverage together with heterogeneous valuations allows for an elevated level of asset prices. It also lays the groundwork for a collapse in values and defaults if bad news arrives. A worsening of fundamentals necessarily lowers the valuation of each individual (both lenders and owners) and hence lowers the asset price. This makes it impossible for the owners to repay their debt, forcing them to default. Now the assets have to be purchased by new owners, who were previously among the pessimistic lenders, and they will have to borrow from lenders who are even more pessimistic than the new owners. The amount the new owners are willing to pay and the amount the lenders are willing to lend against the asset are both much less than before, which further reduces the market price of the asset. Thus, a little bad news can lead to a dramatic fall in asset values because of the amplifying effect of leverage.

He and Xiong (2009) have made a similar argument in the case of financial firms facing rollover risk on multiple maturities of short-term debt. In very good states, the firm faces no risk of default; in very bad states, default is certain; in intermediate states, the probability of default depends on the decision to roll over the debt: if the firm cannot refinance and has to default, the costs of bankruptcy will ensure that debt holders lose money, whereas if the firm can refinance its debt there will be no (immediate) risk of default. The decision to roll over at any date depends on the probability that the debt will be rolled over by the other borrowers at subsequent dates. This leads to a coordination problem, but the fact that refinancing decisions are made sequentially ensures that there is a unique equilibrium. Nonetheless, the coordination problem does ensure that the cutoff at which the lenders refuse to refinance is higher than efficiency requires. Fear of future failure of refinancing will cause lenders to refuse to roll over the debt today even though the condition of the firm is good enough to ensure repayment conditional on refinancing.

Gorton (2010) has argued that asymmetric information was at the heart of the market freeze. More precisely, the enormous amount of leverage in the financial system was the result of demand for *information-insensitive* assets. When the prospect of default is remote, debt is information-insensitive because it pays the face value in most states. In a crisis, when the prospect of default is non-negligible, debt becomes information-sensitive and the possibility that some market participants are better informed drives the less informed from the market (cf. the analysis of Gorton and Pennacchi, 1990). The collapse of ABS markets follows. In Section 5, we consider one proposal that might increase the supply of high-quality, information-insensitive assets held by transparent, limited-purpose financial companies.

4.2   Liquidity provision or bailouts?

When markets 'freeze' and liquidity 'dries up', the central bank must step in as the lender of *first* resort to replace the frozen markets. During the crisis, central banks responded by creating a variety of facilities to provide liquidity to the financial system, going beyond the normal lender-of-last-resort function. The Federal Reserve System encouraged banks to make use of the discount window and, when this proved insufficient, set up a Term Auction Facility (TAF) to allow banks to access liquidity without the stigma of the discount window. Subsequently, the FRS went on to set up a variety of facilities that provided loans to banks and non-banks and to assist borrowing by issuing guarantees.[6] Instead of requiring treasuries or agency debt as collateral, a wide range of collateral was accepted. The Bank of England and the ECB took similar steps.

These were emergency measures, forced on policy makers by circumstances. In some cases, the policy makers were quite unwilling. Here, for example, are the views of the Governor of the Bank of England in a letter to the Chairman of the House of Commons Treasury Committee (King, 2007).

---

[6] The traditional facilities operated by the FRS include open market operations, the discount window and the securities lending programme. The new programmes included: the Term Discount Window Program (announced 17 August 2007); the Term Auction Facility (announced 12 December 2007); the Single-Tranche OMO (Open Market Operations) Program (announced 7 March 2008); the Term Securities Lending Facility (TSLF) (announced 11 March 2008); the Primary Dealer Credit Facility (PDCF) (announced 16 March 2008); the ABCP Money Market Fund Liquidity Facility (AMLF) (announced 19 September 2008); the Commercial Paper Funding Facility (CPFF) (announced 7 October 2008); the Money Market Investing Funding Facility (MMIFF) (announced 21 October 2008); and the Term Asset-Backed Securities Loan Facility (TALF) (announced 25 November 2008).

[T]he moral hazard inherent in the provision of ex post insurance to institutions that have engaged in risky or reckless lending is no abstract concept. The risks of the potential maturity transformation undertaken by off-balance sheet vehicles were not fully priced. The increase in maturity transformation implied by a change in the effective liquidity in the markets for asset-backed securities was identified as a risk by a wide range of official publications, including the Bank of England's Financial Stability Report, over several years. If central banks underwrite any maturity transformation that threatens to damage the economy as a whole, it encourages the view that as long as a bank takes the same sort of risks that other banks are taking then it is more likely that their liquidity problems will be insured ex post by the central bank. The provision of large liquidity facilities penalises those financial institutions that sat out the dance, encourages herd behaviour and increases the intensity of future crises.

By contrast, others claimed that providing liquidity is costless for the central bank – and only the central bank – and that liquidity should be provided on demand.

Liquidity is a public good. It can be managed privately (by hoarding inherently liquid assets), but it would be socially inefficient for private banks and other financial institutions to hold liquid assets on their balance sheets in amounts sufficient to tide them over when markets become disorderly. They are meant to intermediate short maturity liabilities into long maturity assets and (normally) liquid liabilities into illiquid assets. Since central banks can create unquestioned liquidity at the drop of a hat, in any amount and at zero cost, they should be the liquidity providers of last resort, both as lender of last resort and as market maker of last resort. There is no moral hazard as long as central banks provide the liquidity against properly priced collateral, which is in addition subject to the usual 'liquidity haircuts' on this fair valuation. The private provision of the public good of emergency liquidity is wasteful. It's as simple as that. (Willem Buiter, as quoted by Cao and Illing, 2010).

The problem of moral hazard as outlined by the Governor is a puzzling one. If King were referring to bailouts of insolvent banks, his concerns about moral hazard would be understandable. As Farhi and Tirole (2009) have shown, the possibility of a bailout does create moral hazard in the sense that banks will hold less liquidity if they anticipate a bailout and, given the government's inability to credibly commit to a 'tough' no-bailout policy, the bailout becomes a self-fulfilling prophecy.

Liquidity provision is another matter, however. What exactly is the cost of providing liquidity to the banks in question? Discussions in the media tend to leave the impression that any action by the central bank constitutes a 'bailout' involving enormous costs to taxpayers. It is an important and often overlooked question whether liquidity provision necessarily constitutes a 'bailout'. The conventional understanding of the lender-of-last-resort function of central banks makes a critical distinction between insolvent and illiquid banks. Only banks that are solvent are entitled to the services of the lender of last resort. In addition, Bagehot's rule allows lending only against good security and at a penalty rate. If the lender-of-last-resort function is interpreted narrowly, there would seem to be no scope for 'bailouts'. Prior to the collapse of Northern Rock, the Bank of England was willing to lend only against gilts. A bank that can put up riskless assets as collateral should not have any problem obtaining as much liquidity as it needs from the market. So it may be questioned whether at that point the Bank was supplementing market liquidity in any meaningful sense. Meanwhile, if the central bank is lending against the security of (somewhat) risky assets, there will be some states of nature in which it makes a loss. Of course, it is all a matter of degree. In circumstances where the market seems excessively or unreasonably risk averse, the central bank may feel that it is reasonable to adopt a more flexible definition of liquidity provision, as the various central banks did beginning in the autumn of 2007. The fact remains, however, that there is still a grey area where it is difficult to distinguish pure liquidity provision from the shadow of a bailout.

Cao and Illing (2010) describe a model in which the operation of the lender of last resort leads to real costs. In their model, banks engage in *real* maturity transformation, issuing short-term deposits in order to invest in assets that have a random payoff date. When output arrives late, there is not enough revenue to pay the claims of the depositors at the intermediate date. The central bank can provide liquidity that allows the banks to meet their nominal obligations, but the amount of goods available in the economy does not increase. Instead, the monetary injections cause inflation, which depreciates the real value of the depositors' nominal claims. So, although the banks avoid default, the loss is borne by the depositors. Anyone with the liquidity to purchase claims on the delayed production can make a profit. Ex post, there is no dead-weight loss from default, just a transfer from depositors to investors and entrepreneurs. The central bank's actions do distort the banks' decisions, however. Anticipating the central bank's liquidity provision in a crisis, the banks will engage in even more of this undesirable transformation. This moral hazard conforms fairly closely to the Governor's vision, but it does not correspond to the way that central banks actually responded to the financial crisis.

The liquidity facilities set up by the central banks allow banks to borrow reserves if they deposit adequate collateral. If the central bank is simply substituting one asset, either reserves or government debt, for another, it is not clear that any cost is imposed on the system. Some economists are concerned about the inflationary implications of expanding the central bank's balance sheet, but so far these fears have not been realised. In any case, new techniques of monetary policy, such as the payment of interest on reserves, are being used to sterilise the effects of these liquidity injections.

Nor does it appear (so far) that central banks have made significant losses on the massive amounts of ABS that were either purchased or accepted as collateral, but there must have been a state of nature in which the outcome could have been (will be?) different. If King's position seemed a trifle extreme, Buiter's may have erred in the other direction.

Of course, once the central bank is seen to make funding available in emergencies, it will encourage the banks to use short-term lending as a source of finance. If there are limits to the central bank's ability to provide liquidity, there may be a threat of dislocation in the financial system if these limits are breached. It is easy to see why a central banker might fear the practical difficulties of providing so much liquidity. But if there is an argument for limiting the extent of maturity transformation, it is probably best achieved through better liquidity regulation, either by setting explicit limits on the asset–liability maturity gap or by linking capital requirements to the asset–liability maturity gap.

4.3   Example

A simple example may make these distinctions clearer. As usual, we assume there are three dates, indexed by $t = 0, 1, 2$, with a single good that can be used for consumption or investment at each date. There are two assets: a short-term safe asset and a long-term risky asset. The short asset is represented by a storage technology: one unit of the good invested at date t yields one unit of the good at date $t + 1$. The long asset produces a random return of $\tilde{R}$ units of the good at date 2 for each unit of the good invested at date 0. We assume that

$$\tilde{R} = \begin{cases} R_H & \text{w. prob. } 1 - \varepsilon \\ R_L & \text{w. prob. } \varepsilon \end{cases}$$

where $R_H > R_L > 0$ and $0 < \varepsilon < 1$ are constants.

There are a large number of risk-averse consumers, each of whom has an endowment of one unit of the good at date 0 and values consumption at date 2 only. Their risk preferences are represented by a vNM utility function having the form $u(c) = \dfrac{1}{1 - \rho} c^{1-\rho}$, where $\tilde{\rho}$ is a random variable defined by

$$\tilde{\rho} = \begin{cases} \rho_H & \text{w. prob. } \delta \\ \rho_L & \text{w. prob. } 1 - \delta \end{cases}$$

where $\rho_H > \rho_L > 0$ and $0 < \delta < 1$. We assume that $\tilde{R}$ and $\tilde{\rho}$ are independent. The information structure is illustrated in Figure 2.1.

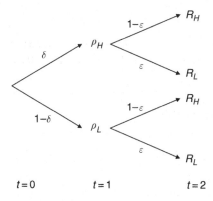

Figure 2.1 Uncertainty about asset returns and risk preferences

The planner's problem is to choose an amount y to invest in storage so as to maximise the expected utility of the typical consumer. The consumer's expected utility can be written as

$$\mathbf{E}\big[u\big(y + (1-y)\tilde{R}; \tilde{\rho}\big)\big] =$$
$$\delta\left\{\frac{1}{1-\rho_H}\Big((1-\varepsilon)(y + R_H(1-y))^{1-\rho_H} + \varepsilon(y + R_L(1-y))^{1-\rho_H}\Big)\right\} +$$
$$(1-\delta)\left\{\frac{1}{1-\rho_L}\Big((1-\varepsilon)(y + R_H(1-y))^{1-\rho_L} + \varepsilon(y + R_L(1-y))^{1-\rho_L}\Big)\right\}.$$

The question is: How can we implement this allocation if the banks use short-term finance, for example, issuing one-period bonds that have to be rolled over at the intermediate date? The problem is that, in the event that risk aversion is high at the intermediate date, it will be impossible to roll over the debt. More precisely, the maximum value of the debt that can be issued will be much less in the high-risk-aversion state than in the low-risk-aversion state.

Suppose that $R_H = 2$, $R_L = 0.5$, $\varepsilon = 0.01$, $\rho_L = 0$, $\rho_H = 20$ and $\delta = 0.01$. The planner's objective function achieves a maximum at $y = 0.22046$. If this allocation can be implemented then consumption will be

$$c_H = y + (1-y)R_H$$
$$= 1.7795$$

in the high-return state and

$$c_H = y + (1-y)R_L$$
$$= 0.61023$$

in the low-return state.

4.4   Asset pricing

The value of the risky asset at date 1 in the event that risk aversion is high will be given by the expected returns, using the usual stochastic discount factor:

$$\frac{(1-\varepsilon)c_H^{-\rho_H}R_H + \varepsilon c_L^{-\rho_H}R_L}{(1-\varepsilon)c_H^{-\rho_H} + \varepsilon c_L^{-\rho_H}} = 0.5,$$

so the total value of the portfolio will be

$$y + (1-y)0.5 = 0.61023.$$

When risk aversion is low, the value of the risky asset is

$$\frac{(1-\varepsilon)c_H^{-\rho_L}R_H + \varepsilon c_L^{-\rho_L}R_L}{(1-\varepsilon)c_H^{-\rho_L} + \varepsilon c_L^{-\rho_L}} = 1.985$$

and the value of the portfolio is

$$y + (1-y)1.985 = 1.7678.$$

At the initial date, it is necessary to issue debt with a high face value of 1.7678 in order to finance the investment in a portfolio consisting of 0.22046 units of the short asset and 0.77954 units of the long asset. But this will ensure a default in the bad state.

Decentralisation of this allocation presents a problem because, when risk aversion is very high, investors do not want to hold even slighty risky assets. What can the central bank do to implement the planner's problem? The central bank can accommodate the flight to quality by selling government bonds to individuals and lending the revenue directly to the banks. The banks are able to pay off their debts and the previous holders of the debt use this repayment to purchase government bonds from the central bank. In the final period, the banks will have to repay their loans to the central bank; or, the central bank will seize the collateral (claims on the output) put up by the banks. In the event that the returns are high, the banks can repay the central bank and the central bank can use this money to repurchase the government bonds. If the returns are low, however, the banks will be unable to repay their loans to the central bank and the government will be forced to bail out the banking system.

If investment in the risky asset is efficient, it seems that a government 'bailout', albeit with very small probability ($p = 0.001$), is necessary to implement the efficient allocation. There is another problem, however. The anticipation of a government 'bailout' will change the investment decision at date 0. Even though the occurrence of a low return in the high-risk-aversion state is very improbable, depending on the size of the haircut, the 'bailout' component of the central bank's liquidity facility may cause the risky asset to dominate the safe asset. For example, if the government guarantees the payoff to the risky asset is at least 0.65 in the bad state, the optimum for the planner's problem is $y = 0$. So the anticipated 'bailout' has the expected effect of increasing the size of the investment that must be bailed out.

4.5   Nominal and real liquidity

We have so far assumed that it makes no difference whether the central bank is providing real or nominal liquidity. If the central bank wants to maintain price stability, it may not matter much whether we model the provision of liquidity in real or monetary terms. The argument that liquidity is costless is based on the notion that the central bank can 'print money' and sooner or later this will produce inflation. Of course, the inflation tax is far from costless, although there are circumstances in which it will not have any distortionary effect. Allen et al. (2009) have investigated the role of the interbank market and central bank intervention in the bond market in achieving an efficient allocation of risk through the financial system. Allen et al. (2010) conduct a similar investigation in a monetary economy in which bank deposits are denominated in terms of money and the central bank can provide liquidity by printing money. In that case, it is possible to achieve the first best through changes in the price level that adjust the real value of deposits in response to real shocks.

We have also seen that excessive asset price volatility arises when markets are incomplete and that this volatility may be exacerbated by incomplete market participation. Whereas some authors (e.g. Taylor, 2009) have argued that loose monetary policy played a role in creating asset price bubbles, monetary policy may have a more beneficial role in preventing fire sales.

There is also an efficiency question lurking behind the moral hazard argument. Is it more efficient to use longer-term finance if it is more expensive? Suppose that banks have two sources of funds, one long-term and expensive, the other short-term and cheap. If the rollover of debt at the same rate of interest is assured, the bank will prefer to use short-term debt. The fact that the two sources of funds both exist suggests that there is some difference between them. Either the interest rate at which the debt can be rolled over is uncertain or the possibility of rolling over the debt is uncertain. If the probability of rolling over the short-term debt and making a profit is sufficiently high, the bank may prefer to choose short-term funding even though it involves some rollover risk. Whether it is more efficient to limit the use of short-term finance in this case requires a cost–benefit analysis that, so far, has not been carried out.

5   The parallel banking system

The universal banks that now dominate the financial systems of the US and the UK are the product of centuries of innovation and evolution. There may have been a reason for combining these disparate activities at one time, but their survival in this form may have more to do with regulation and market power than with efficiency. If we were to invent banks today, starting from scratch, it is unlikely that we would choose to combine the variety of activities that we see in banks today.

Universal banks of the size and scope of Citigroup or J.P. Morgan Chase pose a number of problems for the regulator and the economy. First, their size makes them too big to fail (TBTF) and, hence, subject to moral hazard. Second, they are opaque, which makes them difficult to regulate and difficult for the market to value. Finally, their complexity and size make them potential sources of contagion. This may occur internally, when losses in one activity threaten the rest of the bank, or externally, when the failure of a large bank threatens its counterparties. Complexity also makes the resolution of failed banks difficult and exacerbates the TBTF problem.

For all of these reasons, we would be better off without such gargantuan banks (there is little evidence of economies of scale in banking, even at sizes much smaller than these behemoths). The banks that replace them should be narrower as well as smaller. What follows is a bald summary of a proposal by founders of Gordian Knot for a new model of narrow banking.

5.1   The Gordian Knot proposal

In 1993, Nicholas Sossidis and Stephen Partridge-Hicks left Citigroup (where they had invented the first SIV) and founded Gordian Knot, an investment management company. In 1995, Gordian Knot set up the Sigma Finance Corporation, a limited-purpose finance company (LPFC) that grew to hold $57 billion in assets financed by capital of $4 billion and a mixture of commercial paper, medium-term notes, bonds and repos. Sigma was notable for holding high-quality assets and making use of a sophisticated capital structure for risk and liquidity management. The capital requirements varied with the credit risk of the assets in the portfolio, but they also varied with measures of illiquidity, such as asset–liability maturity gap. In this respect, they were ahead of the Basel committee.

Although Sigma did not survive the crisis, its performance was better than that of SIVs, especially the poorly structured ones set up in the years immediately preceding the crisis.[7]

Despite the problems caused by the sub-prime crisis, the securitisation model has proved itself to be an efficient and stable technology for sharing risk and expanding access to credit. A functioning securitisation market is essential to restore the capacity of the financial system to provide credit for business. The PBS needs to be rebuilt, but it needs to be a different kind of banking system, one based on LPFCs performing the function of a financial utility warehousing high-quality assets rather than a hedge fund or SIV taking large risks in pursuit of high rates of return on equity.

Why are such utility banks needed? Since the early 1990s, banks have earned much higher rates of return on equity (ROE) than the traditional utility bank could achieve. They have done so by taking on much higher leverage, by engaging in proprietary trading and by securitising loans in order to increase the velocity of capital. The increasing complexity of banks has added to their opacity. Capital is expensive for banks because of the combination of risk and opacity. There is a need for narrow banks to provide a lower but safer return from a more transparent business model. These narrow banks are also essential for the functioning of the casino-like universal banks because they provide a demand for high-quality assets that do not require the expertise or expensive capital that universal banks can provide. By offloading high-quality assets to the PBS, universal banks can hold high-risk, high-return and opaque assets and concentrate on information-intensive activities such as origination and securitisation. In the financial ecosystem, narrow banks are somewhere between money market funds on the one hand and traditional banks and investment banks (or universal banks) on the other.

Another reason for wanting to revive the PBS is to allow the central banks to exit from their current role as providers of liquidity directly to banks and market participants. In the last few years, the FRS has instituted a number of facilities to supplement the ABCP market and other sources of liquidity. Most of these lending facilities involve collateral in the form of securities. The danger of providing these services in the longer run is that it will undermine the private sector's provision of credit. What would be lost is the private sector's presumably superior ability to assess and price risk. As Goodfriend and King (1988) persuasively argued, the Fed does not have a comparative advantage in providing credit except to the extent that its control of the money supply makes it easy to obtain loanable funds.

---

[7] This section is based on a presentation by Sossidis and Partridge-Hicks to the Liquidity Working Group at the Federal Reserve Bank of New York on 9 October 2009 (Gordian Knot, 2009).

This suggests that the efficiency of the financial system requires the Fed to find an exit from its current role and that requires a reinvigorated PBS.

The basic building block of the PBS is a narrow bank (LPFC) that holds securities originated by traditional banks and finances them with a combination of capital (equity) and short- and medium-term financing from MMFs, securities lenders, pension and insurance companies, and underexposed banks. The requirements to be a narrow bank are those of a utility company:

- The target returns to capital providers will be low, but stable.
- The activities that the narrow bank can engage in (e.g. the type of securities held) must be fully defined by a charter that is transparent to capital and debt investors and to regulators.
- The capital structure must be responsive to (i) the credit quality of the portfolio; (ii) the maturity of the assets; (iii) the diversification of the portfolio; and (iv) the asset–liability maturity gap. For example, the capital requirements could be based on a Basel-type formula that incorporates measures of credit quality, maturity, diversification and asset–liability gap.
- No off-balance-sheet exposures or contingent risk exposures would be allowed.
- There would be no proprietary trading and most assets would be held to maturity.
- Interest rate and currency exposure would be fully hedged.
- Risk management would be consistent with 'best practice'; in particular, asset quality evaluation would be based on in-house research and would not rely on rating agencies.
- Most importantly, the narrow bank would be regulated by the FRS and would have access to central bank liquidity facilities.

Many of the features of the narrow bank described above are intended to increase stability, but they would also make regulation easier. The fact that the narrow bank does not engage in proprietary trading, does not have complex exposures to counterparties and has a relatively homogeneous and time-invariant portfolio increases transparency. These features are essential to attracting low-cost capital and low-cost and stable funding. It also makes the regulator's job easier because it is possible to distinguish liquidity needs from insolvency.

The key ingredient in this proposal is the highlighted requirement for access to liquidity from the FRS. The extension of liquidity to institutions that are not traditionally recognised as banks will be resisted by many who see any lending, even as a last resort, as a 'bailout'. To the extent that the Fed is accepting risky collateral, it may incur losses in the future; however, to the extent that the Fed is responding to a liquidity crisis and accepts only 'good security', in Bagehot's phrase, the extension of liquidity may be costless or even profitable. If the Fed's intervention is successful and profitable, it may become acceptable to have the monetary authorities providing such facilities on a wider basis, but only as a last resort.

6   Conclusion

The objective of financial regulation should be the growth and stability of a *transparent, efficient* and *innovative* financial system. Recent attempts at 'reform' of financial regulation, such as the Restoring American Financial Stability Act of 2010 (RAFSA), appear to have been hijacked by politicians who had other goals in mind. There have been some minor technical improvements, such as the mandatory use of central clearing platforms for derivatives, but rather than creating a new financial order, the legislation has left the old order largely intact and, in some respects, has reinforced it. Proposals to 'bring back Glass–Steagall' have been watered down and the TBTF institutions, far from being broken up, have been officially sanctioned and promised bailouts in the legislation itself. There remains some hope that the regulators themselves will succeed where the politicians failed, since it is the regulators who will draft the detailed rules governing the financial system and they have considerable latitude since the enabling legislation has little detail.

What, then, should be done? We have seen that, as long as markets are incomplete, private provision of liquidity is not optimal and failure of financial institutions may result in welfare-reducing pecuniary externalities. Theory does not tell us what to do, but it suggests margins along which some regulation may be necessary. What the specific ideas discussed in Section 3 have in common is the *pricing* of illiquidity so that institutions internalise the value of liquidity to the rest of the financial system. In addition, the structural changes entailed by a move to narrow banking, by making banks simpler and more transparent, will make it more likely that regulators have a beneficial effect on the performance of the financial system if and when they choose to intervene. The ideas discussed in this chapter fall short of a blueprint for the future of liquidity regulation, but perhaps they suggest that we can do better than the RAFSA.

Appendix

In this appendix we analyse in more detail the example introduced in Section 3. Recall the crucial assumptions:

$$u_1(c) = c \text{ and } \lambda_1(s) = 0 \text{ for } s = 1, 2;$$

$$u_2(c) = \frac{1}{1-\rho} c^{1-\rho} \text{ and } 0 < \lambda_2(1) < \lambda_2(2) < 1, \text{ where } \rho > 1.$$

A.1   The optimal contract at dates 1 and 2

First, we characterise the optimal contract for type-2 intermediaries at
dates 1 and 2, taking as given the portfolio $(y_{20}, 1 - y_{20})$ chosen at date 0.
Each state $s = 1, 2$ can be considered separately so, for simplicity, we drop
the subscripts and write λ for $\lambda_2(s)$, (x_1, x_2) for $(x_{21}(s), x_{22}(s))$ and q for
$q(s)$. Then consider the problem

$$\max \quad \lambda \frac{1}{1-\rho} x_1^{1-\rho} + (1 - \lambda) \frac{1}{1-\rho} x_2^{1-\rho}$$

$$\text{s.t.} \quad \lambda x_1 + (1 - \lambda) \frac{q}{R} x_2 = w \equiv y + q(1 - y).$$

The first-order condition for a maximum is

$$x_1^{-\rho} = \frac{R}{q} x_2^{-\rho} \Leftrightarrow \left(\frac{R}{q} \right)^{\frac{1}{\rho}} x_1 = x_2.$$

Substituting into the budget constraint gives

$$\lambda x_1 + (1 - \lambda) \frac{q}{R} \left(\frac{R}{q} \right)^{\frac{1}{\rho}} x_1 = w,$$

which can be rewritten as

$$x_1 = \frac{w}{\lambda + (1 - \lambda) \left(\frac{q}{R} \right)^{1 - \frac{1}{\rho}}}.$$

Then the maximum indirect utility is given by

$$V = \lambda \frac{1}{1-\rho} \left(\frac{w}{\lambda + (1 - \lambda) \left(\frac{q}{R} \right)^{1 - \frac{1}{\rho}}} \right)^{1-\rho} + (1 - \lambda) \frac{1}{1-\rho} \left(\frac{w \left(\frac{R}{q} \right)^{\frac{1}{\rho}}}{\lambda + (1 - \lambda) \left(\frac{q}{R} \right)^{1 - \frac{1}{\rho}}} \right)^{1-\rho}$$

$$= \frac{1}{1-\rho} \left(\lambda + (1 - \lambda) \left(\frac{R}{q} \right)^{\frac{1}{\rho} - 1} \right) \left(\frac{w}{\lambda + (1 - \lambda) \left(\frac{q}{R} \right)^{1 - \frac{1}{\rho}}} \right)^{1-\rho}$$

$$= \frac{1}{1-\rho} \left(\lambda + (1 - \lambda) \left(\frac{R}{q} \right)^{\frac{1-\rho}{\rho}} \right)^{\rho} w^{1-\rho}.$$

Now consider the two states $s = 1, 2$ with state-dependent prices $q(s)$ and parameters $\lambda(s)$. The first-period maximisation problem is to choose y to maximise

$$\sum_{s=1,2} \frac{\pi(s)}{1-\rho} \left(\lambda(s) + (1 - \lambda(s)) \left(\frac{R}{q(s)} \right)^{\frac{1-\rho}{\rho}} \right)^{\rho} (y + q(s)(1-y))^{1-\rho}.$$

The first-order condition is

$$\sum_{s=1,2} \pi(s) \left(\lambda(s) + (1 - \lambda(s)) \left(\frac{R}{q(s)} \right)^{\frac{1-\rho}{\rho}} \right)^{\rho} \times$$

$$(y + q(s)(1-y))^{-\rho}(1 - q(s)) = 0$$

$$\sum_{s=1,2} \pi(s) \left(\frac{\lambda(s) + (1 - \lambda(s)) \left(\frac{R}{q(s)} \right)^{\frac{1-\rho}{\rho}}}{y + q(s)(1-y)} \right)^{\rho} (1 - q(s)) = 0.$$

There are three types of equilibrium, depending on the interaction between the two types of intermediaries.

A.2   No-trade equilibrium

The first kind of equilibrium we consider is one in which the type-1 (risk-neutral) intermediaries do not invest in the short asset and hence cannot provide liquidity to the type-2 (risk-averse) intermediaries. This will be the case if the equilibrium prices satisfy

$$\sum_{s=1,2} \frac{\pi(s)}{q(s)} < 1.$$

In that case, the type-2 intermediaries are self-sufficient and equilibrium contract x_2 is defined by

$$x_{21}(s) = \min\left\{ \frac{y_{20}}{\lambda_2(s)}, y_{20} + R(1 - y_{20}) \right\}$$

$$x_{22}(s) = \max\left\{ \frac{(1 - y_{20})R}{1 - \lambda_2(s)}, y_{20} + R(1 - y_{20}) \right\}.$$

The equilibrium asset prices are set by the first-order conditions

$$x_{21}(s)^{-\rho} = \frac{R}{q(s)} (x_{22}(s))^{-\rho}$$

for $s = 1, 2$.

In this case, equilibrium is (locally) constrained efficient. There is no way that both types of consumers can be made better off through intervention at date 0. Forcing the risk-neutral intermediaries to hold the short asset will make them worse off; if the risk-averse intermediaries would be better off holding more of the short asset, they would have done so already.

A.3   Interior equilibrium

Next we consider an equilibrium in which there is trade in both states. This occurs if $q(s) < R$ for $s = 1, 2$ and there is no storage between the two dates. The risk-neutral intermediaries exchange their holding of the good y_{10} for the long asset at date 0 in both states and the risk-averse intermediaries sell the long asset to purchase goods in both states. To satisfy the optimality conditions for a risk-neutral investor holding both assets, we must have

$$\sum_{s=1,2} \frac{\pi(s)}{q(s)} = 1.$$

The market clearing requires that

$$y_{20} - \lambda_2(s) x_{21}(s) = y_{10}$$

for $s = 1, 2$ and this can be reduced to

$$\frac{\lambda_2(1)(y_{20} + q(1)(1 - y_{20}))}{\lambda_2(1) + (1 - \lambda_2(1))\left(\frac{q(1)}{R}\right)^{1-\frac{1}{\rho}}} = \frac{\lambda_2(2)(y_{20} + q(2)(1 - y_{20}))}{\lambda_2(2) + (1 - \lambda_2(2))\left(\frac{q(2)}{R}\right)^{1-\frac{1}{\rho}}}$$

for $s = 1, 2$. Substituting this in the first-order condition,

$$\sum_{s=1,2} \pi(s) \left(\frac{k}{\lambda_2(s)}\right)^{\rho} (1 - q(s)) = 0,$$

where

$$k = \frac{\lambda_2(s) + (1 - \lambda_2(s))\left(\frac{q(s)}{R}\right)^{1-\frac{1}{\rho}}}{\lambda_2(s)(y_{20} + q(s)(1 - y_{20}))}$$

for $s = 1, 2$. The constant k can be eliminated from the first-order condition to give

$$\sum_{s=1,2} \pi(s)\lambda_2(s)^{-\rho}(1 - q(s)) = 0.$$

Thus, we have two equations in two prices.

The no-arbitrage condition can be written as

$$\frac{\pi(1)}{q(1)} + \frac{\pi(2)}{q(2)} = 1 = \pi(1) + \pi(2),$$

which can be rearranged to give

$$\pi(1)\left(\frac{1 - q(1)}{q(1)}\right) = -\pi(2)\left(\frac{1 - q(2)}{q(2)}\right),$$

and the first-order condition can be written as

$$\pi(1)\lambda_2^{-\rho}(1)(1 - q(1)) = -\pi(2)\lambda_2(2)^{-\rho}(1 - q(2)).$$

Dividing the two equations gives

$$\frac{\lambda(1)^{-\rho}}{q(1)} = \frac{\lambda(2)^{-\rho}}{q(2)} \quad \text{or} \quad \frac{q(2)}{q(1)} = \left(\frac{\lambda(1)}{\lambda(2)}\right)^{\rho}$$

so that

$$\log\left(\frac{q(2)}{q(1)}\right) = \rho \log\left(\frac{\lambda(1)}{\lambda(2)}\right).$$

This gives Proposition 5.

Proposition 6
Consider an economy in which $u_1(c) = c, u_2(c) = \frac{1}{1-\rho}c^{1-\rho}, \lambda_1(s) = 0$ for $s = 1, 2$ and $0 < \lambda_2(s) < 1$ for $s = 1, 2$. Let $(\mathbf{x}_1, \mathbf{y}_1, \mathbf{x}_2, \mathbf{y}_2, \mathbf{q})$ be an equilibrium and suppose that $q(s) < R$ for $s = 1, 2$ and $y_{10} > 0$. Then

$$\log\left(\frac{q(2)}{q(1)}\right) = \rho \log\left(\frac{\lambda(1)}{\lambda(2)}\right).$$

Note that there is a second solution to the pair of equations above, namely $\mathbf{q} = (1, 1)$, but this implies that $x_{11}(s)$ is independent of s and that in turn contradicts the market-clearing conditions $\lambda_1(s)x_{11}(s) = y_{10} + y_{20}$.

What happens if we increase y? To achieve an increase in welfare, we need the asset price to rise in the low state and fall in the high state. This is a necessary, not sufficient, condition, of course.

A.4   Boundary equilibrium

Finally, we have the boundary case where the high price is equal to its maximum, R, in the high state and there is storage of the good in the high state. The prices must satisfy the condition

$$\frac{\pi(1)}{R} + \frac{\pi(2)}{q(2)} = 1,$$

which implies that

$$q(2) = \pi(2)\left(\frac{R}{R - \pi(1)}\right)$$

is uniquely determined independently of other endogenous variables. With this constraint, the decision of the risk-averse types determines the equilibrium values of the other endogenous variables, via the maximisation of the objective function

$$\frac{\pi(1)}{1-\rho}(y + R(1-y))^{1-\rho} +$$

$$\frac{\pi(2)}{1-\rho}\left(\lambda(2) + (1 - \lambda(2))\left(\frac{R - \pi(1)}{\pi(2)}\right)^{\frac{1-\rho}{\rho}}\right)^{\rho}\left(y + \pi(2)\left(\frac{R}{R - \pi(1)}\right)(1-y)\right)^{1-\rho}.$$

In this case, the equilibrium prices are determined by the no-arbitrage condition of the risk-neutral types. A regulation that forces the risk-averse intermediaries to hold a large amount of the short asset will have no effect on prices. In fact, it will simply cause the risk-neutral intermediaries to hold less of the short asset, with the result that nothing essential changes in equilibrium. Of course, if this policy is pushed far enough, the risk-neutral intermediaries will not need to hold any of the short asset, the no-arbitrage condition will not be satisfied and then we will be in a no-trade equilibrium. The conclusion that welfare cannot be improved will still hold, of course.

References

Acharya, V., Gale, D. and Yorulmazer, T. (2010) Rollover risk and market freezes, New York University, unpublished.

Allen, F. and Gale, D. (2004) Financial intermediaries and markets, *Econometrica*, 72(4), 1023–61.

(1998) Optimal financial crises, *Journal of Finance*, 53, 1245–84.

(1994) Liquidity preference, market participation and asset price volatility, *American Economic Review*, 84, 933–55.

Allen, F., Carletti, E. and Gale, D. (2010) Money, financial stability and efficiency, Florence: European University Institute, unpublished.

(2009) Interbank market liquidity and central bank intervention, *Journal of Monetary Economics*, 56, 639–52.

Arthur, B., Durlauf, S. and Lane, D. (eds.) (1997) *The Economy as an Evolving Complex System II*, SFI Studies in the Sciences of Complexity, Vol. XXVII, New York: Addison-Wesley.

Bryant, J. (1980) A model of reserves, bank runs, and deposit insurance, *Journal of Banking and Finance*, 4, 335–44.

Cao, J. and Illing, G. (2010) Endogenous systemic liquidity risk? University of Munich, unpublished.

Cohan, W. D. (2009) *House of Cards: A Tale of Hubris and Wretched Excess on Wall Street*, New York: Knopf Doubleday.

Cone, K. (1983) Regulation of depository institutions, Stanford University PhD. dissertation.

Cornett, M., McNutt, J., Strahan, P. and Tehranian, H. (2010) Liquidity risk management and credit supply in the financial crisis, Boston College, unpublished.

Diamond, D. and Dybvig, P. (1983) Bank runs, liquidity, and deposit insurance, *Journal of Political Economy*, 91, 401–19.

Farhi, E. and Tirole, J. (2009) Collective moral hazard, maturity mismatch and systemic bailouts, Fondazione Eni Enrico Mattei Working Paper 318, Rome.

Fostel, A. and Geanakoplos, J. (2008) Leverage cycles and the anxious economy, *American Economic Review*, 98, 1211–44.

Geanakoplos, J. (2009) The leverage cycle, Cowles Foundation Discussion Papers, Rome.

(1997) Promises, promises, in Arthur, B., Durlauf, S. and Lane, D. (eds.) *The Economy as an Evolving Complex System II*, SFI Studies in the Sciences of Complexity, Vol. XXVII, New York: Addison-Wesley, 285–320.

Geanakoplos, J. and Polemarchakis, H. (1986) Existence, regularity, and constrained suboptimality of competitive allocations when the asset market is incomplete, in Heller, W., Starr, R. and Starrett, D. (eds.) *Essays in Honor of Kenneth J. Arrow: Volume 3, Uncertainty, Information, and Communication*, Cambridge University Press, 65–95.

Goldsmith-Pinkham, P. and Yorulmazer, T. (2010) Liquidity, bank runs and bailouts: spillover effects during the Northern Rock episode, *Journal of Financial Services Research*, 37(2–3), 83–98.

Goodfriend, M. and King, R. (1988) Financial regulation, monetary policy and central banking, *Federal Reserve Bank of Richmond Economic Review*, May/June, 3–22.

Goodhart, C. (2008) Liquidity risk management, *Banque de France Financial Stability Review – Special Issue on Liquidity*, 11, 39–44.

Gordian Knot (2009) Levered ABS investors, Presentation to Liquidity Working Group, Federal Reserve Bank of New York, 9 October.

Gorton, G. (2010) *Slapped by the Invisible Hand: The Crisis of 2007*, Oxford University Press.

Gorton, G. and Pennacchi, G. (1990) Financial intermediaries and liquidity creation, *Journal of Finance*, 45, 49–72.

He, Z., Khang, I. and Krishnamurthy, A. (2010) Balance sheet adjustment during the 2008 crisis, NBER Working Paper No. 15919, Evanston, IL: Northwestern University.

(2010) Dynamic bank runs, Princeton University, unpublished.

He, Z. and Xiong, W. (2009) Rollover risk and credit risk, NBER Working Paper No. 15653.

Heller, W., Starr, R. and Starrett, D. (eds.) (1986) *Essays in Honor of Kenneth J. Arrow: Volume 3, Uncertainty, Information, and Communication*, Cambridge University Press.

Jacklin, C. (1986) Demand deposits, trading restrictions, and risk sharing, in Prescott, E. and Wallace, N. (eds.) *Contractual Arrangements for Intertemporal Trade*, University of Minnesota Press.

King, M. (2007) Letter of the Governor of the Bank of England to the Rt Hon John McFall MP, 12 September.

Prescott, E. and Townsend, R. (1984) Pareto optima and competitive equilibria with adverse selection and moral hazard, *Econometrica*, 52, 21–45.

Taylor, J. (2009) *Getting Off Track: How Government Actions and Interventions Caused, Prolonged, and Worsened the Financial Crisis*, Stanford, CA: Hoover Institution Press.

3 Interest rate policies and stability of banking systems

Hans Gersbach and Jan Wenzelburger

1 Introduction

The frequency of severe banking crisis has increased significantly over the last few decades, with the current global crisis likely to be the most costly so far. A banking crisis occurs when a large number of banks fail to meet regulatory capital requirements, are illiquid, or even insolvent. There are at least four empirical facts concerning banking crises which are important from a macroeconomic perspective.

First, banking crises are most often caused by economic downturns. In differentiating between the sunspot view and the business cycle view of banking crises, Gorton (1988) shows in a seminal empirical investigation that bank panics are systematically linked to business cycles. Subsequent work by Demirgüç-Kunt and Detragiache (1998), González-Hermosillo et al. (1997) and Kaminsky and Reinhart (1999) identify a number of factors causing financial fragilities which may ultimately lead to a systemic banking crisis. These results suggest that banking crises tend to occur when the macroeconomic environment is weak, particularly when output growth is low.

Second, the literature provides ample evidence that the costs of banking crises in terms of GDP losses may become very large, even if banks are allowed to continue to operate (e.g. see Caprio and Honohan (1999), Caprio and Klingebiel (1997), Lindren et al. (1996), or Peter (1999)). Further negative real output effects of banking crises beyond economic downturns have been identified in Dell'Arriccia et al. (2008).

Third, many contributions (e.g. see Dekle and Kletzer (2003) and Hoshi and Kashyap (2004)) suggest that the persistent weakness of the

An earlier version of this chapter was entitled 'The dynamics of deposit insurance and the consumption trap' and has been published as CESifo Discussion Paper No. 509, 2001. We would like to thank Volker Böhm, Jagjit Chadha, Domenico Delli Gatti, Ulrich Erlenmaier, Jean-Charles Rochet, Gilles Saint-Paul, Oz Shy, Lars Siemers, Peter Sinclair, Rune Stenbacka, Eva Terberger-Stoy, Jean Tirole, Anne Villamil and participants of seminars in Bielefeld, Heidelberg, Helsinki, Milan and Toulouse, of the CESifo conference in Munich 2001 and of the CIMF/MMF conference in Cambridge 2010.

Japanese banking sector has been responsible for Japan's long-lasting recession after 1990. According to Dekle and Kletzer (2003), four important characteristics are held responsible for this dismal development: the predominance of commercial bank intermediation characterising Japan as a bank-centred financial system; the prospect of deposit insurance implicitly guaranteed by the government; regulatory forbearance that allowed banks to operate without fulfilling regulatory requirements; and the low profitability of the Japanese banking sector for more than ten years.

Finally, some countries have responded to banking crises and the associated economic downturns by lowering short-term interest rates. This has long been advocated by Hellman et al. (2000), Krugman (1998) and many others. Indeed, the US Federal Reserve Bank, the Bank of England and the European Central Bank have responded to the recent sub-prime crisis by lowering short-term interest rates. The Bank of Japan lowered nominal interest rates quite drastically in the 1990s, which led to gradual reduction of the real interest rate, cf. Hoshi and Kashyap (2004). The nominal short-term interest rate reached virtually zero in February 1999 and remained close to zero for many years except for a brief period. Real interest rates, which were high in the first half of the 1990s, declined and fluctuated between zero and two per cent in the second half of the decade.

The empirical findings motivate this chapter, in which we develop a dynamic macroeconomic model with financial intermediation. This model allows us to investigate the interdependence between banking competition, financial stability and a central bank's interest policy. It complements earlier business cycle models with financial intermediation, e.g. contributions of Boyd and Prescott (1986) and Williamson (1987) or more recent approaches by Schreft and Smith (1997) and Uhlig (1995).

We consider an overlapping generations (OLG) model in which each generation consists of two types of agents – consumers and entrepreneurs – who live for two periods. In each period, the output of entrepreneurs is subject to an exogenous macroeconomic productivity shock. Entrepreneurs are financed by banks which offer deposit and loan contracts. Banks are delegated monitors in the sense of Diamond (1984), that is, they monitor borrowers and alleviate the moral hazard problems of entrepreneurs. According to Hellwig (1994), alleviating such agency problems constitutes a major market friction that necessitates financial intermediation, and this is a core activity of commercial banks which dominate in countries such as Japan. In accordance with current practice, we assume that deposit contracts are implicitly insured by the government and, following Hellwig (1998), that deposit contracts cannot be conditioned on macroeconomic events. Furthermore, we assume that depositors believe that deposits are implicitly guaranteed by the government. Banks face double-sided Bertrand competition capturing a situation in which the profitability of a banking industry is low. There is regulatory forbearance that allows banks to operate without fulfilling capital requirements. The central bank may cut interest rates, thereby lowering deposit rates, which, in turn, increases the intermediation margin and fosters the recapitalisation of banks.

Two key notions are of central importance for the model of this chapter: banking crisis and banking collapse. A state of the economy will be called a *banking crisis* when the capital basis of the banking system is below some well-specified regulatory level. In such a state banks can continue to operate as their capital basis is still positive and they have enough funds to pay back depositors. A state of the economy in which banks are unable to pay back depositors is called *banking collapse*. We choose an OLG economy as a convenient setting in which deposit withdrawals to finance old-age consumption occur naturally, allowing the investigation of the effects of a banking crisis and interest rate policies on later generations.

This chapter contains three main results. First, without interest rate cutting, the banking system faces the risk of collapsing. This risk is caused by the asymmetric impact of unobservable macroeconomic shocks on bank capital and the inability of the banking system to accommodate credit losses. Adverse shocks may cause a decline in the repayment capacity of entrepreneurs and incur credit losses for banks. These may increase over time in such a way that a banking collapse becomes inevitable, as banks are unable to recapitalise sufficiently with positive macroeconomic shocks.

Second, we establish conditions under which a banking crisis can be resolved by cutting interest rates. Such cuts may recapitalise the banking system as they lower refinancing costs of banks, increase intermediation margins and therefore increase banks' profits.[1]

Third, even with the most drastic interest rate policy which is obtained by setting interest rates to zero, an economy with a banking crisis may experience a long-lasting recession. As a large share of new funds from the young generation must be used to fulfil old liabilities, aggregate investment and hence aggregate income in subsequent periods will be suppressed. The banking system can recover from the crisis only gradually because its earnings are low. As a consequence, the economy may remain in a state of low aggregate income for many periods. We identify a critical level of bank capital below which the lowering of deposit interest rates by the central bank is necessary to ensure that no banking crisis

---

[1] We do not consider banking crises caused by panic deposit withdrawals. In such circumstances, interest rate cuts alone cannot prevent a banking collapse.

occurs. This level of bank capital is determined by the fundamentals of the economy and might serve as a guideline for determining bank capital requirements.

Overall, our results may help to explain why banking systems with characteristics similar to those of the Japanese system might exhibit persistent weakness and to what extent interest rate policies are capable of resolving banking crises. So far the issue of banking crises in the presence of repeated macroeconomic productivity shocks has received relatively little attention in the literature. One important contribution is that of Blum and Hellwig (1995), who show that strict capital adequacy rules may reinforce macroeconomic fluctuations. Our analysis suggests that capital requirements can serve as an indicator of when to intervene with measures that promote recapitalisation of banks.

There is a large microeconomic literature on bank runs building on the seminal contributions of Allen and Gale (1998, 2004) and Diamond and Dybvig (1984). It is therefore important to emphasise that banking crises in our model are not triggered by bank runs as, for example, in Ennis and Keister (2003). While bank runs may explain banking crises such as the one in Argentina in 2000, the banking crisis in Japan in the 1990s as well as the current global banking crisis cannot be attributed to bank runs and for this reason require a different explanation. In our model, bank runs cannot occur, since informational externalities are absent and deposit contracts last for one period only so that there is no uncertainty about deposit withdrawals.

The chapter is organised as follows. After the introduction of our model in Section 2, Section 3 treats the evolution of the banking system. We discuss measures to avoid a banking collapse in Section 4 and focus on the consumption trap in Section 5. Feasible policy measures that resolve and prevent banking crises are discussed in Section 6. Alternative forms of interventions are discussed in the concluding Section 7. All technical proofs are found in the appendices. Appendix C contains an analytically tractable example.

2   Model

2.1   Entrepreneurs and depositors

Consider an overlapping generations model with one physical good that can be used for consumption or investment. The OLG structure can also be viewed as an economy in which agents with infinitely long lives optimise myopically.

Time is infinite in the forward direction and divided into discrete periods indexed by t. Each generation consists of a continuum of agents with two-period lives, indexed by [0, 1]. Each agent of each generation receives an endowment e of goods when young and none when old. The endowment may be thought of as being obtained from short-term production with inelastically supplied labour. Generations are divided into two classes. One fraction of agents, indexed by [0, η], are potential entrepreneurs. The other fraction, indexed by (η, 1], are consumers. Potential entrepreneurs and consumers differ in that only the former have access to investment technologies.

Consumers are endowed with intertemporal preferences over consumption, with c_t^1, c_t^2 denoting youthful and old-age consumption of a typical consumer born in period t, respectively. For simplification, let $u(c_t^1, c_t^2) = \ln(c_t^1) + \delta \ln(c_t^2)$ be the intertemporal utility function of a consumer, where $\delta (0 < \delta < 1)$ is the discount factor. Each young consumer is a depositor at commercial banks. If a consumer faces a particular deposit rate and assumes that deposits including interest rates will be paid with certainty, the well-known solution of the consumer's intertemporal optimisation problem yields inelastic savings: $s = \frac{\delta e}{1+\delta}$. Aggregate savings of the consumer sector is $S = (1 - \eta)s$.

Potential entrepreneurs are assumed to be risk-neutral and consume only when old. Each entrepreneur has to decide whether to save their endowment or to invest in a production project that converts period-t goods into period-$t + 1$ goods. The funds required for each investment project are fixed to $e + I$ so that an entrepreneur must borrow I additional units of the good from banks to undertake the investment project. Entrepreneurs are heterogeneous in the quality of their investment projects, which depends on their index $i \in [0, \eta]$. The quality parameter of entrepreneur i is assumed to be private information. If entrepreneur i obtains additional resources I and decides to invest, their output y_i in the next period is determined by

$$y_i = q(1 + i)f(e + I).$$

Here f denotes a standard atemporal neoclassical production function and the parameter $q \geq 0$ describes the unobservable macroeconomic shock which affects the productivity of each entrepreneur and thus causes fluctuations of aggregate output.

The depositors of the economy in an arbitrary period t consist of all consumers and those entrepreneurs who save; its borrowers consist of entrepreneurs who invest. In an OLG economy, deposit withdrawals of the old generation occur naturally to finance old-age consumption and banks may use new funds from a young generation of depositors to balance old liabilities. Banks in an OLG economy may thus continue to operate even when their equity is negative.

2.2   Banking sector

As depositors cannot observe the quality parameters of entrepreneurs and cannot verify whether or not an entrepreneur invests, our economy faces market frictions that according to Hellwig (1994) necessitate financial intermediation. To alleviate these market frictions, we assume that there are $n > 1$ (commercial) banks, indexed by $j = 1, \ldots, n$. Banks finance investment projects as delegated monitors in the sense of Diamond (1984) as they ensure that entrepreneurs invest and as they secure repayments which in case of a default is the liquidation value of an investment project. For simplicity, monitoring is assumed to be costless.[2] Banks maximise profits accruing to current shareholders which are the old entrepreneurs. Bank ownership is transferred to the next generation of entrepreneurs through bequests.[3] The interaction between depositors, entrepreneurs and banks within a typical period t is depicted in Figure 3.1.

In each period, a (financial) intermediation game takes place in the form of a *double-sided Bertrand competition* between banks which offer deposit and loan contracts. Each bank j can sign deposit contracts $D(r_j^d)$, where $1 + r_j^d$ is the repayment offered for 1 unit of resources. Loan contracts of bank j are denoted by $C(r_j^c)$, where $1 + r_j^c$ is the repayment required from entrepreneurs for 1 unit of funds. All deposits and loan contracts last for one period. The balance sheet of a bank at the beginning of a typical period consists of liabilities in the form of deposits, assets in the form of loan repayments, and bank capital.

Entrepreneurs are contract takers operating under limited liability. Given a loan interest rate r^c, the expected profit of an entrepreneur i investing is

$$\Pi(i, r^c) := \int_{\mathbb{R}_+} \max\{q(1 + i)f(e + I) - I(1 + r^c), 0\}h(q)\mathrm{d}q,$$

where $h(q)$ denotes the probability density function describing the distribution of the unobservable macroeconomic shocks. Note that as in Stiglitz

---

[2] Monitoring may be thought of as inspecting entrepreneurs' cash flow when customers pay, or efforts to collateralise assets created in the process of investing. The simplest way to model such a technology explicitly is to assume that banks, at the monitoring costs of $m \geq 0$ per loan, can secure a repayment of γI, $0 < \gamma < 1$ from entrepreneurs who received a loan of size I and renege. For sufficiently high γ, entrepreneurs who borrow will invest. In equilibrium, the interest rate spread will then cover the monitoring costs. To simplify the exposition, we assume that monitoring outlays per credit contract are negligible.

[3] This feature will be further discussed at the end of Section 2.4.

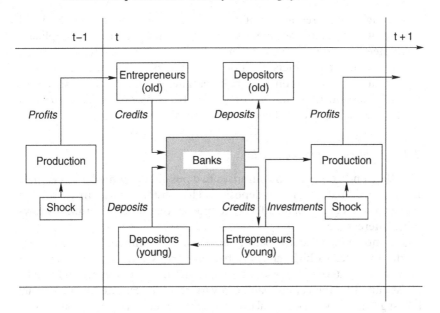

Figure 3.1 Sectors of the economy

and Weiss (1981), $\Pi(i, r^c)$ is non-decreasing in quality levels i and non-increasing in loan rates r^c. Risk-neutral entrepreneurs will choose the most profitable contract offered. Given loan and deposit contracts of banks, an entrepreneur i will apply for a loan at bank j_0, if

$$r^c_{j_0} = \min_{1 \leq j \leq n} \{r^c_j\} \quad \text{and} \quad \Pi(i, r^c_{j_0}) \geq e \max_{1 \leq j \leq n} \{1 + r^d_j\}. \tag{1}$$

Otherwise they will choose the bank with the best deposit contract and save their endowments. Since banks are able to secure repayments, they do not have to worry about low-quality entrepreneurs applying for loans. Low-quality entrepreneurs are always better off with saving endowments.[4] Depositors and entrepreneurs choose randomly between banks which offer the same contract. We assume that aggregate uncertainty in these choices is cancelled out such that banks which offer the same contract obtain the same market share of loans or deposits, respectively.[5]

---

[4] The case in which banks are allowed to screen applicants and to price loan risk contingent on default risk is left for future research.

[5] The exact construction of individual randomness so that this statement holds can be found in Al-Najjar (1995) and Alós-Ferrer (1999).

Throughout the remainder of the chapter we presume two institutional features which are in place in most countries. First, deposits are implicitly guaranteed by the government and depositors trust these guarantees. Second, deposit contracts are not conditioned on productivity shocks such that the macroeconomic risk remains on the balance sheets of banks. These institutional features have been discussed extensively in the literature, e.g. see Hellwig (1998). We take them as given.

2.3   Intermediation equilibria

The Bertrand competition comprises two possible intermediation games. In the first scenario, bank set deposit and loan interest rates. In the second scenario, the central bank affects the intermediation equilibrium by lowering interest rates.

The modelling of central bank policy deserves comments. We built a real model in order to highlight how banking crises can occur and may be alleviated by interest rate policies. In line with the New Keynesian models, we assume that the central bank can vary real interest rates as prices only adjust gradually when nominal interest rates are set. Changes in real interest rates by the central bank translate into changes in financing costs of banks and thus into changes in deposit rates. We therefore associate changes in the real deposit rate with changes in the central bank interest rate policy. We call r_{CB}^d the deposit rate induced or set by the central bank.[6]

In view of Figure 3.1, the time line of actions within a typical period t is as follows:

1. Old entrepreneurs pay back with limited liability.
2. In the first scenario, banks set interest rates on deposits and loans. In the second scenario, banks' realised profits are too low or they have made losses. Then the central bank lowers interest rates. Banks will set interest rates on loans. In both scenarios, banks offer deposit contracts to consumers and deposit and credit contracts to entrepreneurs.
3. Consumers and entrepreneurs decide which contracts to accept. Resources are exchanged and banks pay back depositors. The current level of bank capital is determined. Excess bank capital is distributed among shareholders.
4. Young entrepreneurs produce subject to an unobservable macroeconomic productivity shock.

---

[6] For simplicity we assume that the interest rate set by the central bank coincides with the deposit rates. This, in turn, relies on the assumption that it is not profitable for banks to offer a higher deposit rate than the rate set by the central bank if they can refinance themselves unboundedly at the central bank. Competition among banks will ensure that they do not offer lower deposit rates than the one set by the central bank.

The solution of the intermediation game in an arbitrary period t will be referred to as a (temporary) intermediation equilibrium. The economically meaningful and interesting situation is when aggregate savings of consumers are never sufficient to fund all entrepreneurs. Since the interest rate elasticity of aggregate savings of consumers is zero, this condition takes the form

$$S := (1 - \eta)s < \eta I.$$

Let d denote the current capital level of the banking system. Assume, for a moment, that there exists a marginal entrepreneur i_* such that all entrepreneurs $i \in [0, i_*)$ save their endowments whereas all entrepreneurs $i \in [i_*, \eta]$ invest. The fundamental balance between total bank savings and the loan volume then is

$$S + i_* e + d = [\eta - i_*]I. \tag{2}$$

Total bank savings are composed of aggregate savings of consumers S, aggregate savings of entrepreneurs who do not invest $i_* e$, and the capital of the banking system d.

These three sources of funds are used to finance investing entrepreneurs. Aggregate investments in the economy consists of the loan volume and the equity of investing entrepreneurs $[\eta - i_*]e$.[7]

The balance equation (2) imposes two boundary values for d. We use $\bar{d} := \eta I - S > 0$ to denote the value of bank capital that would allow all entrepreneurs $i \in [0, \eta]$ to invest, since $S + \bar{d} = \eta I$. If $d > \bar{d}$, then banks have more capital than is needed to finance all entrepreneurs, and excess resources are available independent of any interest rates. Similarly, let $\underline{d} := -[S + \eta e]$ denote the lowest level of (negative) bank capital that still allows for a balance of liabilities in a particular period. If $d = \underline{d}$, then all entrepreneurs $i \in [0, \eta]$ are required to save in order to pay back obligations to the previous generation. This prevents any financing of new investment projects. $d > \underline{d}$ ensures that there are enough funds to meet the liabilities of the previous generation and to finance new investment projects. If $d < \underline{d}$, then the banking system can no longer fulfil its obligations and is declared bankrupt. This situation will be referred to as a *banking collapse*.

An intermediation problem arises when $d \in [\underline{d}, \bar{d}]$. For each $d \in [\underline{d}, \bar{d}]$ there exists a unique $i_* \in [0, \eta]$, referred to as the *marginal entrepreneur* and given by

---

[7] Note that aggregate savings in the economy are composed of the sum of total bank savings and the equity of investing entrepreneurs.

$$i_* = i_E(d) := \frac{\overline{d} - d}{e + I} = \frac{\eta I - S - d}{e + I}, \tag{3}$$

such that loans are balanced by total bank savings as expressed in equation (2). In Theorem 6, Appendix A, we establish existence and uniqueness of two types of *intermediation equilibria*. In an intermediation equilibrium *without interest rate cutting*, all banks set the same loan and deposit interest rate $r_* = r_*(d) > 0$ depending solely on the capital level d such that for each bank $j = 1, \ldots, n$,

$$r_j^{d*} = r_j^{c*} = r_*. \tag{4}$$

In an intermediation equilibrium *with interest rate cutting*, the central bank lowers deposit interest rates $r_{CB}^d < r_*$ when the banking system violates certain capital requirements, which will be made explicit below. Theorem 6 in Appendix A states that in this case all banks set the same loan interest rate $r_*^c = r_*^c(d, r_{CB}^d)$, which depends on the capital level d as well as on the interest rate r_{CB}^d, so that for each bank $j = 1, \ldots, n$,

$$r_j^{d*} = r_{CB}^d < r_* \quad \text{and} \quad r_j^{c*} = r_*^c > r_*. \tag{5}$$

Theorem 6 states that in both intermediation games total bank savings and loan volume are balanced, such that all entrepreneurs with quality levels $i < i_*$ save, while all those with quality levels $i \geq i_*$ invest.[8]

The model has two critical features. The first one is that without interest rate cutting, banks receive no premium for the macroeconomic risk of their loans, so that $r_j^{c*} - r_j^{d*} = 0$ for all banks j. Without interest rate cutting, (4) shows that the intermediation game yields the competitive outcome in which total bank savings and loans are balanced at a common interest rate for loans and deposits. The reason for this effect is double-sided Bertrand competition, which allows entrepreneurs to switch market sides and save their endowments when offered unfavourable loan contracts.

The second one is that interest rate cutting increases banks' profits. The key prerequisite for this effect is a low interest rate elasticity for deposits which, for simplicity, is assumed to be zero throughout this chapter. This implies that in equilibrium the marginal entrepreneur i_*, as given in (3), is independent of interest rates. Thus, there are always enough entrepreneurs willing to invest at large intermediation margins. Low refinancing costs and high loan interest rates combined with a sufficiently high equilibrium loan

---

[8] The intermediation game will be further discussed in Appendix A.

volume then allow the banking system to increase its profits which, in turn, recapitalise banks. This feature will be further discussed in Section 2.5.

The next lemma summarises all important properties of equilibrium interest rates.

Lemma 1

Equilibrium interest rates of the intermediation game satisfy the following:

(i) $r_*(d)$ is decreasing in capital levels $d \in [\underline{d}, \overline{d}]$;

(ii) $r_*^c(d, r_{CB}^d)$ is decreasing in capital levels d for each $r_{CB}^d \in [0, r_*(d)]$;

(iii) $r_*^c(d, r_{CB}^d)$ is decreasing in $r_{CB}^d \in [0, r_*(d)]$ for each $d \in [\underline{d}, \overline{d}]$;

(iv) for each $d \in [\underline{d}, \overline{d}]$, $r_*^c(d, r_*(d)) = r_*(d)$ and $r_*^c(d, r_{CB}^d) > r_*(d)$ for all $r_{CB}^d \in [0, r_*(d))$.

The assumption of Bertrand competition captures a benchmark situation of a banking industry with low profitability as, for example, has been the case in Japan or in the recent worldwide banking crisis in 2008 when many banks in Europe and in the US had low and even negative profits. Gersbach and Wenzelburger (2008) show that the initial result of this chapter, namely that interest rate cutting may become necessary to avoid a banking collapse, does not depend on the fact that banks' intermediation margins are zero. It carries over to the case when intermediation margins reflect positive but too low premia on macroeconomic risks. In order to investigate how a central bank's interest policy may help to avoid and resolve banking crises, we use the current, simpler framework.

Observe that an interest rate cutting with $r_{CB}^d = 0$ is equivalent to allowing the banking industry to form a cartel. In such a cartel, aggregate profits are maximised, which is equivalent to setting $r_*^d = 0$ and r_*^c such that total bank savings and loans are balanced. We focus directly on controlling short-term real interest rates. During the Japanese banking crisis, the short-term nominal interest rates had been set at zero. During deflation, the real interest rate in Japan was, of course, higher than zero, but declined considerably in the second half of the 1990s. During the recent worldwide banking crisis, the major central banks have substantially lowered short-term nominal interest rates, thereby lowering short-term real interest rates as inflation expectations remained low.

2.4 Profits and capital of banks

As an immediate consequence of Theorem 6, all banks are identical and adopt the same strategies in an intermediation equilibrium. We can therefore focus directly on the banking system and proceed by calculating its profits and the amount of capital at the end of a period. We present the key economic equations for the case in which the central bank sets r_{CB}^d.

The case without interest rate cutting is then obtained as a special case by setting $r^d_{CB} = r_*(d)$, which in turn implies $r^c_* = r_*(d)$.

Let $d \in [\underline{d}, \overline{d}]$ be the current capital level at the beginning of an arbitrary period and $r^d_{CB} \le r_*(d)$ and $r^c_*(d, r^d_{CB})$ be the corresponding equilibrium interest rates. Since loans are balanced by total bank savings, the banking system raises funds $S + ei_E(d)$ that have to be paid back with interest at the end of the subsequent period. The loan volume of the banking system is given by $[\eta - i_E(d)]I$.

At the end of the period, banks will receive repayments from all entrepreneurs who have invested. These will be denoted by $P = P(d, q, r^d_{CB})$ and are given by

$$P(d, q, r^d_{CB}) = \int_{i_E(d)}^{\eta} \min\{q(1+i)f(e+I), I[1 + r^c_*(d, r^d_{CB})]\} \, \mathrm{d}i.$$

(6)

The repayments P depend significantly on the macroeconomic productivity shock q. Given a macroeconomic shock q, the *capital function G* of the banking system is defined by

$$G(d, q, r^d_{CB}) = P(d, q, r^d_{CB}) - [S + ei_E(d)](1 + r^d_{CB}).$$

(7)

$G(d, q, r^d_{CB})$ is the level of bank capital (or equity) of the banking system at the end of the period *before* dividends are paid out to current shareholders. The end-of-period profits of the banking system are given by the change in capital that the banking system experiences in the period under consideration and hence are $G(d, q, r^d_{CB}) - d$. To focus on the evolution of bank capital, it is convenient to work with the capital function rather than with the profit function.

Aggregate losses of the banking system are determined by the difference between full repayments of all entrepreneurs and actual repayments P and are given by

$$L(d, q, r^d_{CB}) = [\eta - i_E(d)]I[1 + r^c_*(d)] - P(d, q, r^d_{CB}).$$

(8)

Using (2), the capital function (7) now takes the convenient form

$$G(d, q, r^d_{CB}) = d + dr^d_{CB} + [\eta - i_E(d)]I[r^c_*(d, r^d_{CB}) - r^d_{CB}] - L(d, q, r^d_{CB}).$$

(9)

Thus capital of the banking system at the end of a period consists of its initial capital d and its profits, which are represented by the last three terms in (9). The profits are composed of interest rate earnings on d, the intermediation margin times the loan volume $[\eta - i_E(d)]I$, and losses L. Observe that in the case without interest rate cutting, the third term in (9) vanishes due to zero intermediation margins.

Finally, we specify how banks distribute positive capital among old entrepreneurs who are the shareholders of the banks. If $d \leq \bar{d}$, we assume that no capital is distributed. If $d > \bar{d}$, then excess capital $d - \bar{d}$ is distributed as dividends. This assumption gives the banking system the best chance to accumulate reserves against adverse macroeconomic shocks. It could be further justified in two ways. First, when current owners are altruistic regarding their children in the sense of a warm glow model, they may refrain from withdrawing their capital. Second, the bank regulator might impose a zero payout ratio in order to enhance the recapitalisation of the banking system. Since excess capital is distributed among old entrepreneurs, dividend prospects alter neither their savings nor their investment decisions and hence do not affect our intermediation results.

2.5   Regulatory instruments

In this section we describe how regulatory instruments are used and when the regulator intervenes. We assume that the banking system is subject to a capital adequacy rule.[9] Here, a capital adequacy rule is defined as a threshold for the ratio between the capital of a bank and its loan volume. Since the banks in our model behave symmetrically, this capital requirement will be formulated for the whole banking system. A *(prospective) capital adequacy rule* is the requirement that the banking system fulfils

$$\frac{d}{[\eta - i_E(d)]I} \geq \alpha, \tag{10}$$

where $0 \leq \alpha \leq 1$. The capital requirement (10) defines a threshold for the capital level of the banking system as a percentage α of the current loan volume $[\eta - i_E(d)]I$. In the first Basel Accord, α was set at 0.08. The capital level d_{reg} below which (10) is violated is given by

$$d_{\text{reg}} := \frac{-\alpha I \underline{d}}{e + I - \alpha I} \geq 0. \tag{11}$$

[9] The pros and cons of capital adequacy rules in the presence of bank moral hazard have been hotly debated in the literature, e.g. Dewatripont and Tirole (1994), Gehrig (1996), Hellwig (1995), and Holmström and Tirole (1997). The welfare costs associated with capital requirements may be quite high when costs of a possible banking collapse are not taken into account – see the recent contribution by Van den Heuvel (2008).

We distinguish between two forms of banking crises: *critical states*, when capital in the banking sector is below regulatory capital d_{reg} but still positive so that $d \in (0, d_{\text{reg}})$, and *bad states*, when $d \leq 0$ and the banking system is insolvent.

We assume that a bank regulator suspends strict enforcement of the capital adequacy rule and the central bank lowers the deposit interest rate as soon as d_{reg} is reached.[10] Such a rule is referred to as an *interest rate cutting*. We note that strict enforcement of capital adequacy rules would force all banks to reduce loans and hence could trigger a credit crunch.[11] Formally, an *interest rate policy rule* is defined by a function

$$\psi : [\underline{d}, \overline{d}] \longrightarrow \mathbb{R}_+, \quad r^d_{\text{CB}} = \psi(d), \tag{12}$$

such that $\psi(d) = r^d_{\text{CB}} \leq r_*(d)$ in the case with interest rate cutting when $d \in [\underline{d}, d_{\text{reg}})$ and $\psi(d) = r_*(d)$ in the case without interest rate cutting when $d \in [d_{\text{reg}}, \overline{d}]$. The latter corresponds to an intermediation equilibrium without interest rate cutting. The policy rule ψ thus describes an intervention whereby the central bank reduces interest rates as soon as banks violate regulatory capital requirements.

The intuition for this regulatory response is as follows. The important feature of the model is that by Lemma 1, low deposit rates will induce high loan interest rates and thus large intermediation margins. This, in turn, relies on the assumption that the interest rate elasticity of the savings function S is inelastic, which implies that in equilibrium, the marginal entrepreneur i_* is independent of deposit rates. Indeed, by Theorem 6, the marginal entrepreneur i_* in any intermediation equilibrium (r^d_{CB}, r^c_*) is indifferent between investing and saving, i.e.

$$\Pi(i_*, r^c_*) = e(1 + r^d_{\text{CB}}). \tag{13}$$

Since $i_* = i_E(d)$ as given in (3) is independent of r^d_{CB} and $\Pi(i, r^c)$ is decreasing in r^c, lowering deposit rates r^d_{CB} will lead to positive intermediation margins $r^c_* - r^d_{\text{CB}} > 0$. This will increase banks' profits as the equilibrium amounts of loans $[\eta - i_*]I$ and deposits $S + i_* e$ depend only on bank capital and not on interest rates.

Positive intermediation margins will still obtain for elastic savings functions. However, as the equilibrium loan volume will decrease, interest rate cutting may not increase banks' profit sufficiently if the interest rate elasticity of S is too high. Qualitatively, all that matters is that banks'

---

[10] In the recent worldwide banking crisis, bank regulators relaxed capital requirements and central banks responded by lowering interest rates.

[11] Further comments on this regulatory option are found in Section 7.

profits increase sufficiently. Any alternative intervention policy must therefore aim at increasing banks' profits.[12]

As discussed in Gersbach and Wenzelburger (2003), at least two other types of intervention policies could be fitted into this framework. The first measure is *financial support* to a bank in financial distress. This measure would directly recapitalise banks and could be financed by taxing endowments of consumers and entrepreneurs. Financial support should preferably be provided in the form of equity to enable future generations of taxpayers to benefit from a recovery of the banking system. The second measure is *random bailouts* when only a randomly selected group of banks is rescued. This could be applied when the banking system is insolvent.

It should be noted that taxing endowments reduces not only consumers' savings but also entrepreneurs' equity and thus will create further feedback effects. In the current crisis, central banks have responded by both cutting interest rates and providing additional funds. Our model would predict that additional funds for banks will lower intermediation margins. The investigation of these more comprehensive intervention policies is left for future research.

3 Evolution of the banking system

We are now ready to describe the evolution of the capital of the banking system. We allow the banking system to start with an arbitrary capital level $d_0 \in (\underline{d}, \overline{d}]$. The case of an initially positive level $d_0 > 0$ may be interpreted as follows. In previous periods, either capital requirements have forced the banking system to accumulate d_0 or the banking system has operated in an oligopolistic or monopolistic manner. In period $t = 0$ a liberalisation shock occurs and the banking system encounters tough price competition.

3.1 Bank capital

The stochastic difference equation which drives the evolution of bank capital is now set up as follows. Let $\underline{d} < d_t < \overline{d}$ denote the level of bank capital at the beginning of period t. Then banks raise funds $S + i_E(d_t)e$ that have to be paid back with interest in the subsequent period $t + 1$. Given

---

[12] Equations (2) and (13) reveal that an excessive reduction of deposits, which in this model could be incorporated by an exogenous drastic reduction of S and e, can make it impossible to increase banks' profits by just raising intermediation margins. Although banks may obtain high intermediation margins, a decline in the amount of loans on which these margins can be earned may be so severe that banks' profits decline.

the capital function G as defined in (7) and a policy rule ψ as defined in (12), the new level of bank capital d_{t+1} is thus determined by

$$d_{t+1} = \min\{\bar{d}, G(d_t, q_t, \psi(d_t))\}, \tag{14}$$

where q_t is the macroeconomic shock in period t. Equation (14) is a stochastic difference equation, where, for simplicity, we assume from now on that the sequence of shocks $\{q_t\}_{t\in\mathbb{N}}$ follows an i.i.d. process.[13]

As long as the capital at the end of period t is below $\bar{d}$, no dividends are paid out to shareholders, and the level of bank capital d_{t+1} at the beginning of the subsequent period $t+1$ is equal to the level of capital at the end of period t. If, on the contrary, capital at the end of period t is above $\bar{d}$, then $d_{t+1} = \bar{d}$ and excess capital is paid out to old shareholders. If $\underline{d} \leq d_{t+1} < 0$, then banks have incurred losses, and d_{t+1} is the amount of liabilities that could not be covered by loan repayments from entrepreneurs. In this case, banks in period $t+1$ must raise enough funds to reimburse the amount $-d_{t+1}$ to the depositors born in period t who withdraw their deposits for old-age consumption. For $d_t = \underline{d}$ we have $i_E(d_t) = \eta$ such that all funds are needed to meet previous obligations. The banking system is bankrupt and defaults for $d_{t+1} < \underline{d}$, since previous obligations can no longer be met and (2) is violated.

It will turn out that the crucial quantity governing the evolution of bank capital is the return on loans of the banking system, which is given by

$$\frac{P(d, qr_{CB}^d)}{[\eta - i_E(d)]I} - 1, \quad d > \underline{d}. \tag{15}$$

Three observations are of central importance. The first one is equation (9), which shows that the capital base of the banking system can increase only if the intermediation margin on the loan volume $[\eta - i_E(d)]I$ and the earnings on capital d exceed losses L. This is equivalent to saying that the capital base increases only if the return on loans exceeds the deposit interest rate times the deposit–loan ratio. This observation follows immediately from (7) and is formalised in the following lemma.

Lemma 2
For each $d \in (\underline{d}, \bar{d}]$, each $0 \leq r_{CB}^d \leq r_*(d)$, and each $q \in \mathbb{R}_+$, the following holds:

$$G(d, q, r_{CB}^d) \gtreqqless d \Leftrightarrow \frac{P(d, qr_{CB}^d)}{[\eta - i_E(d)]I} - 1 \gtreqqless \left(\frac{S + i_E(d)e}{[\eta - i_E(d)]I}\right) r_{CB}^d.$$

[13] This implies that the sequence of bank capital levels $\{d_t\}_{t\in\mathbb{N}}$ generated by (14) is a Markov process, see Lasota and Mackey (1994).

The second observation is that banks' capital $G(d, q, r^d_{CB})$ at the end of a period is non-decreasing in macroeconomic shocks q, since their repayments from entrepreneurs P are non-decreasing in macroeconomic shocks. The last observation, formally stated in Lemma 7 of Appendix B, is that bank capital can be increased if the central bank lowers deposit interest rates as repayment obligations to depositors are reduced.

In the next section we focus on the repayment behaviour of entrepreneurs.

3.2   *Repayments of entrepreneurs and aggregate income*

Let $\underline{d} \leq d \leq \overline{d}$ be the current level of bank capital at the beginning of an arbitrary period. Assume that the central bank has set the deposit interest rate at some value $r^d_{CB} \leq r_*(d)$ and that entrepreneurs have encountered the shock q. An entrepreneur with quality level i enters bankruptcy if they are unable to fully pay back their credit, that is, if

$$I[1 + r^c_*(d, r^d_{CB})] > q(1 + i)f(e + I). \tag{16}$$

Clearly, if the lowest-quality entrepreneur $i_E(d)$ is able to fully repay their credit, then all higher-quality entrepreneurs will also be able to do so. The critical shock above which no entrepreneur enters bankruptcy is thus given by

$$q_{NB}(d, r^d_{CB}) := \frac{I[1 + r^c_*(d, r^d_{CB})]}{(1 + i_E(d))f(e + I)}. \tag{17}$$

In other words, no entrepreneur enters bankruptcy if shocks are sufficiently positive, i.e. $q \geq q_{NB}(d, r^d_{CB})$, while for shocks below $q_{NB}(d, r^d_{CB})$ entrepreneurs with insufficient quality levels enter bankruptcy. We infer from (6) that repayments of entrepreneurs are maximal and aggregate losses (8) of the banking system vanish for sufficiently positive shocks, i.e.

$$L(d, q, r^d_{CB}) = 0 \quad \text{for all} \quad q \geq q_{NB}(d, r^d_{CB}). \tag{18}$$

By Lemma 1 (iv), the loan interest rate r^c_* increases when r^d_{CB} is lowered. Given a capital level d, this has two consequences for banks. First, entrepreneurs' repayments P defined in (6) increase, as they increase with r^c_*. This is illustrated in Figure 3.2, in which P corresponds to the grey shaded area. Second, the critical shock (17) will be raised, thus forcing more entrepreneurs into bankruptcy. As a consequence, by lowering $r^d_{CB} \geq 0$

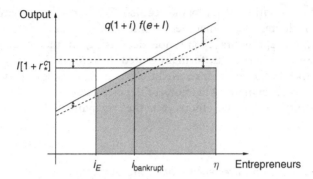

Figure 3.2 Repayments of entrepreneurs

the central bank can only increase banks' repayments at the expense of an increasing number of bankruptcies.[14]

The return on loans, as introduced in equation (15), has the important property that it is non-increasing in bank capital. The reason is that higher levels of d allow banks to finance a larger portion of entrepreneurs, thus causing the average quality level of investments to decline. This important observation is expressed in Lemma 3. The formal proof is given in Appendix B.

Lemma 3

Let $r_{CB}^d \geq 0$ *be an arbitrary deposit interest rate. Then for each* $q \in \mathbb{R}_+$, *the return on loans (15) is non-increasing in d.*

Finally, we introduce aggregate income of the economy, which is given by

$$Y(d,q) = e + \int_{i_E(d)}^{\eta} q(1+i)f(e+I)di. \tag{19}$$

Since $i_E(d)$ is decreasing in d, aggregate income Y is increasing in d and q. High capital levels of the banking system allow for a high loan volume that enables many entrepreneurs to invest.

A critical state of our economy is $\underline{d} = -[S + \eta e]$ in which all available funds are needed to meet previous obligations. Equilibrium interest rates are such that even the highest-quality entrepreneur $i_E(\underline{d}) = \eta$ saves their endowment. Profitable but risky investments can no longer be financed, aggregate income Y is minimal and equal to e. We therefore refer to $\underline{d}$ as the *consumption trap* of the economy.

---

[14] The fact that higher loan rates simultaneously increase repayments to banks and the fraction of bankrupt entrepreneurs is a property of many intermediation models. The subtle point here is that this effect is caused by interest rate cutting of the central bank.

4   Banking collapse and prevention

In this section we discuss scenarios in which the banking system collapses and introduce *feasible policy rules* that will prevent such a banking collapse. We start with the observation that interest rate cutting may be necessary to prevent a banking collapse.

4.1   Banking collapse without interest rate cutting

Consider the case without interest rate cutting in which loan and deposit interest rates coincide. In this case, the capital function of the banking system (9) takes the form

$$G(d, q, r_*(d)) = d[1 + r_*(d)] - L(d, q, r_*(d)). \tag{20}$$

The most favourable situation is when all entrepreneurs meet their obligations. This occurs for all shocks $q \geq q_{\mathrm{NB}}(d, r_*(d))$. Then aggregate losses L as given in (18) are zero and repayments to banks (6) are maximal and equal to

$$P(d, q, r_*(d)) = [\eta - i_E(d)]I[1 + r_*(d)].$$

In view of (14), the evolution of bank capital is now given by the following lemma.

Lemma 4
Let $d_\tau \in (\underline{d}, \overline{d}]$ be the capital base in some period τ, and suppose that no bankruptcies occur, i.e. $q_\tau \geq q_{\mathrm{NB}}(d_\tau, r_*(d_\tau))$. Then $d_{\tau+1} = \min\{d_\tau[1 + r_*(d_\tau)], \overline{d}\}$.

Lemma 4 shows that if aggregate productivity shocks are sufficiently positive, bank capital grows according to the interest rate that banks earn on capital invested in the last period. Whether or not the banking system can sustain a sufficiently high level of bank capital will now depend on the evolution of bank capital in bad times, when adverse shocks cause aggregate losses.

Suppose, for a moment, that negative macroeconomic shocks have caused $d_{T_0} < 0$ in some period T_0. To cover these losses, banks need new deposits on which they have to pay interest. Since intermediation margins are zero, it follows from (20) that bank capital in the subsequent period $T_0 + 1$ is at most equal to $d_{T_0}[1 + r_*(d_{T_0})]$, provided that no bankruptcies occur. Since, by Theorem 6, Appendix A real interest rates are positive, $d_{T_0}[1 + r_*(d_{T_0})] < d_{T_0}$ and bank capital will decline.

This argument shows also that the future bank capital can at most be zero, once it has been depleted in period T_0 so that $d_{T_0} = 0$, and that it becomes negative as soon as losses occur. The statistical property of ergodicity of the i.i.d. sequence of macroeconomic shocks implies that losses occur in finite time with probability one.[15] Hence, once $d_{T_0} \leq 0$, bank capital decreases until the banking system collapses. This result is stated in the following lemma.

Lemma 5

Suppose that the central bank does not lower interest rates. Then the banking system collapses with probability one, if one of the following conditions holds:

(i) *The banking system has accumulated negative bank capital $d_{T_0} < 0$ in some period T_0.*

(ii) *Bank capital has been depleted such that $d_{T_0} = 0$ in some period T_0, and bankruptcies of entrepreneurs occur with positive probability, that is, $\text{Prob}(q < q_{\text{NB}}(0, r_*(0))) > 0$.*

A formal proof of Lemma 5 is given in Appendix B. The next crucial issue is whether an initial level of bank capital can be sufficient to prevent a banking collapse. Suppose to this end that the capital level of the banking system is $d_0 > 0$ at some given point in time, say $t = 0$. Suppose further that there exists a critical shock $q_{\text{crit}} > \underline{q}$ that reduces entrepreneurs' repayments in such a way that the capital base will decrease for shocks below q_{crit}, i.e.

$$G(d, q, r_*(d)) < d \text{ for all } d \in [0, \overline{d}], q \leq q_{\text{crit}}. \tag{21}$$

Then a series of sufficiently many shocks $q_0, \ldots, q_t$ below q_{crit} will lead to a series of decreasing capital bases

$$d_1 = G(d_0, q_0, r_*(d_0)) > \cdots > d_{t+1} = G(d_t, q_t, r_*(d_t))$$

that will finally take on values below zero. Let T_0 denote the first time that negative bank capital occurs, i.e. $d_{T_0} < 0$. It follows from the ergodicity of the shock process that this event will occur within finite time T_0 with probability one, if shocks below q_{crit} occur with positive probability, i.e. if $\text{Prob}(q \leq q_{\text{crit}}) > 0$. As a consequence of Lemma 5, the banking system will then collapse with probability one. The intuition for this result is qualitatively illustrated in Figure 3.3, showing that the banking system starting with initial bank capital d_0 collapses after encountering two successive adverse shocks $q_{\text{low}} \leq q_{\text{crit}}$.[16] In view of Lemma 2, condition (21) can be rephrased in terms of a productivity condition to yield the following theorem.

---

[15] This is a consequence of the Birkhoff Ergodic Theorem, e.g. see Lasota and Mackey (1994).

[16] For uniformly distributed shocks, it will be shown in Appendix C that G is non-decreasing in d.

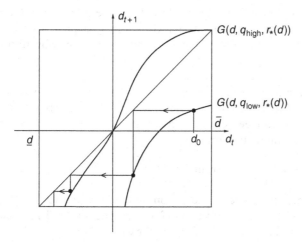

Figure 3.3 Collapse of the banking system

Theorem 1

Suppose that there exists a critical shock q_{crit} such that the return on loans satisfies

$$\frac{P(d, q, r_*(d))}{[\eta - i_E(d)]I} - 1 < \left(\frac{S + i_E(d)e}{[\eta - i_E(d)]I}\right) r_*(d)$$

for all $d \in [0, \bar{d}]$ and all $q \leq q_{\text{crit}}$. If $\text{Prob}(q \leq q_{\text{crit}}) > 0$*, then the banking system collapses with probability one for each initial capital level $d_0 \in [0, \bar{d}]$.*

Adrian and Shin (2008) identified excessive procyclical leverage of banks as a cause for the recent banking crisis. In our model, leverage is given by the ratio of total loans to bank capital $\frac{[\eta - i_E(d)]I}{d}$, which is decreasing in bank capital d. Therefore, leverage is relatively low in good times when banks have accumulated high levels of capital.

Theorem 1 now states that, independently of the initial level of bank capital, a banking collapse will occur if the return on loans is lower than the deposit interest rate times the deposit–loan ratio with positive probability. Whether or not this condition holds depends essentially on the interplay between the productivity of entrepreneurs, the distribution of macroeconomic shocks and the interest rate levels set by the banking system.

4.2   Preventing a banking collapse

Under the hypotheses of Theorem 1 the banking system will collapse with certainty. In this section we show that a collapse of the banking system in which the capital base has fallen below $\underline{d}$ may be prevented by capping deposit interest rates appropriately. By capping deposit interest rates $r_{CB}^d = \psi(d) < r_*(d)$, the central bank will enhance recapitalisation of the banking system as banks are able to ask for higher loan interest rates $r_*^c(d, r_{CB}^d) > r_*(d)$.

The ultimate goal of any central bank policy must be to keep bank capital above $\underline{d}$ with certainty. Since, as argued above, bank capital is increasing in shocks (see Lemma 7, Appendix B), it suffices to implement a policy rule ψ which guarantees

$$G(d, \underline{q}, \psi(d)) \geq \underline{d} \text{ for all } d \in [\underline{d}, \overline{d}], \tag{22}$$

where $\underline{q}$ denotes the lowest macroeconomic shock. In view of (20), the monotonicity of the capital function G with respect to shocks implies that a critical capital level $d_{crit} \in [\underline{d}, \overline{d}]$ exists for which

$$G(d_{crit}, \underline{q}, r_*(d_{crit})) = \underline{d}. \tag{23}$$

This implies that for any capital base $d \leq d_{crit}$, the probability that the banking system will collapse in the next period is positive unless the central bank lowers interest rates. Without restriction, let $d_{crit} \in [\underline{d}, \overline{d}]$ be the highest level satisfying (23).

To obtain a cap for the deposit interest rates which prevents a banking collapse, consider the extreme case in which $\underline{q} = 0$ and repayments to banks are zero, i.e. $P = 0$. Recalling that $\underline{d} = -(S + e\eta)$, it then follows from the capital function G as given in (7) that condition (22) holds if banks' liabilities are below the total amount of resources in the economy, i.e. if

$$(S + ei_E(d))[1 + \psi(d)] \leq S + e\eta \text{ for } d \in [\underline{d}, d_{crit}).$$

We thus obtain a cap for the policy function $r_{CB}^d = \psi(d)$, which is given by

$$r_{CB}^d = \psi(d) \leq \frac{S + e\eta}{S + ei_E(d)} - 1 \text{ for all } d \in [\underline{d}, d_{crit}). \tag{24}$$

Summarising, we obtain the following.

Theorem 2
Let $d_{crit} \leq d_{reg}$ with d_{crit} as defined by (23). Then any policy rule ψ with $\psi(d) = r_*(d)$ for all $d \in [d_{crit}, \overline{d}]$ which satisfies (24) prevents a banking collapse with probability one.

Theorem 2 shows that the central bank may always fulfil (24) and thus prevent a banking collapse by directly setting $r_{CB}^d = 0$ once the capital base is below the critical level d_{crit}. Observe that the critical capital level d_{crit} is determined by the fundamentals of the economy as is expressed by equation (23). Therefore, only if regulatory capital is above the critical capital level, $d_{crit} \leq d_{reg}$, will the central bank be able to reduce interest rates early enough to avoid the risk of a banking collapse.

5   The consumption trap

Let us take a closer look at interest rate cutting rules that just avoid a banking collapse. Such a scenario could occur when the young generation determines the interest rate policy of the central bank. Suppose that the only interest of a young generation is to secure its own investments. Acting solely on their behalf, the central bank will not cut interest rates as long as bank capital is above d_{crit}, with d_{crit} denoting the largest level satisfying (23). For capital levels below d_{crit}, the central bank will set the highest possible deposit interest rate, denoted by $r_{crit}(d)$, that avoids the risk of a banking collapse. Assume, for a moment, that this critical interest rate $r_{crit}(d)$ exists such that $\underline{d} = G(d, \underline{q}, r_{crit}(d))$ for $d \in [\underline{d}, d_{crit}]$. An interest rate cutting rule that merely avoids a banking collapse then takes the form

$$\psi_{crit}(d) = \begin{cases} r_{crit}(d) & \text{if } d \in [\underline{d}, d_{crit}), \\ r_*(d) & \text{if } d \in [d_{crit}, \overline{d}]. \end{cases} \tag{25}$$

Less reduction of interest rates would run the risk of a banking collapse; more reduction of interest rates would lower interest rates on savings and raise loan rates, thus decreasing the utility of consumers and entrepreneurs of the young generation.

Theorem 3 states conditions under which the interest rate cutting rule (25) will lead the economy into the consumption trap $\underline{d}$. Analogously to the reasoning leading to Lemma 5, a series of sufficiently adverse shocks $q_0, \ldots, q_t$ below a critical level q_{crit} will deplete the capital base of the banking system, so that it finally ends up with a capital base below d_{crit}. By the same reasoning as for Lemma 5, the ergodicity of the shock process then implies that the consumption trap is reached with probability one. This argument is illustrated in Figure 3.4, showing that an economy may converge to the consumption trap for a sequence of four successive shocks $\underline{q}$. In this case the interest rate policy fails to recapitalise the banking system sufficiently and the consumption trap is reached. Using Lemma 2, we obtain the following.

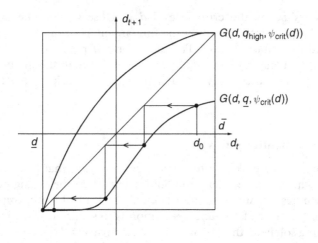

Figure 3.4 Convergence to the consumption trap

Theorem 3

Suppose that the policy rule ψ_{crit} defined by (25) is applied. Assume, in addition, that there exists a critical shock $q_{\text{crit}} \geq \underline{q}$ such that

$$\frac{P(d, q, \psi_{\text{crit}}(d))}{[\eta - i_E(d)]I} - 1 < \left(\frac{S + i_E(d)e}{[\eta - i_E(d)]I} \right) \psi_{\text{crit}}(d)$$

for all $d \in [d_{\text{crit}}, \overline{d}], q \leq q_{\text{crit}}$. If $\text{Prob}(q = \underline{q}) > 0$, then for any initial level $d_0 \in [\underline{d}, \overline{d}]$, the economy converges to the consumption trap with probability one.

The formal proof of Theorem 3 is given in Appendix B. Theorem 3 shows that an interest rate policy may not recapitalise a banking system sufficiently to prevent a consumption trap in which aggregate income is minimal. In order to avoid the trap, the central bank must be able not only to keep bank capital strictly above $\underline{d}$ with certainty but also to prevent bank capital from converging to $\underline{d}$. Thus, a policy rule ψ is needed that allows the banking system to recapitalise in such a way that

$$G(d, q, \psi(d)) > d \tag{26}$$

with positive probability at least for levels d close to $\underline{d}$. Setting deposit interest rates to zero, it follows from Lemma 2 that a sufficient condition for (26) is that the return on loans is positive, i.e.

$$\frac{P(d, q, \psi(d))}{I[\eta - i_E(d)]} - 1 > 0 \tag{27}$$

with positive probability for capital levels d close to $\underline{d}$. As will be shown in the proof of the following Theorem 4, a sufficient condition for (27) is that the entrepreneur with the highest quality level is sufficiently productive.

Theorem 4

Let $r_*(0) > 0$, $d_{\text{crit}} \leq d_{\text{reg}}$, and suppose there is positive probability that the entrepreneur with the highest quality level fully pays back their loan at zero loan interest rates, i.e. $q^*(1 + \eta)f(e + I) > I$ for some $q^* \in \mathbb{R}_+$ with $\text{Prob}(q \geq q^*) > 0$. Then there exists a policy rule ψ that prevents the consumption trap with probability one.

A formal proof of Theorem 4 is given in Appendix B. It shows that setting sufficiently low deposit interest rates $r_{\text{CB}}^d = \psi(d)$ creates high enough intermediation margins to prevent the economy from converging to the consumption trap, provided that the productivity of the economy is high enough.

Theorems 3 and 4 have important implications for the design of interest rate cutting rules. Even if each young generation lowers interest rates sufficiently to avoid a collapse of the banking system, the economy still faces the risk of running into a consumption trap. Although depositors are fully protected, this outcome may be highly inefficient because in the consumption trap aggregate income is minimal.

Since aggregate output Y is monotonically increasing in d, no matter what shock is encountered, later generations will always benefit from their predecessors' interest rate cutting to prevent the decline of d. An old generation, however, is indifferent between interest rate cutting rules as long as a banking collapse is avoided. Therefore, incentives to enforce interest rate cutting rules which prevent the consumption trap must be triggered by concerns for future generations. To avoid the consumption trap, the discretion of a generation to determine central bank policy must be limited. This could be implemented through constitutional political arrangements, for example by restricting the government's freedom to alter previously adapted fiscal policies (e.g. see Azariadis and Galasso, 1998). Such an analysis necessitates a welfare analysis, which is beyond the scope of this chapter. However, before such an analysis can be carried out, the nature of feasible interest rate cutting rules that resolve and prevent banking crises must be understood. We will consider this next.

6   Resolving and preventing banking crises

In this section we discuss *feasible interest rate cutting rules* that resolve and prevent a banking crisis. To prevent a banking crisis, interest rate cutting must preserve *good states* of the banking system in which its capital levels lie within the interval $[d_{\text{reg}}, \overline{d}]$. To resolve a banking crisis, interest rate policy must reverse bad or critical states of the banking system to good states. *Critical states* are those in which the capital requirements are violated but in which the banking system still has positive capital that lies within $(0, d_{\text{reg}})$. In *bad states*, the banking system has accumulated negative capital whose levels lie within the interval $[\underline{d}, 0]$.

Preserving good states requires the banking system to sustain bank capital above regulatory capital d_{reg}. To reverse bad and critical states, the central bank must be capable of inducing a recapitalisation of the banking system in such a way that the economy eventually returns to a good state.

6.1   Resolving a banking crisis

Suppose that $d_{T_0} < d_{\text{reg}}$ has been realised at time T_0 so that the central bank takes action. The central bank's task must be to compensate potential losses due to bad shocks by creating positive intermediation margins. In order to resolve the banking crisis, the central bank must set lower interest rates to promote a sufficient recapitalisation of the banking system. To this end we seek a policy rule ψ such that

$$G(d, q, \psi(d)) > d, \quad d \in (\underline{d}, d_{\text{reg}}] \qquad (28)$$

with positive probability. Suppose that there exists a critical shock q_{crit} such that the capital base will increase in such a way that (28) holds for shocks above q_{crit}. Then at some point in time τ, a series of sufficiently many shocks $q_\tau, \ldots, q_{\tau+t}$ above q_{crit} will lead to a series of increasing capital bases

$$d_{\tau+1} < \cdots < d_{\tau+t+1}$$

that will finally take on a value above d_{reg}. If $\text{Prob}(q \geq q_{\text{crit}}) > 0$, then the ergodicity of the shock process guarantees the existence of the required series of positive shocks such that bad times are reversed. The intuition for this argument is provided in Figure 3.5, in which a series of three successive positive shocks q_{high} leads to a capital level above regulatory capital d_{reg} after a series of three negative shocks q_{low} has caused a serious decline of the initial capital base d_0.

In view of Lemma 2, condition (28) can be rephrased in terms of a productivity condition guaranteeing a recapitalisation of the banking system so that it satisfies regulatory capital requirements within finite time. The following theorem stating conditions under which a banking crisis can be resolved is now straightforward.

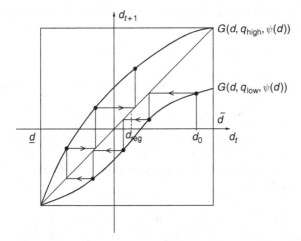

Figure 3.5 Resolving a banking crisis

Theorem 5

Let the assumptions of Theorem 4 be satisfied such that a policy rule ψ exists which prevents a banking collapse. Suppose that there exists a critical shock q_{crit} such that the return on loans satisfies

$$\frac{P(d,q,\psi(d))}{[\eta - i_E(d)]I} - 1 > \left(\frac{S + i_E(d)e}{[\eta - i_E(d)]I}\right)\psi(d) \tag{29}$$

for all $d \in (\underline{d}, d_{\text{reg}}], q \geq q_{\text{crit}}$. If $\text{Prob}(q \geq q_{\text{crit}}) > 0$, then for any initial capital level $d_0 \in (\underline{d}, \bar{d}]$, ψ will resolve a banking crisis as bad and critical states will be reversed with probability one.

Since by Lemma 3 the return on loans is non-increasing in d, a sufficient condition for (29) is that the return on loans is positive at the regulatory capital level, i.e.

$$\frac{P(d_{\text{reg}}, q, 0)}{[\eta - i_E(d_{\text{reg}})]I} - 1 > 0 \quad \text{for all } q \geq q_{\text{crit}}.$$

Setting deposit interest rates to zero, $\psi(d) = 0$, for capital levels d below regulatory capital d_{reg} then suffices to resolve a banking crisis as condition (29) is satisfied.

6.2   Preventing a banking crisis

We complete our analysis by stating necessary conditions that allow a banking system to sustain bank capital d above regulatory capital d_{reg}

without interest rate cutting, thus preserving good states. Formally this requirement reads

$$G(d, q, r_*(d)) \geq d_{\mathrm{reg}}, \quad \text{for all } d \in [d_{\mathrm{reg}}, \overline{d}], \quad q \geq \underline{q}. \tag{30}$$

Replacing the capital function G by (9), condition (30) is equivalent to

$$d(1 + r_*(d)) - d_{\mathrm{reg}} \geq L(d, \underline{q}, r_*(d)), \quad d \in [d_{\mathrm{reg}}, \overline{d}].$$

This shows that in the worst case when the lowest macroeconomic shock $\underline{q}$ occurs, losses must not exceed banks' earnings on capital minus regulatory capital. An argument similar to the one leading to Lemma 2 shows that (30) is equivalent to

$$\frac{P(d, \underline{q}, r_*(d))}{[\eta - i_E(d)]I} - 1 \geq \left(\frac{S + i_E(d)e}{[\eta - i_E(d)]I}\right) r_*(d) - \frac{d - d_{\mathrm{reg}}}{[\eta - i_E(d)]I} \tag{31}$$

for all $d \in [d_{\mathrm{reg}}, \overline{d}]$.

This demonstrates that in the worst-case scenario, the return on loans must be greater than the deposit–loan ratio times the interest rate minus the ratio between 'excess capital' $d - d_{\mathrm{reg}}$ and loan volume. Note, moreover, that the lowest shock $\underline{q}$ must be sufficiently positive in order to guarantee condition (31). Summarising, we obtain the following result.

Lemma 6
Suppose that equilibrium interest rates $r_*(d)$ satisfy (31). Then the banking system preserves good states with certainty and thus is capable of preventing a banking crisis without interest rate cutting by the central bank.

Lemma 6 complements Theorem 1. A situation in which the productivity of entrepreneurs is high enough for bank capital to never fall below regulatory capital d_{reg} is illustrated in Figure 3.6. If, on the contrary, repayments from entrepreneurs P and thus the return on loans becomes too small, then a banking system may not be able to preserve good states on its own. Apart from the regulatory policy and the level of regulatory capital, we see again here that the capability of entrepreneurs to cope with adverse shocks in relation to the interest rate levels is a crucial factor determining whether or not an economy can prevent a banking crisis without interest rate cutting.

In Appendix C, we will illustrate some of the key properties of the banking system with a tractable example in which the shocks are i.i.d. and uniformly distributed.

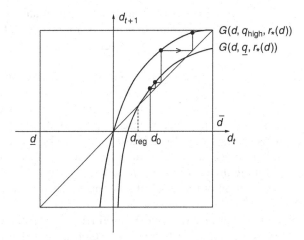

Figure 3.6 Preventing a banking crisis

7   Conclusion

We investigated a model in which a series of adverse macroeconomic shocks may trigger a downward spiral of bank capital. This downward spiral will end up in a banking collapse in which the banking system has insufficient capital to carry out the intermediation services for future generations. If the return on loans of banks is too low, this banking collapse occurs with certainty unless interest rate cutting takes place.

The main conclusion is that given a certain level of productivity of entrepreneurs, interest rate cutting can always avoid a banking collapse. However, the central bank must induce large enough interest rate margins in order to prevent an economy from running into long periods with low aggregate income, that is, a consumption trap.

In future research, alternative intervention policies that foster recapitalisation of a banking system under financial distress should be considered. There are at least two policies that could be incorporated into our framework. The first one is a strict enforcement of capital requirements. This would force banks to reduce their loan volume in critical times, thereby lowering aggregate production. Indeed, the example in Appendix C indicates that the reduction of the loan size required to restore loan/capital ratios when capital has fallen below the threshold level will cause a credit crunch and lowers aggregate production. The second type of intervention would be a direct transfer of resources to a troubled banking system. These funds could be obtained by taxing consumers and entrepreneurs. While such an intervention again decreases aggregate investment and hence production, it would, unlike interest rate policy, not enhance banks' intermediation margins. The examination of the economic costs of these alternative intervention policies opens up important avenues for further research.

The banking system in our model plays a dominant role in economies with emerging markets or in commercial bank-based industrial countries. In future research one should allow for financial markets that exist parallel to banks. In this case, banks may recapitalise themselves by issuing new equity. On the one hand, this could lower the likelihood of banking crises. On the other hand, interest rate policy may become less powerful, as depositors may withdraw their bank deposits when deposit interest rates are capped. An investigation of these countervailing effects is a matter for future research.

In view of the new regulatory framework Basel III, commercial banks will invest more in screening of entrepreneurs. Gehrig and Stenbacka (2001) show that uncoordinated screening behaviour of competing financial intermediaries creates a financial multiplier and may be an additional source of fluctuations. Screening activities are low or zero once the economy is hit by a sufficiently adverse macroeconomic shock. These negative consequences for investment and GDP are likely to reinforce the vulnerabilities of the banking system in our model and may entail stronger interest rate cuts. This is again left for future research.

Appendix A Bertrand competition between banks

This appendix elaborates on the intermediation game introduced in Section 2.2. In accordance with current regulation policies in most countries, we assume that banks cannot ration deposit contracts and that interest rates on deposits are guaranteed by the government. Entrepreneurs face a binary decision problem as they are required to invest all their equity e in order to receive a loan contract of size I. Entrepreneurs are contract-takers.[17]

Formally, an intermediation equilibrium is a *subgame-perfect equilibrium* of the intermediation game, given by a tuple $\left\{ \left\{ r_j^{d*} \right\}_{j=1}^n, \left\{ r_j^{c*} \right\}_{j=1}^n \right\}$, such that entrepreneurs[18] take optimal credit application and saving decisions,

---

[17] Hence, entrepreneurs apply for loans under the assumption that they will not be rationed by banks. If entrepreneurs are rejected nevertheless, they will turn to a bank with the highest deposit interest rate and save. Other rationing schemes are discussed in Gersbach (1998).

[18] Recall that monitoring of banks is assumed to be sufficiently efficient, so that entrepreneurs who obtained a loan will choose to invest.

and no bank has an incentive to offer different deposit or loan interest rates.

Theorem 6

Let $d \in [\underline{d}, \overline{d}]$ be arbitrary and $i_* = i_E(d)$ the marginal entrepreneur as given in (3). Assume that $\Pi(0, 0) > e$ such that the entrepreneur with the lowest quality level $i = 0$ will invest for zero loan interest rates.

A. *Suppose that banks set deposit and loan interest rates. Then there exists a unique subgame-perfect equilibrium of the intermediation game with*

    (i) $r_* = r_j^{c*} = r_j^{d*}, j = 1, \ldots, n;$

    (ii) $r_* = r_*(d) > 0$ *is determined by* $\Pi(i_*, r_*) = e(1 + r_*).$

B. *Suppose that the central bank sets the interest rate $r_{\mathrm{CB}}^d \leq r_*(d)$. Then there exists a unique equilibrium of the intermediation game with*

    (i) $r_*^c = r_j^{c*}, j = 1, \ldots, n;$

    (ii) $r_*^c = r_*^c(d, r_{\mathrm{CB}}^d) > 0$ *is determined by* $\Pi(i_*, r_*^c) = e(1 + r_{\mathrm{CB}}^d).$

In both scenarios, all entrepreneurs $i \in [0, i_*)$ save, while all $i \in [i_*, \eta]$ invest.

Proof of Theorem 6

We start with Part B. In this case, the central bank fixes the refinancing costs of banks. The interest rate r_{CB}^d set by the central bank is identical to the deposit rate offered by banks. Since banks can refinance themselves unboundedly at the central bank, it is not profitable to offer higher deposit rates than the interest rate set by the central bank. Moreover, competition among banks will induce that they do not offer a lower deposit rate than the one set by the central bank.

At r_*^c, banks can exactly provide the amount of loans demanded because total bank savings and loans are balanced. By setting $r_j^c < r_*^c$, bank j attracts all borrowers. Since deposit interest rates are fixed, the only means of increasing savings is by rejecting borrowers. These will then switch banks in order to save. The associated increase in the amount of loans for bank j will not outweigh the decrease in profits per loan. Thus, the deviation is not profitable. The case $r_j^c > r_*^c$ is also not profitable. Since all borrowers would choose the bank offering r_*^c, no borrowers would apply and bank j would simply face an excess of resources. The logic and intuition for Part A are similar, but much more complicated. We have to show that no bank deviates by offering higher deposit interest rates, or by offering higher deposit and loan rates – see Gersbach (1998).[19]   ∎

---

[19] The tedious and lengthy calculations are available upon request.

Appendix B   Technical appendix

We preface the formal proofs of the lemmas and theorems of the main text by a straightforward technical lemma.

Lemma 7

For each $d \in [\underline{d}, \overline{d}]$ and each $0 \le r_{CB}^d \le r_*(d)$, we have:

(i) $G(d, q, r_{CB}^d)$ *is non-decreasing in realisations of shocks $q \in \mathbb{R}_+$ and for each $q \in \mathbb{R}_+$,*

$$\underline{d}(1 + r_{reg}^d) \le G(d, q, r_{CB}^d)$$
$$\le [\eta - i_E(d)]I[r_*^c(d, r_{CB}^d) - r_{CB}^d] + d(1 + r_{reg}^d);$$

(ii) $G(d, q, r^d)$ *is decreasing in r^d and for each $q \in \mathbb{R}_+$,*

$$G(d, q, r_*(d)) \le G(d, q, r_{CB}^d) \le G(d, q, 0).$$

Proof of Lemma 3

Let $d_0 < d_1 \in (\underline{d}, \overline{d}]$ and $r_{CB}^d \ge 0$, $q > 0$ be arbitrary but fixed. By the mean value theorem for integrals there exists $i_0 \in [i_E(d_0), \eta]$ and $i_1 \in [i_E(d_1), \eta]$ with

$$\frac{P(d_0, q, r_{CB}^d)}{[\eta - i_E(d_0)]} = \min\{q(1 + i_0)f(e + I), I[1 + r_*^c(d_0, r_{CB}^d)]\},$$

and

$$\frac{P(d_1, q, r_{CB}^d)}{[\eta - i_E(d_1)]} = \min\{q(1 + i_1)f(e + I), I[1 + r_*^c(d_1, r_{CB}^d)]\},$$

respectively. Since $i_E(d)$ is decreasing, $i_1 \le i_0$. The assertion then follows from Lemma 1 (ii).   ∎

Proof of Lemma 5

(i)   It follows from (20) and the monotonicity of $r_*(d)$ stated in Lemma 1 (i) that

$$G(d, q, r_*(d)) \le d(1 + r_*(d)) \le d(1 + r_*(0)) < d, \; d \in [\underline{d}, 0), q \in \mathbb{R}_+.$$

This implies that $d_{t+1} = G(d_t, q_t, r_*(d_t)) < d_t$ for all subsequent periods $t \ge T_0$. Therefore, if $d_{T_0} < 0$ in period T_0, then the bank capital will be below $\underline{d}$ after a sufficient number of periods, and the banking system collapses with probability one.

(ii) It follows from (18) that losses are positive $L(0, q, r_*(0)) > 0$ for $q < q_{NB}(0, r_*(0))$, which occurs with positive probability. By virtue of the Birkhoff ergodic theorem (see e.g. Lasota and Mackey, 1994), the ergodicity of the shock process implies that this event will occur in some finite time $T_1 > T_0$ with probability one. Then (20) implies $d_{T_1} < 0$ and, as shown in (i), the banking system collapses with probability one.

∎

Proof of Theorem 3

For simplicity, let $\underline{q} = 0$. The proof of the case $\underline{q} > 0$ is more tedious but follows the same lines. We first have to show that (25) is well defined. Since $r_*(d)$ is decreasing by Lemma 1 (i), it follows from Lemma 7 and the definition of d_{crit} in (23) that for each $d \in [\underline{d}, d_{crit}]$,

$$- [S + i_E(d)e][1 + r_*(d)] = G(d, 0, r_*(d)) \leq \underline{d} < G(d, 0, 0)$$
$$= -[S + i_E(d)e].$$

Since G is continuous with respect to r_{CB}^d, there exists a critical interest rate $r_{crit}(d)$ satisfying $\underline{d} = G(d, 0, r_{crit}(d))$ for $d \in [\underline{d}, d_{crit}]$. The rest of the proof is analogous to that of Lemma 5: since $\text{Prob}(q = \underline{q}) > 0$, the ergodicity of the shocks implies that $\underline{d}$ will be reached with probability one. ∎

Proof of Theorem 4

We have to show that there exists $d^* > \underline{d}$ such that (27) holds for all $d \in (\underline{d}, d^*]$ and all $q \geq q^*$. By the mean value theorem for integrals, there exists $i_0(d) \in [i_E(d), \eta]$ with

$$\frac{P(d, q, \psi(d))}{[\eta - i_E(d)]} = \min\{q[1 + i_0(d)]f(e + I), I[1 + r_*^c(d, \psi(d))]\}.$$

$$(32)$$

By Lemma 1, $r_*^c(d, \psi(d)) > r_*(d) > 0$. Therefore, condition (27) is equivalent to $q[1 + i_0(d)]f(e + I) > I$. By assumption there exists q^* such that $q^*[1 + \eta]f(e + I) > I$. By continuity of (32) there exists d^* sufficiently close to $\underline{d}$ such that (27) can be guaranteed for $q > q^*$. The ergodicity of the shock process then implies that the event $q_\tau > q^*$ for some finite time τ will occur with probability one. Hence, $d_t > \underline{d}$ for all times t with probability one and bank capital d_t will never converge to $\underline{d}$. ∎

Appendix C An example

Consider an example in which the shock process $\{q_t\}_{t \in \mathbb{N}}$ is i.i.d. and uniformly distributed on the compact interval $[\underline{q}, \bar{q}] \subset \mathbb{R}_+$ with $\underline{q} > 0$.

Set $\underline{r}(i) = (1+i)\underline{q}f(e+I)/I - 1$ and $\bar{r}(i) = (1+i)\bar{q}f(e+I)/I - 1$. Then the expected profit $\Pi(i, r)$ of entrepreneur i is

$$\Pi(i,r) = \begin{cases} (1+i)f(e+I)\frac{\bar{q}+\underline{q}}{2} - I(1+r) & \text{if } r \le \underline{r}(i), \\ \frac{(1+i)f(e+I)}{2(\bar{q}-\underline{q})}\left[\bar{q} - \frac{I(1+r)}{(1+i)f(e+I)}\right]^2 & \text{if } \underline{r}(i) < r < \bar{r}(i), \\ 0 & \text{if } \bar{r} \le r(i). \end{cases}$$

(33)

In view of Theorem 6, solving the equation $\Pi(i_E, r_*) = e(1 + r_*)$ for the equilibrium interest rate $r_* = r_*(d)$ gives

$$1 + r_* = \begin{cases} \frac{(1+i_E)f(e+I)}{e+I}\frac{\bar{q}+\underline{q}}{2} & \text{if } \frac{I}{e} \le \frac{2\underline{q}}{\bar{q}-\underline{q}}, \\ \frac{(1+i_E)f(e+I)\bar{q}}{I}\left[1 + \frac{\bar{q}-\underline{q}}{\bar{q}}\frac{e}{I} - \sqrt{\left(1 + \frac{\bar{q}-\underline{q}}{\bar{q}}\frac{e}{I}\right)^2 - 1}\right] & \text{otherwise,} \end{cases}$$

(34)

where $i_E = i_E(d)$ denotes the critical entrepreneur as before. It is straight-forward to see that $r_* \le \underline{r}(i_E)$ if $I/e \le 2\underline{q}/(\bar{q} - \underline{q})$ and it follows from (33) that in this case bankruptcies of entrepreneurs are ruled out. This implies in particular that good times can be preserved by reducing the credit size I, provided that $\underline{q} > 0$.

Therefore, interest rate cutting is meaningful only if $I/e > 2\underline{q}/(\bar{q} - \underline{q})$ and entrepreneurs can default with positive probability. When the central bank sets $r_{CB}^d \le r_*(d)$, the loan interest rate $r_*^c = r_*^c(d, r_{CB}^d)$ is given as

$$1 + r_*^c = \frac{(1 + i_E(d))f(e+I)q_{NB}(d, r_{CB}^d)}{I},$$

(35)

where the critical shock $q_{NB} = q_{NB}(d, r_{CB}^d)$ above which no bankruptcies occur takes the form

$$q_{NB} := \begin{cases} \bar{q}\left[1 + \frac{\bar{q}-\underline{q}}{\bar{q}}\frac{e}{I} - \sqrt{\left(1 + \frac{\bar{q}-\underline{q}}{\bar{q}}\frac{e}{I}\right)^2 - 1}\right] & \text{if } r_{CB}^d = r_*(d), \\ \bar{q}\left[1 - \sqrt{\frac{2(\bar{q}-\underline{q})e}{(1+i_E(d))f(e+I)\bar{q}^2}(1 + r_{CB}^d)}\right] & \text{if } r_{CB}^d < r_*(d). \end{cases}$$

Notice that $q_{NB} < \bar{q}$ and that q_{NB} is independent of the capital level in the case without interest rate cutting. Using (35), the bankruptcy condition (16) yields an entrepreneur with the lowest quality level who is not bank-rupt after encountering a shock q. This entrepreneur is given by

$$i_B := \begin{cases} \eta & \text{if } q \leq q_{\text{TB}}, \\ \frac{q_{\text{NB}}(d, r_{\text{CB}}^d)}{q}[1 + i_E(d)] - 1 & \text{if } q_{\text{TB}} < q < q_{\text{NB}}, \\ i_E(d) & \text{if } q \geq q_{\text{NB}}, \end{cases} \qquad (36)$$

where

$$q_{\text{TB}} := q_{\text{NB}}(d, r_{\text{CB}}^d)\left(\frac{1 + i_E(d)}{1 + \eta}\right).$$

If shocks are sufficiently positive $q \geq q_{\text{NB}}$, then no entrepreneur defaults and aggregate losses of banks are zero. For shocks $q_{\text{TB}} \leq q < q_{\text{NB}}$, all investing entrepreneurs with quality levels $i \geq i_B$ fully default, whereas entrepreneurs with quality levels $i \geq i_B(q)$ fully pay back their loans. All entrepreneurs default if $q < q_{\text{TB}}$ and losses are maximal. This event will occur with positive probability whenever $\underline{q} < q_{\text{TB}}$.

Using (36), repayments to banks $P = \bar{P}(d, q, r_*^c)$ as given by (6) take the form

$$P = \begin{cases} q_{\text{NB}}(1 + i_E)f(e + I)[\eta - i_E] & \text{if } q_{\text{NB}} \leq q, \\ q_{\text{NB}}(1 + i_E)f(e + I)\left[1 + \eta - \frac{1 + i_E}{2}\left(\frac{q_{\text{NB}}}{q} + \frac{q}{q_{\text{NB}}}\right)\right] & \text{if } q_{\text{TB}} < q < q_{\text{NB}}, \\ qf(e + I)\frac{1}{2}[(1 + \eta)^2 - (1 + i_E)^2] & \text{if } q \leq q_{\text{TB}}. \end{cases}$$

$$(37)$$

It is straightforward to verify that (37) is non-increasing in i_E for $i_E \in [0, \eta]$ in the case without interest rate cutting. Since banks' liabilities

$$(S + i_E e)\frac{(1 + i_E)f(e + I)q_{\text{NB}}}{I}$$

are increasing in i_E, we see that future capital G is non-increasing in $i_E \in [0, \eta]$. Since $i_E(d)$ is decreasing in $d \in [\underline{d}, \overline{d}]$, it follows that without interest rate cutting, $G(d, q, r_*(d))$ as given in (20) is non-decreasing in capital levels d.

Notice, finally, that an interest rate policy $r_{\text{CB}}^d = \psi(d)$ could be defined by setting

$$1 + \psi(d) := g(d)[1 + r_*(d)], \quad d \in [\underline{d}, \overline{d}]$$

with a non-decreasing function g which satisfies $g(\underline{d}) = 0$ and $g(d) = 1$ for $d \geq d_{\text{reg}}$. It can be verified that g may be chosen such that the resulting capital function G is non-decreasing in d.

References

Adrian, T. and Shin, H. S. (2008) Liquidity and leverage, Discussion Paper, Federal Reserve Bank of New York Staff Reports, No. 328.

Al-Najjar, N. I. (1995) Decomposition and characterisation of risk with a continuum of random variables, *Econometrica*, 63, 1195–224.

Allen, F. and Gale, D. (2004) Financial intermediaries and markets, *Econometrica*, 72(4), 1023–61.

(1998) Optimal financial crises, *The Journal of Finance*, 53(4), 1245–84.

Alós-Ferrer, C. (1999) Individual randomness in economic models with a continuum of agents, Working Paper No. 9807, University of Vienna.

Azariadis, C. and Galasso, V. (1998) Constitutional rules and intergenerational fiscal policy, *Constitutional Political Economy*, 9(1), 64–74.

Blum, J. and Hellwig, M. F. (1995) The macroeconomic implications of capital adequacy requirements, *European Economic Review*, 39, 733–49.

Boyd, J. H. and Prescott, E. C. (1986) Financial intermediary-coalitions, *Journal of Economic Theory*, 38, 211–32.

Caprio, G. and Honohan, P. (1999) Restoring banking stability: beyond supervised capital requirements, *Journal of Economic Perspectives*, 13(4), 43–64.

Caprio, G. and Klingebiel, D. (1997) Bank insolvency: bad luck, bad policy or bad banking?, in World Bank Annual Conference on Development Economics, 1996, ed. by Bruno, M. and Pleskovic, B.

Dekle, R. and Kletzer, K. (2003) The Japanese banking crisis and economic growth: theoretical and empirical implications of deposit guarantees and weak financial regulation, unpublished.

Dell'Arriccia, G., Detragiache, E. and Rajan, R. (2008) The real effects of banking crises, *Journal of Financial Intermediation*, 17(1), 89–112.

Demirgüç-Kunt, A. and Detragiache, E. (1998) The determinants of banking crises in developing and developed countries, *IMF Staff Papers*, 45(1), 81–109.

Dewatripont, M. and Tirole, J. (1994) *The Prudential Regulation of Banks*, Cambridge, MA: MIT Press.

Diamond, D. (1984) Financial intermediation and delegated monitoring, *Review of Economic Studies*, 51, 393–414.

Diamond, D. and Dybvig, P. (1984) Bank runs, deposit insurance, and liquidity, *Journal of Political Economy*, 3, 401–19.

Ennis, H. and Keister, T. (2003) Economic growth, liquidity, and bank runs, *Journal of Economic Theory*, 109, 220–45.

Gehrig, T. (1996) Market structure, monitoring and capital adequacy, *Schweizerische Zeitschrift für Volkswirtschaft und Statistik*, 132(4/2), 685–702.

Gehrig, T. and Stenbacka, R. (2001) Screening cycles, CEPR Discussion Paper No. 2915.

Gersbach, H. (1998) Financial intermediation, regulation and the creation of macroeconomic risks, Working Paper, University of Heidelberg.

Gersbach, H. and Wenzelburger, J. (2008) Do risk premia protect against banking crises? *Macroeconomic Dynamics*, 12(S2), 100–11.

(2003) The workout of banking crises: a macroeconomic perspective, *CESifo Economic Studies*, 49(2), 233–58.

González-Hermosillo, B., Pazarbaşioğlu, C. and Billings, R. (1997) Determinants of banking system fragility: a case study of Mexico, *IMF Staff Papers*, 44(3), 295–314.

Gorton, G. (1988) Banking panics and business cycles, *Oxford Economic Papers*, 40, 751–78.

Hellman, T., Murdock, K. and Stiglitz, J. (2000) Liberalization, moral hazard in banking, and prudential regulation: are capital requirements enough? *American Economic Review*, 90(1), 147–65.

Hellwig, M. F. (1998) Banks, markets, and the allocation of risks, *Journal of Institutional and Theoretical Economics*, 154, 328–45.

(1995) Systemic aspects of risk management in banking and finance, *Schweizerische Zeitschrift für Volkswirtschaft und Statistik*, 131, 723–37.

(1994) Banking and finance at the end of the twentieth century, WWZ-Discussion Paper No. 9426, University of Basel.

Holmström, B. and Tirole, J. (1997) Financial intermediation, loanable funds, and the real sector, *The Quarterly Journal of Economics*, 112(3), 663–91.

Hoshi, T. and Kashyap, A. (2004) Japan's economic and financial crisis: an overview, *The Journal of Economic Perspectives*, 18(1), 3–26.

Kaminsky, G. L. and Reinhart, C. M. (1999) The twin crises: the causes of banking and balance-of-payments problems, *American Economic Review*, 89(3), 473–500.

Krugman, P. (1998) It's baaack! Japan's slump and the return of the liquidity trap, *Brookings Papers on Economic Activity*, 2, 137–87.

Lasota, A. and Mackey, M. (1994) *Chaos, Fractals and Noise: Stochastic Aspects of Dynamics*, Applied Mathematical Sciences, 97, New York: Springer.

Lindren, C.-J., Garcia, G. and Saal, M. (1996) Bank soundness and macroeconomic policy, Discussion Paper, International Monetary Fund, Washington, DC.

Schreft, S. L. and Smith, B. D. (1997) Money, banking, and capital formation, *Journal of Economic Theory*, 73(1), 157–82.

Stiglitz, J. E. and Weiss, A. (1981) Credit rationing in markets with imperfect information, *American Economic Review*, 71(3), 393–410.

Uhlig, H. (1995) Transition and financial collapse, Discussion Paper Series No. 66, CentER.

Van den Heuvel, S. (2008) The welfare cost of bank capital requirements, *Journal of Monetary Economics*, 55(2), 298–320.

von Peter, G. (1999) The banking system as a wealth redistribution device, Working Paper, Columbia University.

Williamson, S. D. (1987) Financial intermediation, business failures, and real business cycles, *Journal of Political Economy*, 95, 1197–216.

4   Handling liquidity shocks: QE and Tobin's q

John Driffill and Marcus Miller

> *These extraordinary methods are, in fact, no more than an intensification of normal procedures of open market operations. [But] I do not know of any case in which the method of open market operations has been carried out à **outrance**.*
>
> J. M. Keynes, *A Treatise on Money* (1930)

1   Introduction

In *Lords of Finance: The Bankers who Broke the World*, Liaquat Ahamed (2009) provides a graphic account of the ill-designed and uncoordinated response by central bankers, in the US and elsewhere, to the US stock market collapse of 1929. Prior to the bust, the US had enjoyed a substantial investment boom – with the real capital stock increasing by more than 3 per cent a year since 1925 – but the value of the stock market, as measured by Tobin's q, had increased much faster, more than doubling over the same period (see Figure 4.1).[1] Then, in two short years, the US stock market fell by more than 70 per cent and the capital stock began literally to contract. These were the years of the Great Depression, when the US banking system collapsed and unemployment grew to more than 20 per cent – leading Roosevelt to declare war on unemployment and Keynes to develop the theory of demand-determined output, published in 1930.

Faced with what Charles Bean (2009) describes as 'The Great Panic' following the collapse of Lehman Brothers in September 2008, the Federal Reserve, the ECB and the Bank of England were determined to avoid a repeat of the 1930s. The slogan – according to Wessel (2009) – was to do 'whatever it takes', be this slashing interest rates to almost zero, dishing out widespread loan guarantees, recapitalising major banks and conducting quantitative easing, with open market operations (QE) involving either

We are most grateful to Nicholas Dimsdale and Stephen Wright for guidance on historical references and data, and to Han Hao Li for research assistance funded by the Department of Economics at the University of Warwick.

[1] Tobin's q is the ratio of the stock market valuation to the current replacement cost of capital – see Blanchard and Fischer (1989, p. 62).

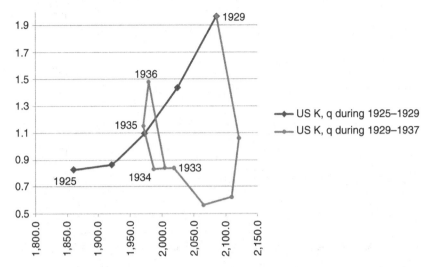

Source: (US) Bureau Economic Analysis and Wright (2004): note that the capital stock is valued at 2005 replacement cost $ billion

Figure 4.1 Capital accumulation and real equity prices before and after the 1929 stock market crash

long-term government debt and/or frozen money market assets. Central bank balance sheets ballooned sharply as never before – doubling in the US, tripling in the UK (see Figure 4.2) – and Treasury backing had to be sought for the quasi-fiscal nature of some of these operations. In the event, output did fall in the US and elsewhere, but there was no Great Depression.

Can recent events be understood in terms of a macroeconomic model, one which includes the effects of QE in particular? In this chapter, we first sketch how the model of Kiyotaki and Moore (2008), hereafter KM, can be used to illustrate the threat posed by the liquidity crunch and the role of policy to inject liquidity. Then we report the results of the numerical exercise by the New York Fed, which uses this framework to calibrate the effect of QE in avoiding severe economic contraction in the US.

2   Kiyotaki and Moore on liquidity and investment

Why should entrepreneurs hold money if other assets – equity in particular – offer higher yields? The answer offered by KM is that these other assets may become illiquid: if limits to equity sales and new equity finance become binding, for example, shares will not provide the purchasing power needed by entrepreneurs who come up with new ideas for investment. Knowing

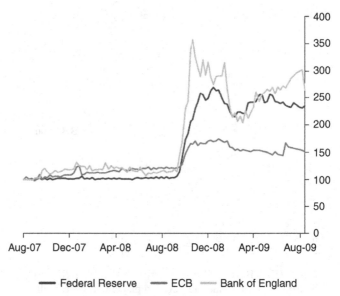

Source: Bank of England Financial Stability Report (2009, June)

Figure 4.2 Central bank total liabilities in the crisis (August 2007=100)

that future investment initiatives may be thwarted in this way generates *a precautionary demand for money* among forward-looking entrepreneurs.

What determines the rate of capital formation? The model of investment behaviour KM adopt is that of James Tobin: given new ideas, entrepreneurs will have an incentive to go ahead if the market value of investing exceeds the cost of the resources required, i.e. so long as Tobin's q is bigger than one. The margin required between market value and replacement cost is usually explained by the need to cover increased costs of installation; for KM, however, the margin is due to the presence of credit constraints that bind more heavily as investment increases.

One can express these ideas in terms of the equilibrium conditions for portfolio balance and capital accumulation. Because the KM model is dynamic, the relevant equlibria will be those implying stationary values for prices and quantities respectively. We take as given the aggregate price level, the wage rate and the stock of money,[2] so the stationarity conditions apply to the real price of equity and the stock of capital, as illustrated in Figure 4.3.

---

[2] As in Driffill and Miller (2010).

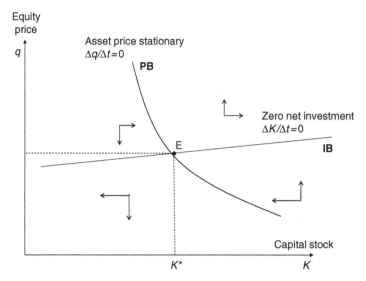

Figure 4.3 Portfolio balance and zero net investment

The schedule labelled *IB, Investment Balance,* is where gross investment just matches depreciation, so the capital stock is stationary. It is an increasing function of Tobin's q measured on the vertical axis, as more capital implies more replacement investment, and this calls for higher q. The schedule for *Portfolio Balance, PB,* is where the real price of equity is stationary. This schedule slopes downwards because, given constant real balances, an increase in the quantity of capital requires a fall in its value for portfolio equilibrium. Equilibrium is at E where both these schedules intersect.

The dynamics associated with these lines of stationarity are that q rises above PB and falls below, while capital expands above IB and contracts below. This implies saddle-point dynamics with a unique convergent path, as discussed in Driffill and Miller (2010) and illustrated in Figure 4.4.

3   Comparative statics

How can the effect of a credit crunch on the economy be analysed using this framework? What if entrepreneurs find to their shock that the re-saleability of non-money assets (equity) has fallen dramatically? In this case, both schedules will move to the left: the shift of IB because tighter

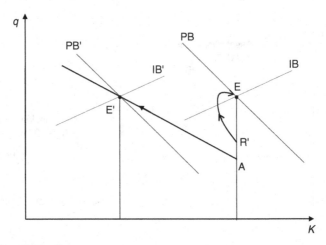

Figure 4.4 Liquidity shock shifts equilibrium from E to E′: stock market falls in the short run

credit chokes off investment; the shift of PB as the fall in the price of equity at any given level of capital mirrors the reduction in its saleability. As a result, equilibrium capital stock contracts as it did in the Great Depression; but the steady state value of q remains virtually unchanged as equilibrium shifts from E to E′.

What about the dynamics of adjustment? They depend crucially on the duration of the liquidity squeeze. If this is prolonged, the adjustment will be as indicated by the path AE′ in Figure 4.4, with the initial fall in the stock market leading to a gradual contraction of the capital stock. Where credit conditions are expected to return to normal, however, the economy should move back to equilibrium: the path R′E sketched in the figure reflects expectations of mean-reversion to normal credit conditions.

This is the crucial prediction of the model constructed by Kiyotaki and Moore: that, in the absence of price flexibility, a tightening of liquidity will promptly lower the value of the stock market and also cut investment and entrepreneurial consumption, with adverse effects on employment and national output. Unless liquidity is restored, the capital stock will contract in the long run, even though the asset price recovers.

4   Policy

What if policy makers take 'prompt corrective action' to avert recession? The form this might take was discussed by Keynes in 1930 as follows:

I suggest, therefore, that bolder measures are sometimes advisable, and that they are quite free of danger whenever there has developed on the part of a capitalist public an obstinate 'bullishness' or 'bearishness' towards securities. On such occasion the central bank should carry its open market operations to the point of satisfying to saturation the desire of the public to hold saving deposits, or of exhausting the supply of such deposits in the contrary case ... My remedy in the event of obstinate persistence of a slump would consist, therefore, in the purchase of securities by the central bank until the long-term market rate of interest has been brought down to the limiting point. Keynes (1930, p. 332)

While the Bank of England in its quantitative easing has proceeded along the lines that Keynes suggests, the Fed went a good deal further in effectively purchasing private-sector ABSs and mortgage-backed securities (MBSs). The effect of open market operations, which consist in purchasing private-sector assets, can be analysed in the KM model and it is the issue specifically addressed in Del Negro et al. (2010), a calibrated model with sticky prices and credit constraints, much the same as considered here – Kiyotaki is indeed a co-author of the paper.

What do they find? First, as regards the persistence of the liquidity shock, they make a 'conservative' assumption that the expected duration of the credit crunch was only eight quarters. Even so, they find that an unanticipated tightening of credit constraints leads to a serious recession. Specifically, a temporary shock which reduces the re-saleability of equity by about three-quarters, and reduces Tobin's q by 10 per cent, would, in the absence of intervention, lead to a roughly proportional cut in investment, consumption and output, as shown by the dashed lines in Figure 4.5.

It is clear from the structure of the KM model that a swap of money for illiquid equity in the hands of entrepreneurs would act directly to ease the liquidity constraint: *the effect of this 'open market operation' is to reverse the leftward shifts of the PB and IB schedules induced by the liquidity squeeze*, as discussed earlier. This explains the claim made by the team from FRBNY: that, by injecting $1 trillion to buy illiquid financial assets in 2008–9, the Federal Reserve engineered a 'Great Escape' for the US economy. The fruits of prompt action to offset the liquidity squeeze are shown by the solid lines in Figure 4.5: the drop in output is limited to 6 per cent, with investment falling by 7 per cent and consumption by 5 per cent.

What the KM model fails to explain is why there should be a sudden contraction of liquidity in the first place. But history may help here. According to Ahamed (2009), the contraction of bank portfolios in the 1930s came about largely because banks had been lending to stock market speculators who got wiped out and the banks became insolvent when the stock market fell. In 2006–8, there was another collapse of asset prices – this time house prices – with the same disastrous effects on banking.

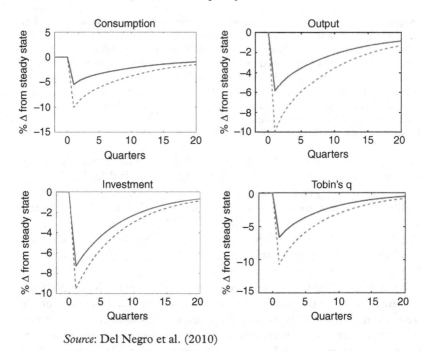

Source: Del Negro et al. (2010)

Figure 4.5 Effect of a liquidity shock that is expected to last for eight quarters (dashed lines without intervention, solid lines with QE)

Morgan Stanley and Goldman Sachs survived only by a timely switch to the status of bank holding companies, but the other major independent investment banks were either taken over or, in the case of Lehman Brothers, went into liquidation, leading to the 'Great Panic'.

In both cases, therefore, a collapsing asset bubble triggered a crisis of liquidity. The KM model assumes that entrepreneurs who have investment opportunities raise funds directly from those who do not, without banks acting as the intermediaries. Nevertheless, the liquidity squeeze may be thought of as 'reduced-form' representation of a banking crisis following the collapse of an asset bubble. In Figure 4.6, for example, where the asset bubble is shown by the divergent path at the top of the figure, the bursting of the bubble puts the economy at point E and acts as the trigger for a liquidity squeeze that causes the economy to follow the path AE' into a 'Great Depression'. Note that Del Negro et al. (2010) also report the outcome under a more extreme scenario where the liquidity shock is expected to last for eight years instead of two (i.e. be of similar duration as the shocks perturbing the Japanese economy during the Great Recession or the US during the Great Depression). They observe:

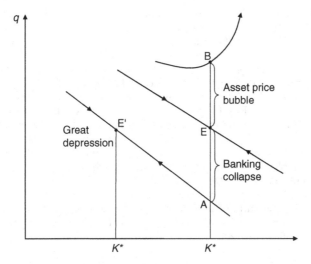

Figure 4.6 Bursting of asset bubble leading to liquidity contraction

Without intervention the equilibrium is a disaster. Output collapses by about 20 per cent and deflation reaches double digits. In short, the equilibrium outcome starts looking a bit like the Great Depression.

5   Conclusion

During the Great Moderation, the sticky price DSGE paradigm proved an attractive framework for policy makers, but it had little traction at the time of the Great Panic, as Charles Bean (2009) ruefully observed. The stylised model of precautionary demand for liquidity developed by Kiyotaki and Moore (2008) offers an alternative perspective, however. Though there is no debt and no explicit role for financial intermediation, it demonstrates the downside risk to the economy – when investment-driven financial transfers between entrepreneurs are suddenly choked off – and highlights the value of injecting liquidity to avert disaster.

References

Ahamed, L. (2009) *Lords of Finance: The Bankers who Broke the World*, London: William Heinemann.

Bean, C. (2009) The Great Moderation, the Great Panic and the Great Contraction, Schumpeter Lecture presented at Annual Congress of the European Economic Association, Barcelona, August.

Blanchard, O. J. and Fischer, S. (1989) *Lectures on Macroeconomics*, Cambridge, MA: MIT Press.

Del Negro, M., Eggertsson, G., Ferrero, A. and Kiyotaki, N. (2010) The Great Escape? A quantitative evaluation of the Fed's non-standard policies, FRBNY Working Paper (www.frbsf.org/economics/conferences/1003/delne-gro_eggertsson_ferrero_kiyotaki.pdf, accessed on 21 October 2010).

Driffill, J. and Miller, M. (2010) When money matters: liquidity shocks with real effects, presented at Royal Economic Society Annual Meeting, April.

Gale, D. (2010) Liquidity and monetary policy, Chapter 2, this volume.

Keynes, J. M. (1930) *A Treatise on Money*, Vol. II, London: Macmillan.

Kiyotaki, N. and Moore, J. (2008) Liquidity, business cycles, and monetary policy, unpublished, Princeton, Edinburgh and LSE.

Wessel, D. (2009) *In Fed We Trust*, New York: Random House.

Woodford, M. (2003) *Interest and Prices*, Princeton University Press.

Wright, S. (2004) Measures of stock market value and returns for the U.S. non-financial corporate sector, 1900–2002, *Review of Income and Wealth*, Blackwell Publishing, 50(4), 561–84.

5   Asset purchase policies and portfolio balance effects: a DSGE analysis

Richard Harrison

1   Introduction

The recent global recession has prompted significant policy responses to support aggregate demand in many countries. A number of central banks have deployed a broader range of policy tools than usual, including so-called 'unconventional' monetary policies that involve the purchase of assets by the central bank. There are several potential approaches to unconventional monetary policy depending on, among other things, whether the assets are purchased from the government or the private sector and whether the purchases are associated with an expansion of the monetary base.[1] In general, however, these policy actions affect the size and/or composition of the central bank's balance sheet.

As noted by Meier (2009), different approaches to unconventional monetary policy can be motivated by alternative views of the transmission channels through which they affect activity and inflation. This chapter considers a 'portfolio balance' transmission mechanism, in which purchases of assets held by the private-sector increase the prices of those assets. As asset prices increase, yields fall and private-sector borrowing costs are reduced, stimulating aggregate demand. Importantly, such asset purchases may provide the policy maker with a policy instrument that can be operated even during periods where the short-term nominal interest rate typically used to implement monetary policy reaches a lower bound.

For asset purchases to have an effect on activity and inflation requires a deviation from the assumptions underlying the 'canonical' New Keynesian model.[2] In standard models, a single asset price (a short-term interest rate)

The views expressed in this chapter are those of the author and should not be taken to represent the views of the Bank of England or its Monetary Policy Committee. I would like to thank Jagjit Chadha, Mike Wickens, an anonymous referee and seminar participants at the Bank of England and the CIMF conference on 'New Instruments of Monetary Policy: The Challenges' for useful comments on an earlier draft. All errors are mine.

[1]   Benford et al. (2009) discuss the approaches taken by a number of central banks.

[2]   See Clarida et al. (1999) for an early review and Woodford (2003) and Galí (2008) for recent comprehensive treatments.

is sufficient to incorporate all of the information relevant for consumption and saving decisions. Price stickiness means that changes in the short-term nominal interest rate by the policy maker can have effects on real interest rates and activity. In such a model, the only policy instrument available is the short-term nominal interest rate. And so monetary policy is typically modelled in terms of a policy rule that guides the current and future settings for the short-term nominal interest rate.

This chapter deviates from the canonical assumptions by incorporating 'portfolio balance effects' using a simple approach similar to that of Andrés et al. (2004).[3] The model includes a simple financial intermediary that lends to the government at both long and short maturities and accepts one-period deposits from households. Portfolio adjustment costs are introduced into financial intermediaries' profit functions so that, at the margin, the larger their holdings of short-term bonds, the more they value *long-term* bonds. This assumption is motivated by the notion that financial intermediaries are more willing to hold relatively illiquid assets if they have ample holdings of liquid assets. The result is that the rate of return faced by households is a weighted average of the market yields on long-term and short-term debt. The market yield on long-term bonds depends on the portfolio mix of financial intermediaries.

This stylised modification to the canonical New Keynesian model provides a channel through which asset purchases by the policy maker can affect aggregate demand. The policy maker can use asset purchases to alter the relative supplies of assets and hence asset prices. To the extent that asset purchases reduce long-term interest rates (over and above the effect of expected future short rates), aggregate demand can be stimulated, leading to higher inflation through a conventional New Keynesian Phillips curve.

This approach is motivated by both theoretical and empirical perspectives. From a theoretical perspective, this setup creates a wedge between the market rates of return on long and short bonds. This approach is a simple way to capture the notion that assets are imperfectly substitutable, so that relative asset prices depend on their relative supply. This idea was part of the monetary theory put forward by Tobin (1956), Tobin and Brainard (1963) and Tobin (1969), among others. Tobin and Brainard (1963) define the imperfect substitution assumption as follows:

[A]ssets are assumed to be imperfect substitutes for each other in wealth-owners' portfolios. That is, an increase in the rate of return on any one asset will lead to an

---

[3] Of course, earlier literatures have explored the implications of adjustment costs in asset markets, for example Branson and Henderson (1985) consider these issues from an international perspective.

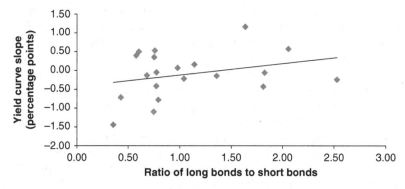

Figure 5.1 UK government bond portfolio and yield curve slope 1991–2010

increase in the fraction of wealth held in that asset, and to a decrease or at most no change in the fraction held in every other asset.

From the empirical perspective, there is a range of evidence that the relative asset prices may be related to relative asset supplies as suggested by the portfolio balance approach. Figure 5.1 presents some suggestive evidence for this effect in UK data. The y-axis measures the slope of the yield curve for successive fiscal years, defined as the difference between the instantaneous forward rate on twenty and four-year bonds.[4] The x-axis measures the ratio of long-term (fifteen years and longer) to short-term (three to seven years) conventional government bonds.[5] Each dot in the chart represents a fiscal year from 1991–2 to 2009–10. The chart shows a mild relationship between the ratio of long-term debt to short-term debt and the slope of the yield curve. As relatively more long-term debt is issued, its relative price falls and so the yield curve slopes up. The slope of the regression line plotted in Figure 5.1 is around 0.3. But the R^2 of the regression is less than 0.1, so the evidence is indicative at best.[6]

Indeed, Figure 5.1 presents very simple average relationships between asset supplies and returns, which will be influenced by many factors.[7]

[4] The underlying data are available from the Bank of England website: www.bankofengland. co.uk/statistics/yieldcurve/index.htm.
[5] The data are from the UK debt management office website: www.dmo.gov.uk/index.aspx? page=Gilts/Data.
[6] More sophisticated time-series analysis for US government debt in the post-war period suggests statistically significant relationships between relative bond supplies and relative returns. See Greenwood and Vayanos (2010).
[7] In normal times, debt financing policies will be used to manage the government debt portfolio to achieve objectives such as minimising financing costs and associated risks. To the extent that debt management policies exploit an imperfect substitution effect in bond markets, the relationship between relative asset supplies and returns will be obscured.

Careful case studies of the effects of asset purchase policies suggest that significant, policy-motivated, purchases of government debt can have substantial effects on bond yields. Bernanke et al. (2004) found that a (roughly) 10 per cent reduction in the stock of long-term US bonds (associated with US Treasury buybacks in the late 1990s) reduced long yields by around 100 basis points. For the Bank of England's quantitative easing programme, for the period 2009–10, Joyce et al. (2010) argue that 'QE may have depressed gilt yields by about 100 basis points. On balance the evidence seems to suggest that the largest part of the impact of QE came through a portfolio rebalancing channel'. Similarly, Gagnon et al. (2010) argue that the Federal Reserve's 'large-scale asset purchases' (LSAP) over the period since 2008 had significant effects on asset prices:

LSAP announcements reduced the 10-year term premium by between 50 and 100 basis points. Little of the observed declines in longer-term yields appears to reflect declining expectations of future short-term interest rates associated with FOMC communications about the likely future path of the federal funds rate.

The 'unconventional' policy responses to the recent global recession have stimulated research into constructing models in which such policies can be analysed. A number of recent papers have examined other extensions to the canonical model that provide a role for unconventional monetary policies. Gertler and Karadi (2011) construct a model with a banking sector that is subject to financial frictions that resemble the financial accelerator mechanism developed for firms by Bernanke et al. (1999). Cúrdia & Woodford (2009) present a model with heterogeneous households that differ in their intertemporal preferences over consumption. This gives rise to an endogenous division between households into savers and borrowers. Financial intermediation between households creates a wedge between borrowing and lending rates that affects aggregate activity and welfare. By intervening in the market for loans, monetary policy can improve welfare. In contrast to these papers, the modelling of financial intermediation here is deliberately more stylised so as to incorporate portfolio balance effects with only a minimal departure from the canonical model.

2   The model

This section provides an overview of the model. Section 2.1 discusses the (standard) treatment of household behaviour and Section 2.2 outlines the government budget constraint and asset markets. Section 2.3 presents the simple financial intermediation sector and Section 2.4 presents a brief summary of the supply side of the model (which is standard). Section 2.5

explains the role and behaviour of monetary policy and Section 2.6 presents the market clearing conditions. Sections 2.7 and 2.8 present the equation listing and baseline parameter values used in the simulations.

2.1   Households

The optimisation problem of the representative household is

$$\max E_0 \sum_{t=0}^{\infty} \beta^t \phi_t \left[\frac{c_t^{1-\frac{1}{\sigma}}}{1-\frac{1}{\sigma}} - \frac{n_t^{1+\psi}}{1+\psi} + \frac{\chi_m^{-1}}{1-\sigma_m^{-1}} \left(\frac{M_t}{P_t} \right)^{1-1/\sigma_m} \right]$$

where c is consumption (of a Dixit–Stiglitz consumption bundle, described below), n is hours worked and M/P are real money balances. Real money balances are given by the ratio of nominal money holdings (M) to the nominal price level (P). The representative household maximises the stream of utility from consumption and money balances, net of the disutility of supplying labour. Utility is discounted by the discount factor β and utility is subject to stochastic shocks ϕ which represent exogenous changes in the household's valuation of current consumption relative to future consumption. As noted below, these shocks generate variations in the natural real interest rate.

Maximisation is subject to a nominal budget constraint given by

$$A_t + M_t = R_{t-1}^A A_{t-1} + M_{t-1} + W_t n_t + T_t + D_t - P_t c_t. \tag{1}$$

The left-hand side of the budget constraint represents the household's holdings of nominal assets. These consist of one-period interest-bearing assets (A) and money (M). The existing asset holdings of the household can be liquidated to purchase new assets. The existing holdings have value $R_{t-1}^A A_{t-1} + M_{t-1}$ reflecting the ex post returns (R^A) on interest-bearing assets A. The remaining terms in the budget constraint capture the household's net income. This is wage income from supplying n_t units of labour at nominal wage rate W_t and lump sum (net) fiscal (T_t) and dividend (D_t) transfers from the government and firms respectively less expenditure on consumption (c_t).

The first-order conditions for the optimisation problem are

$$\frac{\phi_t}{c_t^{1/\sigma}} = \mu_t P_t \tag{2}$$

$$\phi_t n_t^{\psi} = W_t \mu_t \tag{3}$$

$$\phi_t \chi_m^{-1} \left[\frac{M_t}{P_t}\right]^{-1/\sigma_m} \frac{1}{P_t} - \mu_t + \beta E_t \mu_{t+1} = 0 \tag{4}$$

$$- \mu_t + \beta R_t^A E_t \mu_{t+1} = 0 \tag{5}$$

where μ is the Lagrange multiplier on the nominal budget constraint (1).

It is useful to define the real Lagrange multiplier, real money balances and inflation as:

$$\Lambda_t \equiv P_t \mu_t$$

$$m_t \equiv \frac{M_t}{P_t}$$

$$\pi_t \equiv \frac{P_t}{P_{t-1}}.$$

Combining (2) and (5) creates a Euler equation for consumption:

$$-\frac{1}{c_t^{1/\sigma}} + \beta R_t^A E_t \pi_{t+1}^{-1} \frac{\phi_{t+1}/\phi_t}{c_{t+1}^{1/\sigma}} = 0$$

which can be log-linearised to give

$$\hat{c}_t = E_t \hat{c}_{t+1} - \sigma \left[\hat{R}_t^A - E_t \hat{\pi}_{t+1} - r_t^*\right] \tag{6}$$

where $\hat{x}_t \equiv \ln(x_t/x)$ denotes the log deviation of variable x_t from its steady state value x. The 'natural real rate of interest' is defined as[8]

$$r_t^* \equiv -E_t \left(\hat{\phi}_{t+1} - \hat{\phi}_t\right) \tag{7}$$

and is assumed to follow the exogenous process

$$r_t^* = \rho r_{t-1}^* + \varepsilon_t. \tag{8}$$

The labour supply condition (3) can be log-linearised to give

$$\psi \hat{n}_t = \hat{w}_t - \sigma^{-1}\hat{c}_t. \tag{9}$$

A money demand relationship can be constructed by noting that

$$\phi_t \chi_m^{-1} m_t^{-1/\sigma_m} - \Lambda_t + \beta E_t \pi_{t+1}^{-1} \Lambda_{t+1} = 0$$

---

[8] If preference shocks (ϕ) are the only shocks then it is readily verified that, in the absence of sticky prices or bond market imperfections, the real interest rate satisfies equation (7).

which can be log-linearised to give

$$\hat{m}_t = \frac{\sigma_m}{\sigma}\hat{c}_t - \frac{\beta\sigma_m}{1-\beta}\hat{R}_t^A.$$

2.2   The government budget constraint

As is common in many models of this type, fiscal policy does not play an important role in the economy: there is no government spending and net transfers are made to households on a lump-sum basis (so taxation does not distort any economic decisions). This simplification is made to focus attention on the portfolio balance transmission mechanism of monetary policy.

The government budget constraint is

$$\frac{V_t B_{c,t}}{P_t} + \frac{B_t}{P_t} - \frac{[1+V_t]B_{ct-1}}{P_t} - \frac{R_{t-1}B_{t-1}}{P_t} + \frac{\Delta_t}{P_t} = \frac{T_t}{P_t}$$

which states that issuance of bonds (B and B_c, discussed below) plus the change in the central bank balance sheet (Δ, discussed below) finances net transfers to households (T). All items in the budget constraint are deflated by the aggregate price index P (the price of a Dixit–Stiglitz consumption bundle, described below).

The left-hand side of the budget constraint represents the government's net issuance of liabilities. The government issues two types of bonds: one-period bonds (B) and consols (B_c). One-period bonds sell at a unit price and are redeemed at price R in the following period (R is the nominal interest rate on one-period bonds). Consols yield one unit of currency each period for the infinite future. The value (i.e. price) of a consol is denoted V. Consols are infinitely lived instruments and do not have a redemption date.[9]

Modelling long-term bonds as consols is a useful alternative to the assumption in Andrés et al. (2004), who assume that the long-term bond is a zero coupon fixed-maturity bond. The authors also assume that there is no secondary market for long-term bonds so that agents who buy long-term government debt must hold it until maturity. As Andrés et al. (2004) point out, ruling out trades in long-term debt on a secondary market reduces the number of variables in the model, which is a useful simplification.[10] The use

---

[9] Of course, the government may withdraw existing consols from circulation by purchasing them from private agents at the market price.

[10] Suppose the maturity of long-term debt is L periods. Allowing trade on secondary markets would require keeping track of household holdings of debt with $L, L, L-1, L-2, \ldots, 1$ periods to maturity.

of consols as the long-term bond may be viewed as a similar simplification, as it allows both short-term and long-term bonds to be traded each period so that the optimal long-bond holdings depend on the *one-period* return on consols. Nevertheless, as will be demonstrated, with imperfect substitutability between assets this approach still creates a wedge between market rates of return of those assets.

It is convenient to write the government budget constraint in terms of the one-period return on consols. To do so, define

$$B_{L,t}^g \equiv V_t B_{c,t}$$

and rewrite the budget constraint as

$$\frac{B_{L,t}^g}{P_t} + \frac{B_t}{P_t} - \frac{[1+V_t]B_{L,t-1}^g}{V_{t-1}P_t} - \frac{R_{t-1}B_{t-1}}{P_t} + \frac{\Delta_t}{P_t} = \frac{T_t}{P_t}.$$

Defining

$$R_{L,t} \equiv \frac{1+V_t}{V_{t-1}}$$

as the ex post nominal return on consols allows the government budget constraint to be written as

$$\frac{B_{L,t}^g}{P_t} + \frac{B_t}{P_t} - \frac{R_{L,t}B_{L,t-1}^g}{P_t} - \frac{R_{t-1}B_{t-1}}{P_t} + \frac{\Delta_t}{P_t} = \frac{T_t}{P_t}.$$

The effect of changes in the central bank balance sheet on the government budget constraint is given by

$$\frac{\Delta_t}{P_t} = \frac{M_t - M_{t-1}}{P_t} - \left[\frac{Q_t}{P_t} - \frac{R_{L,t}Q_{t-1}}{P_t}\right]$$

where the second term records the net increase in the central bank's holdings of long-term government debt, which are denoted by Q. This setup assumes that asset purchases are concentrated in long-term bonds, in line with the focus of asset purchase schemes recently introduced by central banks.[11] In this simple model, the central bank finances asset

---

[11] For example, the maturity range for gilts eligible for the Bank of England's Asset Purchase Facility was initially set at 5–25 years.

purchases by money creation (taking as given the level of transfers to households and the existing portfolio of government debt).[12]

The asset purchase policy is operated by varying the fraction of bonds held on the central bank balance sheet:

$$Q_t = q_t B_{L,t}^g$$

which means that the consolidated government budget constraint is

$$b_t + m_t + (1 - q_t)b_{L,t}^g = \pi_t^{-1}\left[m_{t-1} + R_{t-1}b_{t-1} + R_{L,t}(1 - q_{t-1})b_{L,t-1}^g\right] + \tau_t$$

where lower-case letters denote nominal quantities deflated by the price index and

$$\tau_t \equiv \frac{T_t}{P_t}$$

is the real net transfer to/from households.

The choice variables for the government are net transfers to households and debt issuance. The real stock of consols is assumed to be held fixed so that the value of long-term bonds is given by

$$b_{L,t}^g = \bar{b}_C V_t$$

where it should be noted that the total value of consols depends on the price V_t and therefore responds to developments in the economy.

Net transfers to households are set according to a simple rule designed to stabilise the total debt stock:

$$\frac{T}{b}\hat{\tau}_t = -\beta^{-1}\hat{R}_{t-1}\theta\hat{b}_{t-1}$$

where the notation $\hat{x}_t \equiv \ln(x_t/x)$ denotes the log deviation of variable x_t from its steady-state value x. The transfer rule responds to the lagged debt stock in a way that ensures that debt issuance is a stable process. The transfer rule also adjusts payments to/from households to offset the cost of financing the previously issued short-term debt. This reduces the feedback from debt financing costs to the debt stock.

---

[12] The fiscal commitments (bond issuance and transfer payments) dictate the level of Δ. So additional purchases of debt by the central bank, which increase the asset side of its balance sheet, must be financed by an expansion of the liabilities side of the balance sheet via money creation.

Taking all of this information together means that the government budget constraint can be log-linearised to give

$$b\hat{b}_t + m\hat{m}_t - \bar{b}_L(q_t + \hat{V}_t) = -\pi^{-1}[m + Rb + R_L\bar{b}_L]\hat{\pi}_t + \frac{m}{\pi}\hat{m}_{t-1} + \frac{Rb}{\pi}\hat{b}_{t-1}$$

$$+ \frac{R_L\bar{b}_L}{\pi}[\hat{R}_{L,t} - q_{t-1} - \hat{V}_{t-1}] - \theta b\hat{b}_{t-1}.$$

(10)

2.3   Financial intermediation

There is a continuum of perfectly competitive financial intermediaries. Since all financial intermediaries are identical, it is sufficient to focus on the maximisation problem of a representative financial intermediary. The financial intermediary accepts one-period deposits from households at rate R^A, financed by investments in short-term and long-term government debt. The maximisation problem of the financial intermediary is

$$\max E_t\left[R_tB_t + R_{L,t+1}B_{L,t} - \left(R_t^A A_t + \frac{\tilde{v}}{2}\left(\delta\frac{B_t}{B_{L,t}} - 1\right)^2 P_t\right)\right]$$

subject to

$$A_t = B_t + B_{L,t}.$$

The financial intermediary acts to maximise profit, which is defined as the difference between the returns earned on its investments and the returns paid to households. The role of the financial intermediary is therefore to allocate household savings among the available financial instruments in the most profitable way.

The profit function incorporates the assumption that financial intermediation entails a cost related to the mix of short- and long-term bonds held in the intermediary's portfolio. The cost is a quadratic function of the deviation of the mix of bonds relative to the steady state mix (δ). The importance of the adjustment costs is controlled by the parameter $\tilde{v}$: the greater this parameter, the more costly are deviations from the steady-state asset mix.

This setup means that assets are imperfectly substitutable, as defined by Tobin and Brainard (1963). In this model, financial intermediaries are the wealth owners and, as shown below, their demand functions for the two (government) assets are a function of the relative returns on those assets. As in Andrés et al. (2004), the assumption that government bonds are the only assets in the economy is a convenient assumption: 'As usual, the government bond market specified in the model is really a stand-in for the markets for loans to both government and large corporations that exist in practice.'

This maximisation problem can be represented as

$$\max E_t \left[R_t B_t + R_{L,t+1} B_{L,t} - \left(R_t^c [B_t + B_{L,t}] + \frac{\tilde{v}}{2} \left(\delta \frac{B_t}{B_{L,t}} - 1 \right)^2 P_t \right) \right].$$

The first-order conditions are

$$R_t - R_t^A - \tilde{v}\delta \left(\delta \frac{b_t}{b_{L,t}} - 1 \right) \frac{1}{b_{L,t}} = 0$$

$$E_t R_{L,t+1} - R_t^A + \tilde{v}\delta \left(\delta \frac{b_t}{b_{L,t}} - 1 \right) \frac{b_t}{b_{L,t}} \frac{1}{b_{L,t}} = 0.$$

Log-linearising gives

$$R\hat{R}_t - R\hat{R}_t^A - \frac{\tilde{v}\delta}{b_L}\delta \frac{b}{b_L} \left(\hat{b}_t - \hat{b}_{L,t} \right) = 0$$

$$RE_t\hat{R}_{L,t+1} - R\hat{R}_t^A + \frac{\tilde{v}\delta b}{b_L^2}\delta \frac{b}{b_L} \left(\hat{b}_t - \hat{b}_{L,t} \right) = 0.$$

Noting that $\frac{b_L}{b} = \delta$ and $R = \beta^{-1}$ in a zero-inflation steady state means that the equations can be rearranged to give

$$\hat{R}_t^A = \hat{R}_t - \beta \frac{\tilde{v}\delta}{b_L} \left(\hat{b}_t - \hat{b}_{L,t} \right)$$

$$\hat{R}_t^A = E_t\hat{R}_{L,t+1} + \beta \frac{\tilde{v}}{\delta b_L} \left(\hat{b}_t - \hat{b}_{L,t} \right).$$

A linear combination of these equations reveals that

$$\hat{R}_t^A = \frac{1}{1+\delta}\hat{R}_t + \frac{\delta}{1+\delta}E_t\hat{R}_{L,t+1}$$

which is the rate of return that appears in the household's Euler equation.

Combining the first-order conditions reveals that

$$\hat{R}_t = E_t\hat{R}_{L,t+1} + \beta \frac{\tilde{v}\delta}{b_L} \left(\frac{1}{\delta^2} + 1 \right) \left(\hat{b}_t - \hat{b}_{L,t} \right)$$

$$= E_t\hat{R}_{L,t+1} + v \left(\hat{b}_t - \hat{b}_{L,t} \right)$$

where

$$v \equiv \beta \frac{\tilde{v}\delta}{b_L}.$$

This shows that relative asset returns are a function of relative asset supplies. An increase in the supply of short bonds will, other things being equal, increase the short rate. So the relative *price* of short bonds falls as relative supply increases, as posited by Tobin and Brainard (1963).

2.4   *Firms*

There is a set of monopolistically competitive firms indexed by $i \in (0, 1)$ that produces differentiated products that form a Dixit–Stiglitz consumption bundle that is purchased by households. The bundle is given by

$$Y_t = \left[\int_0^1 Y_t(i)^{1-\eta^{-1}} di \right]^{\frac{1}{1-\eta^{-1}}}$$

implying a demand curve of the form

$$Y_t(i) = \left(\frac{P_t(i)}{P_t} \right)^{-\eta} Y_t.$$

The demand curve states that the demand for firm i's output $(Y(i))$ depends on the total demand for output (Y) and negatively on firm i's price $(P(i))$ relative to the aggregate price level (P).

Firms produce using a constant returns production function in the single input (labour, n):

$$Y_t(i) = A n_t(i)$$

where A is the productivity parameter.

The firm faces Rotemberg (1982) quadratic price adjustment costs so that the profit maximisation problem is given by

$$\max E_0 \sum_{t=0}^{\infty} \beta^t \left[P_t(i) Y_t(i) - W_t n_t(i) - \frac{\chi_p}{2} \left[\frac{P_t(i)}{P_{t-1}(i)} - 1 \right]^2 P_t Y_t \right]$$

subject to

$$Y_t(i) = \left(\frac{P_t(i)}{P_t} \right)^{-\eta} Y_t$$

$$Y_t(i) = A n_t(i).$$

The importance of the quadratic adjustment costs is dictated by the size of the parameter χ_p, with $\chi_p = 0$ corresponding to the case of flexible prices.

The profit maximisation problem can be represented as

$$\max E_0 \sum_{t=0}^{\infty} \beta^t \left[\left(P_t(i) - \frac{W_t}{A} \right) \left(\frac{P_t(i)}{P_t} \right)^{-\eta} - \frac{\chi_p}{2} \left[\frac{P_t(i)}{P_{t-1}(i)} - 1 \right]^2 P_t \right] Y_t$$

which has first-order condition

$$Y_t \left[(1 - \eta) \left(\frac{P_t(i)}{P_t} \right)^{-\eta} + \eta \frac{W_t}{A} \left(\frac{P_t(i)}{P_t} \right)^{-\eta} \frac{1}{P_t(i)} - \chi_p \left[\frac{P_t(i)}{P_{t-1}(i)} - 1 \right] \frac{P_t}{P_{t-1}(i)} \right]$$
$$= -\beta \chi_p E_t \left[\frac{P_{t+1}(i)}{P_t(i)} - 1 \right] \frac{P_{t+1} P_{t+1}(i)}{P_t(i)^2} Y_{t+1}.$$

In a symmetric equilibrium, this becomes

$$(1 - \eta) + \frac{\eta w_t}{A} - \chi_p [\pi_t - 1] \pi_t = -\beta \chi_p E_t [\pi_{t+1} - 1] \pi_{t+1}^2 \frac{Y_{t+1}}{Y_t}.$$

Noting that in steady state $w/A = (\eta - 1)/\eta$, log-linearising gives

$$\hat{\pi}_t = \beta E_t \hat{\pi}_{t+1} + \frac{\eta - 1}{\chi_p} \hat{w}_t. \tag{11}$$

2.5   Monetary policy

Monetary policy is conducted in terms of the short-term nominal interest rate (R) and the fraction of long-term bonds held on the central bank's balance sheet (q). For simplicity, the policy rate is assumed to follow a Taylor-type rule, with smoothing:

$$\hat{R}_t = \rho_R \hat{R}_{t-1} + (1 - \rho_R)(a_\pi \hat{\pi}_t + a_x \hat{x}_t) + \varepsilon_t^R \tag{12}$$

where $\hat{x}$ is the output gap, defined below.

Asset purchases are assumed to be set according to a simple autoregressive process:

$$q_t = \rho_q q_{t-1} + \varepsilon_t^q \tag{13}$$

2.6   Market clearing

Assuming that profits from firms and financial intermediaries are transferred to households, the resource constraint in a symmetric equilibrium is

$$y_t = c_t - \frac{\chi_p}{2}[\pi_t - 1]^2 y_t - \frac{\nu}{2}\left(\delta\frac{b_t}{b_{L,t}} - 1\right)^2.$$

It is straightforward to show that in the absence of price setting and imperfect asset substitutability frictions, the efficient level of output is constant. This means that, to a first-order approximation, the log-deviations of consumption and output from steady state are equal to the output gap:[13]

$$\hat{c}_t = \hat{y}_t = \hat{x}_t. \tag{14}$$

Bond market clearing requires that the supply of bonds available to private agents is taken up by financial intermediaries:

$$b_{L,t} = (1 - q_t)b_{L,t}^g = (1 - q_t)\bar{b}_C V_t$$

which can be log-linearised to give[14]

$$-q_t + \hat{V}_t = \hat{b}_{L,t}. \tag{15}$$

Equation (15) shows that asset purchases (q) influence the quantity of long bonds available to the private sector and hence long-term bond yields.

2.7   Equation listing

Collecting together the log-linearised model equations and making some substitutions delivers the following equation listing:

$$\hat{x}_t = E_t\hat{x}_{t+1} - \sigma\left[\hat{R}_t^A - E_t\hat{\pi}_{t+1} - \hat{r}_t^*\right] \tag{16}$$

$$\hat{m}_t = \frac{\sigma_m}{\sigma}\hat{x}_t - \frac{\beta\sigma_m}{1-\beta}\hat{R}_t^A \tag{17}$$

---

[13] The quadratic terms in the resource constraint disappear in the log-linear approximation.
[14] A linear (rather than log-linear) approximation is applied to q since the steady-state level of q is assumed to be zero, as discussed later.

$$\hat{R}_t^A = \frac{1}{1+\delta}\hat{R}_t + \frac{\delta}{1+\delta}E_t\hat{R}_{L,t+1} \tag{18}$$

$$\hat{R}_t = E_t\hat{R}_{L,t+1} + v\left(\hat{b}_t - \hat{b}_{L,t}\right) \tag{19}$$

$$\hat{\pi}_t = \beta E_t\hat{\pi}_{t+1} + \kappa\hat{x}_t \tag{20}$$

$$\hat{R}_t = \rho_R\hat{R}_{t-1} + (1-\rho_R)(\alpha_\pi\hat{\pi}_t + \alpha_x\hat{x}_t) + \varepsilon_t^R \tag{21}$$

$$q_t = \rho_q q_{t-1} + \varepsilon_t^q \tag{22}$$

$$\hat{b}_t + \frac{m}{b}(\hat{m}_t - \hat{m}_{t-1}) = \delta q_t - \left[\frac{m}{b} + \frac{1+\delta}{\beta}\right]\hat{\pi}_t + \left(\frac{1}{\beta} - \theta\right)\hat{b}_{t-1}$$
$$- \frac{\delta}{\beta}q_{t-1} \tag{23}$$

$$\hat{b}_{L,t} = -q_t + \hat{V}_t \tag{24}$$

$$E_t\hat{R}_{L,t+1} = \beta E_t\hat{V}_{t+1} - \hat{V}_t \tag{25}$$

$$r_t^* = \rho r_{t-1}^* + \varepsilon_t \tag{26}$$

Equation (16) is derived by combining (6) with the definition of the real interest rate (7) and the market clearing condition (14).

Equation (20) combines the Phillips curve (11) with the labour supply curve (9), market clearing ($\hat{n}_t = \hat{x}_t$) and defines $\kappa \equiv \frac{\eta-1}{\chi_{p_t}}(\psi + \sigma^{-1})$.

Equation (23) combines (10) with the consol valuation equation (25).

2.8   Parameter values

A number of parameters are set in order to pin down the steady state of the model. The productivity parameter A is chosen to normalise output to unity in the steady state. The parameter χ_m is set to ensure that real money balances are a small fraction (0.001) of short-term debt in steady state. The steady-state inflation rate is normalised to zero ($\pi = 1$). The level of asset purchases is also zero in steady state ($q = 0$) in order to implement the efficient equilibrium.

Table 5.1 shows the baseline parameter values. Parameters β, σ, κ and ρ are set in line with Levin et al. (2010), who use these values to show that large negative demand shocks can have significant effects on activity even under optimal commitment policy in a canonical New Keynesian model. The elasticity of money demand is set to ensure a unit income elasticity of money demand.

The monetary policy parameters are set to fairly standard values. The feedback parameters on inflation and the output gap (α_π and α_x) are set in

Table 5.1 *Parameter values*

	Description	Value
σ	Elasticity of intertemporal substitution	6
β	Discount factor	0.9925
κ	Slope of Phillips curve	0.024
ρ	Autocorrelation of natural real interest rate	0.85
σ_m	Money demand elasticity	6
α_π	Interest rate response to inflation	1.5
α_x	Interest rate response to output gap	0.5
ρ_R	Smoothing coefficient in policy rule	0.85
ρ_q	Autocorrelation of asset purchases	0.95
$\frac{m}{b}$	Steady-state money:bond ratio	0.001
δ	Steady-state ratio of long-term bonds to short-term bonds	3
v	Elasticity of long-term bond rate with respect to portfolio mix	0.1
θ	Feedback parameter in tax/transfer rule	0.025

line with the original values used in Taylor (1993). The interest rate smoothing parameter is set in line with recent empirical evidence (e.g. Smets and Wouters (2007)). The persistence of the asset purchase policy (ρ_q) is set to ensure that asset purchases persist for a number of quarters. The feedback parameter in the transfer rule is set to a small value so that the stock of short debt moves persistently in response to shocks.

The steady-state ratio of long-term to short-term bonds (δ) is set to 3 in light of the US data presented in Kuttner (2006). The elasticity of the long-term bond rate with respect to household's portfolio mix is set to $v = 0.1$. There is little guidance in the literature on the appropriate range of values for this parameter. However, Andrés et al. (2004) estimate a similar parameter (relating the long-term bond premium to household's relative holdings of money and long bonds) to be around 0.045 using US data. The evidence presented in Bernanke et al. (2004) (based on a case study of a 10 per cent reduction in the stock of long-term bonds associated with US Treasury buybacks) suggests a value for v of around 0.25.

The value chosen for v lies in the middle of these estimates. The simulations presented in Sections 3 and 4 examine the responses of the model for three parameterisations of v: 0.1 (the baseline assumption), 0 (corresponding to a canonical New Keynesian model with perfectly substitutable assets) and 0.2 (closer to the estimates presented by Bernanke et al. (2004)).

The shocks in the model (ε_t, ε_t^R and ε_t^q) are assumed to be uncorrelated. The shock to the natural real interest rate provides a mechanism to investigate the effects of demand shocks. The policy shocks are included simply to elucidate the transmission mechanisms in the model. In particular, the shock to asset purchases ε^q may be more easily interpreted as a policy instrument to be chosen by the central bank. The representation of the process for asset prices (q) as an AR(1) process is akin to the specification of an exogenous money growth rule and serves as a very simple way to characterise policy choices.

3   The transmission mechanism

This section explores the transmission mechanism of both interest rate policy and asset purchases. In each case, the model is at steady state before the shock arrives.

3.1   Interest rate policy

Figure 5.2 plots the responses to a negative shock to the Taylor rule $(\varepsilon_t^R = -0.5)$ for three parameterisations of the model: $v = (0, 0.1, 0.2)$. The figure plots the impulse responses of the short-term nominal interest rate, the output gap and inflation. The impulse response of the five-year spot rate is also plotted. This rate is the five-year return on consols and is computed using the pricing equation for consols.[15] The figure also plots the consol-based yield curve observed in the period in which the shock materialises. The yield curve is simply computed as the expected sequence of one-period consol returns $E_t \hat{R}_{t+i}^L$.

In all cases, the monetary policy shock reduces the short-term nominal interest rate by around 1 per cent on impact. The reduction in short-term nominal interest rates leads to a fall in real rates because prices are sticky. The fall in real rates stimulates aggregate demand and hence inflation through the Phillips curve.

Despite the generic similarities between the alternative parameterisations of the model, the differences stem from varied degrees of imperfect substitution in asset markets. In the model, implementing a lower policy rate leads to a reduction in debt financing costs for the government. Since the supply of long-term government debt is held fixed, the reduction in debt financing costs induces a reduction in the supply of short-term debt. However, as financial intermediaries reduce their holdings of short-term debt, their portfolio mix shifts towards long-term bonds. The premium on long-term bonds is a decreasing function of the ratio of short-term to long-term government debt, so the premium rises.

---

[15] So the n-period return on consols is $\frac{1}{n}\sum_{i=1}^n E_t \hat{R}_{t+i}^L$.

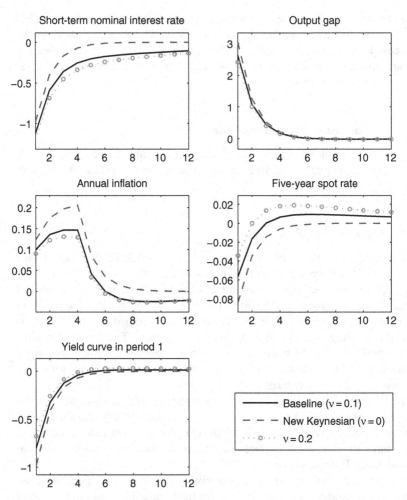

Figure 5.2 Responses to conventional monetary policy shock

One way to think about this effect is in terms of the textbook description of monetary policy implementation in terms of an open market operation in which the central bank finances purchases of short-term government bonds through money creation. In a textbook model, the open market operation increases liquidity (the money/short-bond ratio increases) and depresses the short-term nominal interest rate. In the present model, this mechanism is at work. But alongside that mechanism is the portfolio balance effect arising from the reduction in short-term interest-bearing assets induced by the open market operation.

This mechanism is evident in the responses shown in Figure 5.2. In the cases in which assets are imperfectly substitutable (solid and dotted lines), nominal interest rates are reduced by more than the standard New Keynesian case (dashed lines) but demand and inflation rise by less. This reflects the fact that the rate of return relevant to household decisions is a weighted average of the returns on short-term and long-term bonds. And since the premium on long-term bonds rises, as described above, the average return relevant for spending decisions falls by less than the short-term policy rate.

Indeed, in the case when long-term bond rates are more sensitive to relative asset supplies ($v = 0.2$), five-year spot rates actually rise after a few quarters. So imperfect substitutability between assets may be sufficiently strong that the increase in the premium on long-term bonds completely offsets the effect on long-term yields from lower expected short rates.

This experiment makes it clear that, other things being equal, the presence of portfolio balance effects reduces the efficacy of *conventional* monetary policy compared with the standard New Keynesian model. When portfolio balance effects are present, conventional monetary policy has a smaller effect on activity and inflation, despite a more prolonged period of low interest rates. As explained above, the mechanism giving rise to this result is driven by the effect of the conventional monetary policy actions on the relative quantities of long-term and short-term bonds held by financial intermediaries and, hence, the premium on long-term bonds.

3.2   Asset purchase policy

Figure 5.3 depicts the responses of the model to purchases of long-term bonds by the central bank. The shock applied to the model is $\varepsilon^q = 0.25$ so that asset purchases rise to $q = 0.25$ in period 1, before falling back in line with the asset purchase 'policy rule' (bottom right panel). This calibration implies that the policy maker purchases 25 per cent of the outstanding stock of long-term government debt. This is broadly in line with the scale of asset purchases undertaken by the Bank of England in 2009 and 2010. Joyce et al. (2010) note that, in summer 2010, the Bank's £200 billion of asset purchases amounted to almost 30 per cent of the outstanding stock of eligible government debt.

The purchase of long-term assets from the private sector shifts the portfolio mix of financial intermediaries towards short-term bonds. The increase in the liquidity of financial intermediaries' portfolios reduces the premium on long-term bonds, driving up their price and reducing their yields. The reduction in long-term yields reduces the rate of return at which households can borrow and save, stimulating aggregate demand

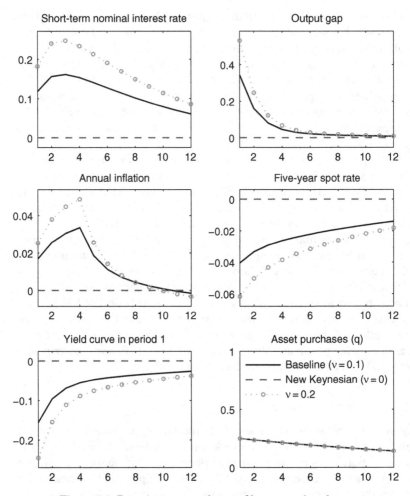

Figure 5.3 Responses to purchases of long-term bonds

and inflation. Of course, in the standard New Keynesian case with perfectly substitutable assets ($v = 0$, dashed red lines), asset purchases have no effect.

Although the transmission of asset purchase policy has the predicted effect on activity and inflation, the size of the effects is much smaller than the empirical estimates reported in Joyce et al. (2010). A key reason for the small magnitude of the responses in Figure 5.3 is that the increase in demand and inflation elicits another policy response: the Taylor rule (12) means that short-term policy rates rise. Just as the imperfect substitutability

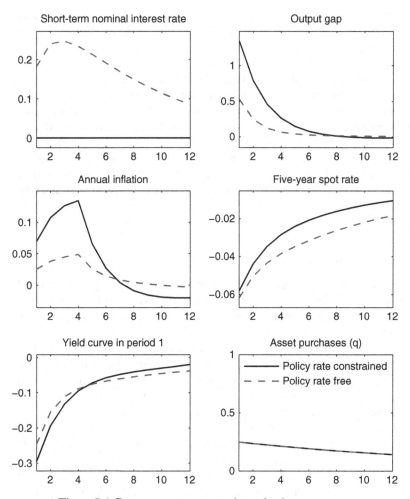

Figure 5.4 Responses to asset purchase shock

of assets partially offsets the effect of short-term nominal interest rate policy, the Taylor rule acts to partially offset the stimulus provided by asset purchases. The empirical evidence in Joyce et al. (2010) relates to a period in which the short-term policy rate did not respond to the asset purchases: the motivation for the asset purchases was to increase the overall level of monetary stimulus.

Figure 5.4 demonstrates that, when the nominal interest rate is prevented from responding to the asset purchase shock, the effects on the output gap and inflation are significantly larger. The figure is constructed for the case in which $v = 0.2$, so that relative asset prices are more responsive to relative asset supplies than in the baseline calibration. The solid lines plot the case in which the nominal interest rate is not permitted to respond to the shock.[16] The dashed lines show the case in which the nominal interest rate does respond (this replicates the circled responses plotted in Figure 5.3). When the nominal interest rate does not respond, the effect of asset purchases is around twice as large as the case in which the short-term nominal interest rate responds to the shock. This provides a motivation for the use of asset purchases when the short-term policy rate is constrained by a lower bound: the effects of asset purchases are significantly larger in this case. Christiano et al. (2009) present a similar argument on the effects of fiscal policy when interest rates are constrained by a lower bound.

4   Demand shocks

This section examines the responses of the model to negative demand shocks. The shock is $\varepsilon = -1$ so that, measured as an annual percentage rate, the natural real interest rate falls by about 4 percentage points on impact.

Figure 5.5 depicts the responses to an unexpected fall in the natural real interest rate, r^*. The fall in demand reduces the output gap and inflation. The Taylor rule means that policy is loosened in response to the reduction in demand and the short-term nominal interest rate falls. The policy response acts to partially offset the reduction in demand.

The differences in responses between the alternative parameterisations is explained by the imperfect substitutability of assets as explained above. The reduction in short rates in response to the fall in demand reduces the average liquidity of the bonds held by the private sector. This acts to increase the term premium on long-term bond rates and so long-term yields increase, partly offsetting the stimulus generated by the reduction in short rates. Indeed, the yield curve (computed using consol yields) is higher in the cases when assets are imperfect substitutes, despite the fact that short rates are reduced by more than in the canonical New Keynesian model (dashed lines). So, as noted in Section 3.1, the presence of imperfectly substitutable assets reduces the efficacy of conventional

---

[16] The simulation is implemented by applying a sequence of *anticipated* monetary policy shocks (ε^r). Bodenstein et al. (2009) show that this is a valid way to compute the effects of shocks when policy rates are constrained (for example, by a lower bound) as long as they do not alter the duration of the period for which the policy rate is constrained.

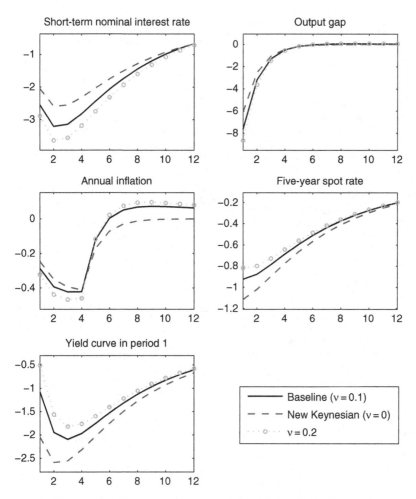

Figure 5.5 Responses to contractionary demand shock

monetary policy somewhat: the output gap and inflation fall by more, despite a greater reduction in short-term interest rates.

This observation suggests that asset purchase policies may be able to partially offset the reduction in efficacy of conventional monetary policy in the presence of imperfectly substitutable assets. This logic is borne out in Figure 5.6, which depicts the responses of the model to a negative demand shock when asset purchase policies are implemented alongside reductions in short-term nominal interest rates. Specifically, the additional policy response is assumed to be $\varepsilon^q = 0.75$ in the period that the demand

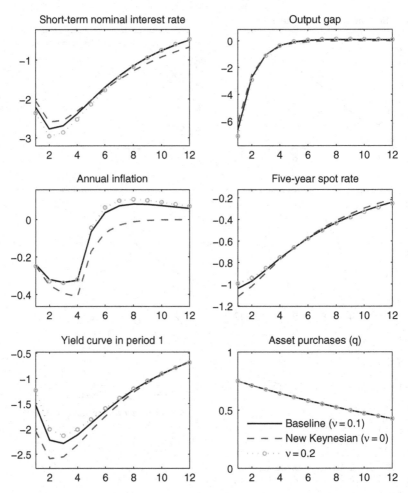

Figure 5.6 Responses to contractionary demand shock with asset purchase policies

shock arrives.[17] These initial purchases are then unwound in line with the asset purchase policy rule.

It is clear from Figure 5.6 that asset purchase policies can partially offset the rise in the premium on long-term bonds generated by the reduction in short-term nominal interest rates. This is sufficient to deliver a yield curve

---

[17] This corresponds to a case in which the policy maker purchases 75 per cent of the stock of long-term bonds.

that is similar to that generated by the canonical New Keynesian model. As a result, the decline in the output gap when asset purchase policies complement conventional monetary policy actions is also closer to the result from the canonical model. In fact, the inflation response is more muted than the standard model because, in the later periods following the shock, the output gap is actually higher. And since inflation is determined by the discounted sum of expected future output gaps, the effect on inflation of a higher output gap in the later periods is sufficient to offset the effect of a (slightly) larger initial decline in the output gap.

5   Conclusion

This chapter has explored a simple extension to a canonical New Keynesian model so that long-term and short-term bonds are imperfect substitutes. Imperfect substitutability is introduced by the assumption that financial intermediaries (which lend to the government at both long and short horizons and offer short-term and long-term bonds) face 'portfolio balance effects'. Deviations of the portfolio mix from the desired allocation are assumed to be costly to the financial intermediary. This approach means that financial intermediaries equate the effective rates of return on short-term and long-term bonds. The effective rates of return consist of the market rates of return adjusted for the costs of deviating from the desired portfolio allocation. The rate of return faced by households is thus a weighted average of the long-term and short-term bond rates. A further implication is that long-term interest rates are a function of both the expected path of short-term rates and the expected deviations of bond holdings from the desired portfolio: long-term interest rates depend on the private sector's relative holdings of short-term and long-term debt.

The chapter uncovers two key results. The first result is that the presence of portfolio balance effects may reduce the effectiveness of conventional monetary policy (implemented by the short-term interest rate). In the model, reducing the short-term policy rate leads to a reduction in the supply of short-term bonds relative to long-term bonds. Since the premium on long-term bonds is a decreasing function of the ratio of short-term to long-term government debt, the premium rises. The increased premium on long-term bonds acts (other things being equal) to increase long-term rates and hence partially offsets the effect of the reduction in short-term rates. The second result is that the portfolio balance effect creates the possibility of using an additional policy instrument – asset purchases – alongside conventional monetary policy. Asset purchases shift the supply of assets available to the private sector and hence the yields on those assets. The experiments with the model indicate that the efficacy of asset purchases is increased substantially when short-term nominal interest rates are not permitted to respond (as would be the case, for example, when they are constrained by a lower bound).

Several issues touched on in this chapter will doubtless be taken further in future research. The interplay between conventional and unconventional monetary policies could be analysed further, particularly in cases where short-term nominal interest rates are constrained by a lower bound. The microfoundations underlying the imperfect substitutability of financial assets are certain to be the subject of considerable interest.

References

Andrés, J., López-Salido, J. D. and Nelson, E. (2004) Tobin's imperfect asset substitution in optimizing general equilibrium, *Journal of Money, Credit & Banking*, 36(4), 665–91.

Benford, J., Berry, S., Nikolov, K., Young, C. and Robson, M. (2009) Quantitative easing, *Bank of England Quarterly Bulletin*, 2, 90–100.

Bernanke, B. S., Gertler, M. and Gilchrist, S. (1999) The financial accelerator in a quantitative business cycle framework, *Handbook of Macroeconomics*, 1, 1341–93.

Bernanke, B. S., Reinhart, V. R. and Sack, B. P. (2004) Monetary policy alternatives at the zero bound: an empirical assessment, *Brookings Papers on Economic Activity*, 2(2004), 1–78.

Bodenstein, M., Erceg, C. J. and Guerrieri, L. (2009) The effects of foreign shocks when interest rates are at zero, Federal Reserve Board of Governors International Finance Discussion Paper No. 983.

Branson, W. H. and Henderson, D. W. (1985) The specification and influence of asset markets, in Jones, R. W. and Kenen, P. B. (eds.), *Handbook of International Economics*, Vol. 2. Amsterdam: Elsevier, pp. 749–805.

Christiano, L., Eichenbaum, M. S. and Rebelo, S. (2009) When is the government spending multiplier large? NBER Working Paper No. 15394.

Clarida, R., Galí, J. and Gertler, M. (1999) The science of monetary policy: a New Keynesian perspective, *Journal of Economic Literature*, 37(4), 1661–707.

Cúrdia, V. and Woodford, M. (2009) Conventional and unconventional monetary policy, Federal Reserve Bank of New York Staff Report No. 404.

Gagnon, J., Raskin, M., Remache, J. and Sack, B. (2010) Large-scale asset purchases by the Federal Reserve: did they work? Federal Reserve Bank of New York Staff Report No. 441.

Galí, J. (2008) *Monetary Policy, Inflation, and the Business Cycle*, Princeton University Press.

Gertler, M. and Karadi, P. (2011) A model of unconventional monetary policy, *Journal of Monetary Economics*, 58, 17–34.

Greenwood, R. and Vayanos, D. (2010) Bond supply and excess bond returns. unpublished, LSE.

Joyce, M., Lasoasa, A., Stevens, I. and Tong, M. (2010) The financial market impact of quantitative easing, Bank of England Working Paper No. 393.

Kuttner, K. N. (2006) Can central banks target bond prices? NBER Working Paper No. 12454.

Levin, A., López-Salido, D., Nelson, E. and Yun, T. (2010) Limitations on the effectiveness of forward guidance at the zero lower bound, *International Journal of Central Banking*, 6(1), 143–89.

Meier, A. (2009) Panacea, curse, or nonevent? Unconventional monetary policy in the United Kingdom, IMF Working Paper No. 09/163.

Rotemberg, J. J. (1982) Monopolistic price adjustment and aggregate output, *The Review of Economic Studies*, 49(4), 517–31.

Smets, F. and Wouters, R. (2007) Shocks and frictions in US business cycles, *American Economic Review*, 97(3), 586–606.

Taylor, J. B. (1993) Discretion versus policy rules in practice, *Carnegie–Rochester Conference Series on Public Policy*, 39, 195–214.

Tobin, J. (1969) A general equilibrium approach to monetary theory, *Journal of Money, Credit and Banking*, 1(1), 15–29.

(1956) Liquidity preference as behavior towards risk, *Review of Economic Studies*, 25(2), 65–86.

Tobin, J. and Brainard, W. C. (1963) Financial intermediaries and the effectiveness of monetary controls, *American Economic Review*, 53(2), 383–400.

Woodford, M. (2003) *Interest and Prices: Foundations of a Theory of Monetary Policy*, Princeton University Press.

6   Financial intermediaries in an estimated DSGE model for the UK

Stefania Villa and Jing Yang

Abstract

Gertler and Karadi (2011) combined financial intermediation and unconventional 'monetary policy' in a DSGE framework. We estimate their model with UK data using Bayesian techniques. To validate the fit of the estimated DSGE model, we evaluate the model's empirical properties. Then, we analyse the transmission mechanism of the shocks, set to produce a downturn. Finally, we examine the empirical importance of nominal, real and financial frictions and of different shocks. We find that banking friction seems to play an important role in explaining the UK business cycle. Moreover, the banking sector shock seems to explain about half of the fall in real GDP in the recent crisis. A credit supply shock seems to account for most of the weakness in bank lending.

1   Introduction

Gertler and Karadi (2009) (GK, henceforth) presented a DSGE model with financial frictions and unconventional monetary policy,[1] calibrated for the US economy. Unlike Bernanke et al. (1999) and Kiyotaki and Moore (1997), the financial frictions directly originate in the financial sector: the financial intermediaries face an agency problem and their balance sheets are endogenously constrained.

The views expressed in this chapter are those of the authors and not necessarily those of the Bank of England. We are indebted to Mark Gertler and Peter Karadi for providing access to their code. We are grateful to Andrew Blake, Jagjit Chadha, Federico Di Pace, Marcelo Ferman, Mark Gertler, Peter Karadi, Giovanni Melina, Haroon Mumtaz, Matthias Paustian, Konstantinos Theodoridis and Stephen Wright, as well as seminar participants at the Bank of England, Birkbeck College, the Cambridge Conference 'New Instruments of Monetary Policy: The Challenges' and at the EEA 2010 for helpful comments and suggestions. The usual disclaimer applies.

[1] Under GK's 'unconventional monetary policy' the policy maker assumes a direct intermediation role. This is clearly not the policy of quantitative easing undertaken by the Bank of England. We note that the effects of unconventional monetary policy cannot be estimated due to the absence of such policies.

GK's paper is particularly interesting because the authors emphasise the role of financial intermediaries in the transmission mechanism of the shocks. In addition, their paper is the first attempt to quantitatively assess direct credit intermediation of the type pursued by the Fed during the financial crisis as an additional tool for monetary policy in a DSGE framework.

As Bean (2009) noted, in most DSGE models with financial frictions, financial intermediaries are simple or non-existent. However, as the current recession has shown, banks play an active role in the real economy and they are not simply a part of the amplification of the transmission mechanism. The aim of this chapter is to examine the empirical properties of the GK model estimated for the UK economy. In particular, we analyse the capability of the model to mimic the path of financial variables. Bayesian estimation techniques are used to estimate the model with financial intermediaries and without unconventional monetary policy.

The Bayesian DSGE approach has become very popular in recent times, both in academia and among policy makers, because it can address a number of key issues in business cycle analysis (see Smets and Wouters (2007), Adolfson et al. (2007), Gertler et al. (2008), among many others).[2]

We first analyse the model's fit for the UK economy. The comparison between model and data will be made along two dimensions: the Kalman filtered estimates of the observed variables, computed at the posterior mode of the estimated parameters, along with the actual variables, and second, the comparison of the unconditional moments, as standard in the real business cycle (RBC) literature (see Cooley and Hansen (1995), among many others). After validating the fit of the model, impulse response functions (IRFs) are used to summarise the predictions of the model. Its baseline specification is compared with a model without respectively nominal, real and financial frictions. Finally, some policy implications are presented via IRFs analysis, when unconventional monetary policy is 'at work'.

The chapter is structured as follows. In Section 2 the main features of the model are briefly presented. Section 3 contains a short description of the data used. Section 4 analyses the estimation procedure: calibrated parameters, prior and posterior distributions of the estimated parameters and model fit; it also provides subsample estimates. Section 5 presents the following estimation results: impulse responses to different shocks; the empirical importance of different frictions; and the relative importance of

---

[2] Fernández-Villaverde (2009) provides a comprehensive survey about Bayesian estimation of DSGE models.

different shocks. Section 6 presents some policy implications. The final section offers some concluding remarks.

2   The model

The GK model combines three different strands of literature. First, the vast literature about financial frictions on non-financial firms, whose seminal paper is Bernanke et al. (1999) (BGG, henceforth). Second, the smaller literature on the role of bank capital, e.g. Aikman and Paustian (2006), Gertler and Kiyotaki (2009) and Meh and Moran (2010). Third, the standard DSGE modelling with frictionless capital markets: Christiano et al. (2005) and Smets and Wouters (2007) (SW, henceforth).

The main novelties of the model regard the setup of the financial intermediaries and of the policy maker. We now briefly present the main features of the GK model. The agents in the GK model are households, financial intermediaries (FIs), intermediate goods firms, capital producers, monopolistically competitive retailers and the policy maker.

Each household consumes, saves and supplies labour. Households do not hold capital directly; they save by lending funds to the FIs. Within each household there are two types of members at any point in time: the fraction f of the household members are workers and the fraction $(1 - f)$ are bankers. GK introduced a finite horizon for bankers in order to avoid the possibility that they can reach the point where they can fund all investment from their own capital. The turnover between bankers and workers is as follows: every banker stays banker next period with a probability θ, which is independent of history. Therefore, every period $(1 - \theta)$ bankers exit and become workers. Similarly, a number of workers become bankers, keeping the relative proportion of each type constant. The family provides its new banker with a start-up transfer, which is a small fraction of total assets, χ. Each banker manages a financial intermediary.

The households maximise utility subject to the budget constraint; the utility function is separable in consumption and labour and exhibits internal habit formation:

$$E_t \sum_{t=0}^{\infty} \beta^t \left[ln(C_t - hC_{t-1}) - \frac{\omega}{1 + \phi} L_t^{1+\phi} \right] \qquad (1)$$

where $\beta > 0$, the parameter h captures habit formation, ω measures the relative weight of leisure and ϕ is the inverse of Frisch elasticity of labour supply.

Financial intermediaries obtain funds from the household at the rate R_t and they lend them to firms at the market lending rate R_t^k. There is perfect information between financial intermediaries and firms and asymmetric information between financial intermediaries and households.

At the beginning of the period the financial intermediary can divert a fraction λ of total assets and transfer them to their family. The cost of doing so is that the FI goes into bankruptcy.

The objective of the banker is to maximise expected terminal wealth, V_t. For the lender to deposit money in the FI, the following incentive compatibility constraint should hold:

$$V_t \geq \lambda Q_t S_t \tag{2}$$

where S_t is the quantity of financial claims on non-financial firms and Q_t is the relative price of each claim. The LHS of equation (2) represents the loss for the FI from diverting funds and the RHS represents the gain from doing so.

When the constraint binds, GK show that the previous equation can be written as

$$Q_t S_t = lev_t N_t \tag{3}$$

where lev_t stands for the FI leverage ratio and N_t is FI capital (or net worth).

According to equation (3), the assets the FI can acquire depend positively on its equity capital. The agency problem introduces an endogenous capital constraint on the bank's ability to acquire assets.

Total net worth is the sum of net worth of existing bankers, N^e, and net worth of new bankers, N^n. The net worth of existing bankers evolves as

$$N_t^e = \{\theta[(R_t^k - R_{t-1})lev_{t-1} + R_{t-1}]N_{t-1}\} \exp\left(-e_t^n\right) \tag{4}$$

where R_t is the riskless interest rate on deposit, R_t^k is the lending rate and e_t^n is a shock to FI capital. Net worth of new bankers is

$$N_t^n = \chi Q_t S_t \tag{5}$$

where χ is the fraction of total assets given to new bankers.

The spread is defined as[3]

$$\hat{SP}_t = \hat{R}_{t+1}^k - \hat{R}_t. \tag{6}$$

---

[3] Variables without time subscripts denote steady-state values and the hat denotes a percentage deviation from steady state.

Each intermediate-good firm finances the acquisition of capital, K_{t+1}, by obtaining funds from the FI. The firm issues S_t state-contingent claims equal to the number of units of capital acquired and prices each claim at the price of a unit of capital Q_t:

$$Q_t K_{t+1} = Q_t S_t. \tag{7}$$

Lending to firms does not involve any agency problem. However, the constraint that FIs face affects the supply of funds to intermediate firms and the lending rate. The firms maximise profits, choosing capital, labour and the utilisation rate. The production function is a standard Cobb–Douglas:

$$Y_t = A_t(u_t K_t \psi_t)^\alpha \ell_t^{1-\alpha} \tag{8}$$

where u_t is the utilisation rate and ψ_t is the shock to the quality of capital (which is meant to capture economic obsolescence).

At the end of each period, competitive capital-producing firms buy capital from intermediate goods firms and then repair depreciated capital and build new capital. They then sell both the new and refurbished capital.

Sticky prices are introduced in the production sector by assuming monopolistic competition at the retail level as in BGG. The Phillips curve is

$$\hat{\pi}_t = \frac{\sigma_p}{1 + \sigma_p \beta} \hat{\pi}_{t-1} + \frac{\beta}{1 + \sigma_p \beta} E_t\{\hat{\pi}_{t+1}\} - \frac{(1 - \beta\sigma)(1 - \sigma)}{(1 + \sigma_p \beta)\sigma} \hat{\mu}_t \tag{9}$$

where σ is the probability of keeping prices constant and σ_p measures indexation to past inflation.

The policy maker conducts both conventional and unconventional monetary policy – a standard Taylor rule:

$$i_t = i_{t-1}^{\rho_i} \left(\pi_t^{\rho_\pi} y_t^{\rho_y}\right)^{1-\rho_i} \exp(\varepsilon_t^i) \tag{10}$$

and the following feedback rule for credit policy:

$$cp_t = cp + v(R_{t+1}^k - R_t) - (R^k - R)] \tag{11}$$

$$\text{with} \quad Q_t S_{pt} = cp_t Q_t S_t$$

where $Q_t S_{pt}$ is the value of assets intermediated via the policy maker, which is a fraction, cp_t, of total assets. In steady state the fraction of publicly intermediated assets is zero. According to equation (11), the degree of intermediation depends on the extent that the spread deviates from its steady-state value.

Unconventional monetary policy works in GK as follows. The policy maker, after obtaining funds from households at the rate R, lends the funds to non-financial firms at the market lending rate R^k. The policy maker always honours its debt, so there is no agency conflict that limits the policy maker's ability to obtain funds from households. In other words, the policy maker does not have a balance sheet constraint that limits its lending capacity.

In the model there are five exogenous disturbances: ε_i, the monetary policy shock; the FI capital (or bank capital) shock; the technology shock; the capital quality shock; and the government shock. The last three shocks evolve exogenously according to the following first-order autoregressive processes:

$$x_t = \rho_x x_{t-1} + \varepsilon_t^x$$

where $\rho_x \in (0, 1)$ with $x = a, \psi, g$ and ε_t^x is an i.i.d. shock with constant variance $\sigma_{\varepsilon^x}^2$.

3 The data

To estimate the model we use quarterly UK data for the period 1979Q2–2010Q1. We match the following five observable variables: real GDP (y), real investment, CPI seasonally adjusted inflation, lending to private non-financial corporations (PNFCs) and corporate bond spread.[4]

The M4 lending data show the business between UK monetary financial institutions and M4 private sector. This is broken into business with other financial corporations, PNFCs and the household sector. The reason we are considering M4 lending to PNFCs is that the GK model is analysing lending to PNFCs only.

The spread is calculated as the yield on BAA-rated corporate bonds over maturity-equivalent risk-free rates.

To make these variables stationary, the logarithm of GDP, of investment, of lending to PNFCs and inflation have been detrended with the HP filter. Inflation is calculated as log difference of seasonally adjusted CPI. Data on the spread have been demeaned and then divided by 100 to make the units compatible with the HP data.

---

[4] We use ONS quarterly series GDP (ABMI) and investment (NPQT), both seasonally adjusted and in constant 2006 prices. The lending series (LPQBC57) come from the Bank of England database and have been deflated with the GDP deflator.

We have chosen this period following DiCecio and Nelson (2007). Notwithstanding, this sample period has been characterised by different monetary policy regimes (Benati, 2004 and Nelson, 2006). Hence, in Section 4 we compare the full-sample estimates with the post-1992 period, when inflation targeting was adopted.

Table 6.1 presents some statistical properties of the data. As far as the full sample is concerned, the series display different volatilities: investment is three times more volatile than GDP. The volatility of inflation is slightly lower than that of GDP, with a relative standard deviation of inflation (std of inflation/std of GDP) equal to 0.93. Lending to PNFCs is more volatile than investment as in Bean et al. (2002), with a relative standard deviation of 3.7. The spread is less volatile than output, with a relative standard deviation of 0.56. As far as cross correlations are concerned, the data reflect the economic properties that output and investment are positively correlated, and the same applies to inflation and output. Lending to PNFCs is also procyclical. The correlation with the spread is negative; this evidence supports the countercyclicality of the spread, as in Aksoy et al. (2009) and Gertler and Lown (1999). The evidence in Table 6.1 suggests that CPI inflation lags the cycle by approximately four quarters, as in Bean et al. (2002); the lending series lags the cycle by approximately two quarters.

These results are in line with Bean et al. (2002), who used a different filtering technique over the sample 1970–2000.

Table 6.1 *Some statistical properties of the data (1979–2009)*

Variable (t)	Std dev	Relative std dev	Cross correlation with GDP_{t+k}				
			$t=-4$	$t=-2$	$t=0$	$t=2$	$t=4$
Full sample							
GDP	0.0146						
Investment	0.0457	3.13	0.28	0.65	0.80	0.57	0.23
Inflation	0.0136	0.93	0.51	0.48	0.08	−0.29	−0.43
Lending	0.0540	3.70	0.35	0.44	0.39	0.16	−0.07
Spread	0.0082	0.56	0.20	0.06	−0.26	−0.36	−0.21
1993Q1–2010Q1							
GDP	0.0121						
Investment	0.0417	3.45	0.01	0.50	0.80	0.60	0.14
Inflation	0.0061	0.50	0.35	0.57	0.42	−0.10	−0.22
Lending	0.0516	4.26	0.34	0.60	0.55	0.28	0.03
Spread	0.0101	0.83	0.39	0.21	−0.33	−0.54	−0.32

The subsample period 1993Q1–2010Q1 includes not only the 'Great Moderation' but also the 'Great Contraction' (Bean, 2009). The volatility of output, investment, inflation and lending fell; the most significant reduction regards the inflation series, whose standard deviation has decreased by more than 50 per cent. On the contrary, the volatility of the spread has increased almost 25 per cent compared with the full-sample value (0.0101 versus 0.0082). The last observations of this sample include the Great Contraction. In the period 1993Q1–2007Q4 the volatility of the spread was 0.003, while it increased more than fourfold (0.0139) when including the period 2008Q1–2010Q1.

The signs of the correlations are the same as those in the full sample, confirming both the cyclical and the leading characteristics of the macro series. Interestingly, the values of the correlation between output and the spread are higher than the full-sample value.

4 Estimation

Bayesian inference starts out from setting the prior distribution of selected parameters; the prior describes the available information prior to observing the data used in the estimation. Then the Kalman filter is used to calculate the likelihood function of the data. Combining prior distributions with the likelihood of the data gives the posterior kernel, which is proportional to the posterior density. The posterior distribution of the model's parameters is summarised by the mode and the mean.

4.1 Calibrated parameters

As standard in Bayesian estimation of DSGE models, some parameters are fixed in the estimation procedure (see, e.g., Christiano et al., 2010). Most of the calibrated parameters are related to the steady-state value of variables observed in the economy. Table 6.2 reports the calibrated parameters.

The calibrated values of the capital income share, the discount factor, the depreciation rate and the price elasticity of demand are standard in the literature. These values reproduce the ratio of investment to GDP of our dataset, equal to 0.18.

The elasticity of labour supply, the relative utility weight of labour and the habit persistence parameter have been calibrated such that the average hours of work is equal to 0.33, a common value in the literature. We have chosen to calibrate these parameters since our dataset do not contain any information on employment and wages.

152   Interest Rates, Prices and Liquidity

Table 6.2 *Calibrated parameters*

Parameter	Value
a, capital income share	0.33
β, discount factor	0.99
δ, depreciation rate	0.025
ε, price elasticity of demand	6
ϕ, inverse of Frisch elasticity of labour supply	0.33
ω, relative utility weight of labour	4.01
h, habit persistence parameter	0.815
χ, fraction of assets given to the new bankers	0.002
θ, survival rate	0.94
λ, fraction of divertable assets	0.19
v, feedback parameter for unconventional mo. po.	0

The three parameters related to the financial sector are calibrated because they pin down some steady-state values of the model economy. In particular, the fraction of assets given to new bankers, the survival rate and the fraction of assets that can be diverted are, respectively, equal to 0.002, 0.94 and 0.19. Those values imply an annual steady-state spread of 118 basis points, consistently with the average value in our dataset, and with a steady-state leverage ratio of 11, as in Gerali et al. (2009). The feedback parameter in the credit policy rule, v, is set equal to zero because what GK describe as unconventional monetary policy cannot be captured in our dataset (see footnote 1).

4.2   Prior and posterior distributions of the estimated parameters

The remaining parameters governing the dynamics of the model are estimated and they mostly pertain to the nominal and real frictions in the model as well as the exogenous shock processes.

Table 6.3 shows the assumptions for the prior distributions of the estimated parameters. The locations of the prior mean correspond to a large extent to those in previous studies on the UK economy, DiCecio and Nelson (2007) and Harrison and Oomen (2010).

The posterior distribution of all estimated parameters is obtained in two steps. First, the posterior mode and an approximate covariance matrix, based on the inverse Hessian matrix evaluated at the mode, is obtained by numerical optimisation on the log posterior density. Second, the posterior distribution is subsequently explored by generating draws using the Random Walk Metropolis–Hastings algorithm with

Table 6.3 *Prior and posterior distributions of structural parameters*

Parameters	Prior distr			Posterior
	Distr	Mean	St. Dev./df	Mean
σ, Calvo parameter	Beta	0.75	0.1	0.81
σ_p, price indexation	Beta	0.5	0.2	0.11
S'', Inv. adj. costs	Gamma	5.5	0.25	5.85
ζ, elasticity of marg. deprec	Gamma	1	0.5	1.88
ρ_π, Taylor rule	Normal	1.5	0.2	1.59
ρ_y, Taylor rule	Normal	0.12	0.2	0.39
ρ_i, Taylor rule	Normal	0.87	0.1	0.64
ρ_a, persist of tech shock	Beta	0.85	0.1	0.98
ρ_k, persist of capital shock	Beta	0.5	0.1	0.40
ρ_g, persistence of gov shock	Beta	0.5	0.1	0.51
σ_a, std of tech shock	IG	0.1	2	0.02
σ_k, std of capital shock	IG	0.1	2	0.02
σ_i, std of monetary shock	IG	0.1	2	0.02
σ_n, std of FI capital shock	IG	0.1	2	0.18
σ_g, std of gov shock	IG	0.1	2	0.05

a sample of 250,000 draws – see Schorfheide (2000) and SW for further details.

We use the inverse gamma (IG) distribution for the standard deviation of the shocks and we set a loose prior with 2 degrees of freedom. We use the beta distribution for all parameters bounded between 0 and 1. For parameters measuring elasticities we use the gamma distribution. And for the unbounded parameters we use the normal distribution. However, for the parameter measuring the response to inflation in the Taylor rule we set a lower bound so that the Taylor principle is satisfied.

The parameter of price stickiness is assumed to follow a beta distribution with mean 0.75, which corresponds to changing prices every four quarters on average and we set a relatively loose prior for the indexation parameter as in SW.

The elasticity of the investment adjustment cost function has a prior mean of 5.5 and a relatively high standard deviation. The elasticity of marginal depreciation with respect to capital utilisation is set at 1, as in GK, and with a high standard deviation, following the previous studies on the UK economy. The Taylor rule coefficient on inflation has a normal distribution with a prior mean of 1.5 and a relatively high standard deviation, following the studies of DiCecio and Nelson (2007), Harrison and Oomen (2010) and SW. The Taylor coefficient on the output gap is set at

0.12, with a standard deviation of 0.2, and the Taylor smoothing parameter has a prior mean of 0.87, as in DiCecio and Nelson (2007) and Harrison and Oomen (2010).

The last column of Table 6.3 shows the posterior mean of all the parameters. The estimated Calvo parameter, σ, implies that firms reoptimise on average every five quarters. The degree of price indexation, σ_p, is lower than its prior mean, similarly to the results obtained by SW for the US economy.

The elasticity of the cost of changing investment is estimated to be higher to that assumed a priori, suggesting a slower response of investment to changes in the value of capital. The elasticity of marginal depreciation with respect to capital utilisation is higher than assumed a priori, suggesting a small response of capital utilisation to the shocks.

Concerning the monetary policy reaction function parameters, the mean of the reaction coefficient to inflation is estimated to be higher to its prior distribution. There is a lower degree of interest rate smoothing, as the mean of the coefficient on the lagged interest rate is estimated to be 0.64. Monetary policy appears to react to the output gap level with a coefficient of 0.39, similar to DiCecio and Nelson (2007).

Finally, turning to the exogenous shock variables, the shock to bank capital is the most volatile, with the second most volatile being the government shock. It is worth noting that in a closed-economy model, government shock might also capture trade movements; its higher value could be interpreted as a signal of the exogenous disturbances from trade. The technology shock is very persistent, with a coefficient of 0.98; the persistence of the shock to the quality of capital is lower than the prior mean, with a coefficient of 0.40.

4.3   Model fit

Following Adolfson et al. (2007), in Figure 6.1 we report the Kalman filtered estimates of the observed variables, computed at the posterior mode of the estimated parameters in the benchmark model along with the actual variables. The lighter line corresponds to the one-step-ahead forecasts implied by the estimated model and the darker line represents the data. Roughly speaking, these estimates correspond to fitted values in a regression.

As evident from Figure 6.1, the in-sample fit of the baseline model is quite satisfactory for inflation, lending and the spread. The fit for investment improves in the last decade while that of output is overall less satisfactory. This result is not surprising for a number of reasons. First, a closed economy model is unlikely to perfectly reproduce the GDP

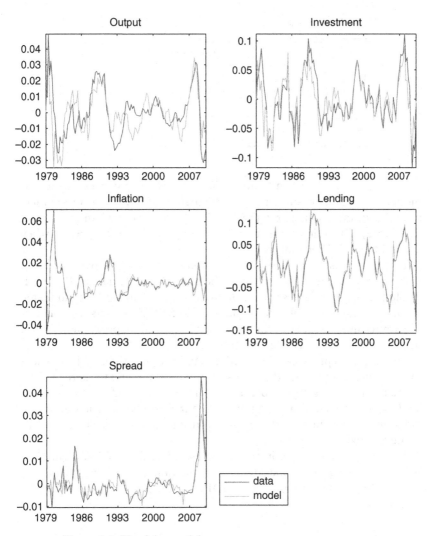

Figure 6.1 Fit of the model

fluctuations for the UK, since external demand is not explicitly modelled. Second, the GK model does not incorporate unemployment or frictions in the labour market, which might be important drivers of GDP fluctuations. Third, since bank capital is explicitly included, the model is able to capture the disruption of financial intermediation, similar to what happened in the recent crisis. Indeed, the fit of the model for GDP is more satisfactory in the most recent period since the onset of the crisis.

Table 6.4 *Simulated moments*

Variable	Std dev	Relative std dev
GDP	0.111	
Investment	0.368	3.32
Inflation	0.054	0.49
Lending	0.239	2.15
Spread	0.072	0.65

There seems to be a support to the empirical properties of the GK model, in particular concerning the financial variables. One of the main novelties of the GK paper is the microfoundation of the banking sector. Therefore, this microfoundation has nice empirical properties when applied to the UK economy.

To further assess the conformity between the data and the model, we compare the moments generated by the model with the data in Table 6.1. Table 6.4 reports some selected moments of the data and the simulated model. Overall, the table shows that the model overpredicts the volatility of output, investment and lending, which is a common problem in DSGE models (see also von Heideken (2009)).

The model reproduces the relative standard deviations of investment (3.32 in the simulated model versus 3.13 in the data) and the spread (0.56 in the model versus 0.65 in the data). The relative standard deviations of lending and inflation are slightly different from the actual values (for inflation 0.49 in the model versus 0.93 in the data and for lending 2.15 in the simulated model versus 3.7).

This result is not surprising given the estimates obtained in Figure 6.1. Notwithstanding, the cyclical feaures of inflation, less volatile than GDP, and lending, more volatile than GDP, are preserved in the estimated model.

4.4   Subsample estimates

The full sample 1979–2010 includes different monetary regimes: monetary targeting in the late 1970s and early 1980s; exchange rate management, culminating in the UK membership of the European exchange rate mechanism (ERM) and the adoption of inflation targeting in October 1992.

We now investigate whether the previous results are sensitive to the chosen sample; our subsample corresponds to the inflation targeting period. Table 6.5 compares the full sample estimates with the post-1992

Table 6.5 *Subsample estimates*

Parameters	Full sample	Subsample
Mode of estimated parameters		
σ	0.81	0.84
σ_p	0.11	0.19
S''	5.85	4.69
ζ	1.88	1.58
ρ_π	1.59	1.66
ρ_y	0.39	0.37
ρ_i	0.62	0.74
ρ_a	0.98	0.98
ρ_k	0.40	0.37
ρ_g	0.51	0.69
σ_a	0.02	0.01
σ_k	0.02	0.02
σ_i	0.02	0.01
σ_n	0.18	0.19
σ_g	0.05	0.05

sample estimates. The comparison between two samples reveals that the Calvo parameter has slightly increased, suggesting that the average duration of price contracts is about six quarters, a quarter more than the full-sample value. The indexation parameter reveals a higher degree of price stickiness in the recent period.

Concerning the two real elasticities, the elasticity of the cost of changing investment is lower than the full-sample value and the elasticity of marginal depreciation with respect to capital utilisation is lower as well. Therefore, on the side of investment the real friction is reduced, while on the side of marginal depreciation the real friction has increased, so that overall the presence of real frictions in the model economy has not changed significantly.

The parameters in the Taylor rule seem to signal a different monetary regime. The policy maker's reaction coefficient to inflation is higher than its full-sample value, revealing that in the post-1992 sample period, UK monetary policy behaviour opted for more weight on inflation. The contrary happens to the policy maker's reaction coefficient to output gap, which has decreased.

Results are quite stable as far as the volatility of the shocks is concerned. The standard error of technology and interest rate shocks have slightly fallen, while the volatility of net worth shock has slightly increased.

5   Estimation results

5.1   *Impulse response function*

In the GK model there are five shocks: while four of them are standard in the literature (the technology, monetary, bank capital and government shock), the shock to the quality of capital is relatively new. In the GK model this last shock is meant to mimic the broad dynamics of the subprime crisis.

Figures 6.2 and 6.3 show the impulse response functions to four shocks. All the shocks are set to produce a downturn, as in GK. We can distinguish the transmission mechanism between the technology and monetary shocks on one hand, and the bank capital and quality of capital shocks on the other.

Contractionary technology and monetary policy shocks determine a fall in investment; this implies a decrease in the asset prices, which deteriorates the bank's balance sheet. Such a deterioration implies that banks push up the premium and this reduces the amount of lending, as is evident from Figure 6.2. The technology shock is a standard supply shock, in the sense that it has a negative effect on output and a positive effect on inflation. The interest rate shock is a standard demand shock, in the sense that it has a negative impact on both output and inflation.

The shock to the quality of capital translates directly into a shock to the bank balance sheet because of the identity between capital and assets. In the GK model, financial frictions are always binding and depositors require that banks do not become over-leveraged; as a result, banks are forced to curtail their lending. The squeeze on credit means that firms are able to buy less capital for use in the following period.

The shock to bank capital directly affects the bank's balance sheet as well: the drop in bank net worth tightens the bank's borrowing constraint because banks are leveraged.

In order to better understand the financial accelerator effect in the transmission mechanism, it is worthwhile to note that three factors drive the growth of bank profit: the size of the spread, the lending volume and the leverage. Following a sharp decline in bank net worth, banks have to cut back lending because of the balance sheet constraint. The more leveraged they are, the larger is the impact of capital losses on the reduction in lending. This retrenchment in lending leads to a fall in banks' profits. Banks can rebuild their profit and capital base only by increasing the lending rate; therefore, the spread rises as shown in the figures. In the face of the sharp increase in financing cost, firms are forced to reduce demand for loans, therefore cut back investment and increase the

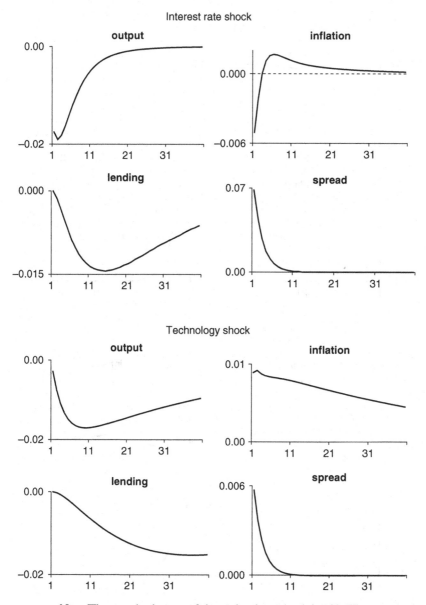

Note: The standard error of the technology shock is 2%. The standard error to the interest rate is 2% as well

Figure 6.2 The estimated IRFs to a technology shock and to an interest rate shock

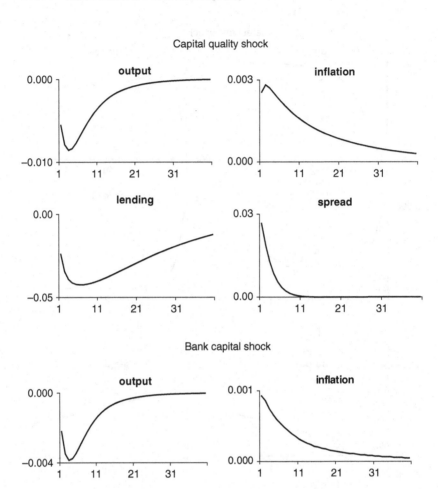

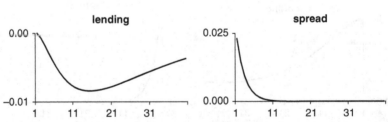

Note: The standard error of the shock to the quality of capital is 2%. The standard error to the FI capital shock is 18%

Figure 6.3 The estimated IRFs to a shock to the quality of capital and to a shock to bank capital

utilisation rate of capital. Both investment and output suffer a protracted decline. Subdued aggregate demand feeds back to the banking sector, resulting in lower profits. This in turn causes banks to further tighten credit supply and raise lending spreads in order to satisfy their endogenous balance sheet constraint. This is the financial accelerator effect. Given the lending volume decline, banks can try to increase profit only by increasing spreads, which is likely to lead to a further fall in lending demand. It can take a long time for banks to rebuild their capital back to their steady-state level. Reflected in lending, the figures show that the slowdown in lending is highly persistent. From a quantitative point of view, the reduction in lending due to the financial shocks is substantial. And the reduction of the credit flow exacerbates the crisis.

As is evident from Figure 6.3, both shocks are supply shocks. This finding is particularly interesting compared with the findings of GK – in their paper both the shock to the quality of capital and the shock to bank capital behave like demand shocks. Aikman and Paustian (2006), Gilchrist et al. (2009) and Meh and Moran (2010) found that a negative shock to bank capital behaves like a supply shock. As Aikman and Paustian (2006) explained, the contraction in the production of intermediate goods is accompanied by higher prices, implying higher marginal costs. The increase in marginal costs is expected to persist and this results in an upward pressure on inflation.

It is not surprising that the shock to the quality of capital behaves like a supply shock, because in the GK model it affects the capital accumulation equation and, therefore, the production function, equation (8). Therefore, the supply-side effect of this shock dominates.

5.2   Model comparison

The introduction of a large number of frictions raises the question of which of those are really necessary to capture the dynamics of the data. Bayesian estimation techniques can address this type of issue. As illustrated by Chang et al. (2002), the marginal data density can be interpreted as maximum log-likelihood values; it provides an indication of the overall likelihood of the model given the data.

In this section, we examine the contribution of each of the frictions to the marginal likelihood of the model. In particular, we analyse three types of frictions: nominal frictions (price stickiness, price indexation), real frictions (investment adjustment, capital utilisation) and financial frictions.

Table 6.6 presents the estimates of the mode of the parameters and the marginal likelihood when each friction is drastically reduced one at a time.

Table 6.6 *The importance of the different frictions*

	Base	$\sigma = 0.1$	$\sigma_p = 0$	$S'' = 0.1$	$\zeta = 3.5$	no FF
Marginal likelihood						
	1231	1122	1224	1087	1244	1076
Mode of estimated parameters						
σ, Calvo parameter	0.80	0.10	0.80	0.83	0.81	0.85
σ_p, price indexation	0.15	0.15	0	0.16	0.15	0.16
S'', Inv. adj.costs	6.00	6.00	6.00	0.10	6.00	5.99
ζ, elasticity of marg. depr.	1.90	1.90	1.90	1.90	3.5	1.91
ρ_π, Taylor rule	1.65	1.66	1.65	1.66	1.65	1.65
ρ_y, Taylor rule	0.31	0.29	0.30	0.40	0.37	0.28
ρ_i, Taylor rule	0.75	0.73	0.76	0.60	0.76	0.77
ρ_a, persist of tech. shock	0.93	0.89	0.94	0.82	0.94	0.85
ρ_k, persist of capital shock	0.51	0.51	0.51	0.43	0.51	0.53
ρ_g, persist of gov. shock	0.48	0.48	0.48	0.49	0.48	0.50
σ_a, std of tech. shock	0.02	0.03	0.01	0.03	0.02	0.06
σ_k, std of capital shock	0.04	0.03	0.03	0.04	0.04	0.05
σ_i, std of monetary shock	0.01	0.02	0.01	0.01	0.01	0.03
σ_g, std of gov. shock	0.05	0.05	0.05	0.05	0.05	0.08

This experiment also makes it possible to analyse the robustness of the parameters under the different specifications.

In order to make a meaningful comparison with the model without financial frictions ('no FF'), we use four observables for all the models described in Table 6.6 and therefore four structural shocks in the model economy. Unlike the BGG framework, removing financial frictions in the GK model is not obtained by setting a certain parameter equal to zero. We have calculated again the equilibrium conditions for the standard DSGE model, where the banking sector has been removed. There is no spread variable and no shock to bank capital in the model 'no FF'. Therefore, the series on the spread are not used as observable for the estimation procedure.

For comparison, the first column reproduces the baseline estimates (mode of the posteriors) and the marginal likelihood based on the Laplace approximation for the model.

Concerning nominal frictions, we reduced the Calvo probability to 0.1; therefore, on average a firm reoptimises its price every quarter. The marginal likelihood of the model is reduced to the value of 1122, while in the baseline model it is 1231. A lower degree of price stickiness does not have a great impact on the mode of the parameters, which are quite stable across the two models.

Removing price indexation to past inflation, that is setting $\sigma_p = 0$, implies a moderate reduction of the marginal likelihood, which decreases to the value of 1224. The values of the estimated parameters are substantially stable under this different model specification.

Concerning real frictions, removing the investment adjustment costs implies a considerable deterioration in the marginal likelihood, whose value becomes 1087. The parameter most affected by the significant reduction of the elasticity of adjustment cost is the persistence of the technology shock, whose mode decreases.

The presence of variable capital utilisation is examined by setting the value of the elasticity of depreciation with respect to capital utilisation to 3.5. A larger ζ implies that variation in capital utilisation is more costly (in terms of higher depreciation rate) and, thus, capital utilisation varies less. Therefore, the elasticity of the marginal depreciation with respect to capital utilisation is a measure of how variable the capital utilisation rate can be. In the standard RBC model, the value of this parameter tends to infinity: the cost of changing the utilisation rate is very high and therefore cost-minimising firms decide not to vary utilisation rate at all. Removing this friction is not costly in terms of marginal likelihood, whose value slightly increases to 1244. This result is in line with SW.

As far as nominal and real frictions are concerned, the most important friction in terms of empirical performance of the model is the investment adjustment costs parameter, similarly to SW.

The last column of Table 6.6 presents the results for the model without financial frictions (FF). The marginal likelihood reveals that the model without FF has the worst empirical performance and the value of the marginal likelihood is 1076. Given the significant deterioration of the marginal likelihood, the data clearly favour the model with financial frictions in the UK economy. The parameters most affected are the Calvo parameter and the standard deviations of technology shock and of government shock, whose modes have increased.

5.3   Historical decomposition

Once we have estimated the model and studied its propagation mechanism, we can now use it to quantify the relative importance of different shocks. Indeed, one advantage of having an estimated DSGE model (as opposed to a calibrated one) is that we can decompose movements in endogenous variables into that part caused by each of the shocks. More specifically, given the starting values of all the endogenous variables in the model, we can run a simulation in which one shock, say the credit supply shock, follows its historical path while the other shocks are set equal to zero in all periods. This simulation shows us the proportion of movements in the endogenous variables that are due to this particular shock. We can repeat this exercise for all the shocks so as to apportion movements in the endogenous variables between them all. Doing that, we can see what shocks have contributed to the movement in macro and financial variables at different stages of the business cycle.

We assume that the economy is driven by five shocks: productivity, bank capital, monetary policy, government spending and a shock to capital quality. We decompose output, inflation, corporate bond spreads and lending for the whole sample period. Figure 6.4 plots the shock decomposition for a more recent period (2006Q1–2010Q1).

The first figure shows which shocks are important in explaining the sharp fall in real output by 6 per cent in the recent crisis. First, a bank capital shock contributes negatively to a decline in output from its trend. Since the onset of the crisis, this shock on its own would be pushing GDP 3 per cent below its trend. Second, what may seem surprising is that the government expenditure shock also pushes down GDP. In fact, this is because the bar here captures both shocks to government expenditure and net trade. Since we apply a closed economy model for the UK, the external sector is not explicitly modelled here. We calibrate the steady-state parameters to let consumption and investment match their shares in GDP. Then we let the share of government expenditure pick up the rest in GDP that is not included in the consumption and investment. This implies that the shock to government expenditure, in effect, reflects both shocks to government expenditure and shocks to external demand. In the recent crisis, the UK economy was hit by a large negative shock in external demand. The negative contribution indicates that the negative external demand shock is more than offsetting the expansionary effect of government spending in the early stages of the crisis. On the whole, this negative effect from external demand also may explain the 2 per cent fall in GDP. However, acting to push up on output is the monetary policy shock.

The second chart in Figure 6.4 shows the shock decomposition for inflation, which may shed some light on why inflation has not fallen as much as we might expect given the size of the fall in GDP. The negative productivity shock together with banking sector shock seems to be the main driver for higher inflation. What may seem surprising is that the contribution of monetary policy shock to inflation has changed from being positive to negative in recent quarters. This could reflect that the monetary policy becomes less stimulating than that implied by a Taylor rule during this period, when the nominal interest rate reached its lower bound.

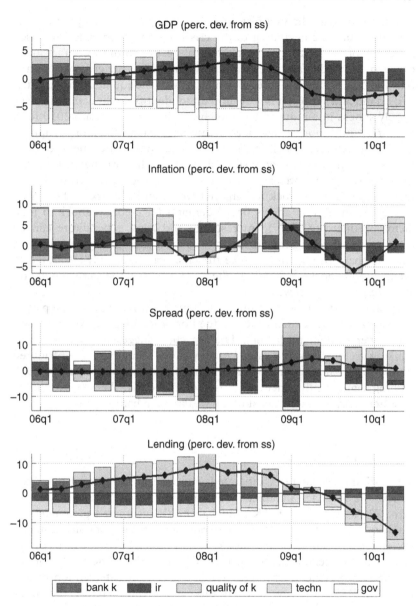

Figure 6.4 Historical decomposition

The third chart shows a historical decomposition for corporate bond spreads. Since the beginning of the crisis, corporate spreads have risen about 400bps from trough to peak. It is interesting to know whether this is driven by credit demand or credit supply conditions. But given we observe only the final price (here spread), which reflects the equilibrium condition of demand and supply, it is very difficult to identify credit demand versus supply shocks in a reduced form analysis (see Chadha et al., 2010 for a similar identification issue applied on money demand and money supply). But the structured model like this offers a natural environment to study this issue. The credit supply shock is the one that originated from the financial sector and affects only banks' ability to extend credit – in this model it includes a shock to bank net worth and a shock to the capital quality. A shock that affects firms' demand for credit, a shock to total factor productivity (TFP), interest rate and fiscal expenditure can be categorised as credit demand shock. The third chart in Figure 6.4 shows that the sharp rise in spread since the crisis can be mainly attributed to credit supply shocks, although in the most recent quarter, credit demand starts to play a role as well.

Finally, we study bank lending behaviour in the recent crisis. In particular, we ask to what extent the subdued bank lending is driven by credit supply versus demand factors. The last chart suggests that as much as banking sector shock and capital quality shock seem to have contributed positively to bank lending before the crisis, they act to drag down bank lending significantly since the onset of the crisis. These two shocks together seem to explain most of the weakness in bank lending.

6   Credit policy

The GK model has been estimated without unconventional monetary policy: the feedback parameter of equation (5) has been set equal to zero. We now solve the GK model using the estimated parameters of Table 6.3 and setting the feedback parameter in the credit policy equal to two different values: $v = 10$ and $v = 50$. In the GK paper, $v = 10$ corresponds to an intervention by the central bank fairly in line with what has occurred in practice in the US. When $v = 50$, the intervention by the policy maker is more aggressive. In this experiment, therefore, the policy maker is now implementing both conventional and unconventional monetary policy: the Taylor rule and the credit policy.

In this counterfactual experiment, the policy maker might offset the contraction shown in Figures 6.2 and 6.3 with the non-standard measure, aimed to increase liquidity provisions.

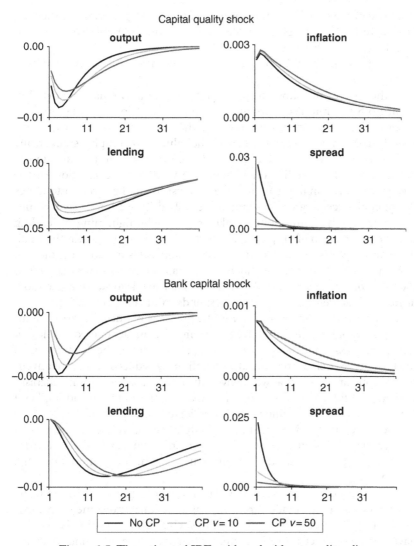

Figure 6.5 The estimated IRFs with and without credit policy

Figure 6.5 reports this experiment. We have analysed the response of output to the two 'financial' shocks: the quality of capital and bank capital. The case of an interest rate shock has not been examined because it is unlikely that the policy maker would increase interest rates and at the same time decide to inject credit in the economy to offset the recession. The same rationale applies to the government shock. The black line is the response of the variable in the absence of the credit policy, while the grey line represents the response of the corresponding variable when $v = 10$ and the red line corresponds to $v = 50$.

The intervention by the policy maker makes the crisis less severe in both cases.

In the case of the shock to the quality of capital, we have reported in Figure 6.5 the impulse responses of output, inflation, lending and the spread. The moderate intervention by the policy maker, $v = 10$, corresponds to the injection of 7 per cent of the value of total capital stock, while the more aggressive intervention, $v = 50$, corresponds to the injection of 11 per cent. The credit policy significantly affects the reaction of the spread, as is evident in the figure. The modest rise in the spread attenuates the financial accelerator mechanism described in Section 5. As a result, the intervention by the policy maker reduces the tightening of lending and the contraction of output. The effect on inflation is significantly small. The more aggressive intervention further moderates the contraction.

In the case of the net worth shock, a moderate intervention corresponds to the injection of 5 per cent of the value of total capital stock, while the more aggressive intervention, $v = 50$, corresponds to the injection of 7 per cent. The contraction of output is lower in the presence of unconventional monetary policy, but it is slightly more persistent. The impact of credit policy on inflation is less prominent. The credit policy reduces the contraction of lending. As expected, the spread is significantly reduced when unconventional monetary policy is at work; given the financial accelerator mechanism explained in the previous section, the moderate rise in the spread implies a lower contraction in lending and a lower fall in banks' profits.

The policy maker intervention directly aimed at reducing the spread weakens the financial accelerator mechanism. Thus, as GK obtain from their calibrated model, the credit policy significantly moderates the contraction.

In the UK, credit easing policy has never been pursued. Instead, the UK government has made direct capital injections into some of its large banks. In this framework, the impact of such a recapitalisation is likely to have a similar effect on real economic activity to credit easing. A direct capital injection at the moment that the banking sector is hit by a negative capital shock can help banks to restore their capital ratios to a desired level. This implies that banks do not have to rely on raising lending spreads – profit margins – to rebuild their capital. As a result, such a policy is likely to prevent sharp rises in spreads at the outset, therefore moderating the decline in investment and output.

In some aspects, the direct recapitalisation may even turn out to be a better policy response than credit easing in this framework. A credit easing policy works through policy makers forcing down lending spreads by directly intermediating funds to firms. Since banks rely on higher profit margins to rebuild their capital, a credit easing policy which reduces lending spreads is likely to slow down the banks' balance sheet adjustment. Thus it is likely to take a long time for banks to rebuild their capital to a desired level. This may be one reason why we observe a persistent weakness in lending in response to a bank capital shock. In this sense, the direct capital injection could be more efficient and effective. But a formal welfare comparison of different unconventional policies must be left for future research.

7   Conclusion

We have estimated Gertler and Karadi's model incorporating financial intermediation and frictions, using Bayesian techniques for the UK economy.

The fit of the model is quite satisfactory, in particular for the financial variables. The estimation seems to suggest that financial friction plays an important role in explaining UK business cycles. The historical decomposition suggests that the banking sector shocks explain around half of the fall in real output from its trend in the most recent crisis. Credit supply shocks seem to explain most of the fall in bank lending and rises in lending spreads.

The chapter finds that financial factors have played a significant role both in the systematic component of business cycle behaviour and in the recent recession. Therefore, financial frictions cannot be ignored in setting systematic monetary policy or in dealing with recovery from recession.

References

Adolfson, M., Laséen, S., Lindé, J. and Villani, M. (2007) Bayesian estimation of an open economy DSGE model with incomplete pass-through, *Journal of International Economics*, 72(2), 481–511.

Aikman, D. and Paustian, M. (2006) Bank capital, asset prices and monetary policy, Working Paper, Bank of England.

Aksoy, Y., Basso, H. and Coto-Martinez, J. (2009) Lending relationships and monetary policy, Birkbeck Working Paper in Economics and Finance No. 0912.

Bean, C. (2009) The great moderation, the great panic and the great contraction, in Schumpeter Lecture, Annual Congress of the European Economic Association, August.

Bean, C., Larsen, J., Nikolov, K. and Street, T. (2002) Financial frictions and the monetary transmission mechanism: theory, evidence and policy implications, Working Paper No. 113, European Central Bank.

Benati, L. (2004) Evolving post-World War II UK economic performance, *Journal of Money, Credit & Banking*, 36(4), 691–718.

Bernanke, B., Gertler, M. and Gilchrist, S. (1999) The financial accelerator in a quantitative business cycle model, *Handbook of Macroeconomics*, 1, 1341–93.

Chadha, J., Corrado, L. and Sun, Q. (2010) Money, prices and liquidity effects: separating demand from supply, *Journal of Economic Dynamics and Control*, 34 (9), 1732–47.

Chang, Y., Gomes, J. and Schorfheide, F. (2002) Learning-by-doing as a propagation mechanism, *American Economic Review*, 92(5), 1498–520.

Christiano, L., Eichenbaum, M. and Evans, C. (2005) Nominal rigidities and the dynamic effects of a monetary policy shock, *Journal of Political Economy*, 113 (1), 1–45.

Christiano, L., Motto, R. and Rostagno, M. (2010) Financial factors in economic fluctuations, ECB Working Paper No. 1192.

Cooley, T. and Hansen, G. (1995) Money and the business cycle, in Cooley, T. F. (ed.), *Frontiers of Business Cycle Research*, Princeton University Press, pp. 175–216.

DiCecio, R. and Nelson, E. (2007) An estimated DSGE model for the United Kingdom, *Federal Reserve Bank of St Louis Review*, 89(4), 215–32.

Fernández-Villaverde, J. (2009) The econometrics of DSGE models, NBER Working Paper No. 14677, National Bureau of Economic Research, Inc.

Gerali, A., Neri, S., Sessa, L. and Signoretti, F. (2009) Credit and banking in a DSGE model, unpublished, Banca d'Italia.

Gertler, M. and Karadi, P. (2011) A model of unconventional monetary policy, *Journal of Monetary Economics*, 58(1), Carnegie-Rochester Conference Series on Public Policy: The Future of Central Banking April 16–17, 2010, 17–34.

Gertler, M. and Kiyotaki, N. (2009) Financial intermediation and credit policy in business cycle analysis, in Friedman, B. M. and Woodford, M. (eds.) *Handbook of Monetary Economics*, Vol. 3, Amsterdam: Elsevier, pp. 547–99.

Gertler, M. and Lown, C. (1999) The information in the high-yield bond spread for the business cycle: evidence and some implications, *Oxford Review of Economic Policy*, 15(3), 132.

Gertler, M., Sala, L. and Trigari, A. (2008) An estimated monetary DSGE model with unemployment and staggered nominal wage bargaining, *Journal of Money, Credit and Banking*, 40(8), 1713–64.

Gilchrist, S., Ortiz, A. and Zakrajšek, E. (2009) Credit risk and the macroeconomy: evidence from an estimated DSGE model, in International Conference on Financial System and Monetary Policy Implementation, Bank of Japan.

Harrison, R. and Oomen, O. (2010) Evaluating and estimating a DSGE model for the United Kingdom, Working Paper No. 120, Bank of England.

Kiyotaki, N. and Moore, J. (1997) Credit cycles, *Journal of Political Economy*, 105 (2), 211–48.

Meh, C. and Moran, K. (2010) The role of bank capital in the propagation of shocks, *Journal of Economic Dynamics & Control*, 34(3), 555–76.

Nelson, E. (2006) UK monetary policy, 1972–97: a guide using Taylor rules, Working Paper No. 120, Bank of England.

Schorfheide, F. (2000) Loss function-based evaluation of DSGE models, *Journal of Applied Econometrics*, 15(6), 645–70.

Smets, F. and Wouters, R. (2007) Shocks and frictions in US business cycles: a Bayesian DSGE approach, *American Economic Review*, 97(3), 586–606.

von Heideken, V. (2009) How important are financial frictions in the United States and the Euro area? *Scandinavian Journal of Economics*, 111(3), 567–96.

7 Central bank balance sheets and long-term forward rates

Sharon Kozicki, Eric Santor and Lena Suchanek

1 Introduction

The global financial crisis has led to dramatic actions by central banks. Initially, many central banks responded to the crisis by rapidly cutting interest rates and undertaking measures to address liquidity issues in interbank funding markets. But the bankruptcy of Lehman Brothers, the threat of failure of AIG and other related events led to a deepening of the crisis. Credit markets that previously had been relatively unaffected by the crisis subsequently froze. At the same time, the global real economy collapsed. Central banks responded by lowering interest rates aggressively. Moreover, as policy rates reached their effective lower bound, some central banks responded with additional initiatives, first via credit easing and then more dramatically, by introducing large-scale asset purchase programmes. These latter measures sought to lower interest rates further out the yield curve and thus stimulate the macro economy.

There is considerable debate with respect to the effectiveness of these interventions by central banks, in terms of both the effect of asset purchases on long-term interest rates and the ultimate impact on the real economy (Borio and Disyatat, 2009). The focus of this analysis is on the former question. On the one hand, the yield on UK ten-year gilts fell substantially on the day of the announcement of the purchase programme (Figure 7.1). Likewise, US long-term interest rates initially responded dramatically to the announcement of large-scale asset purchases, falling nearly fifty basis points (Figure 7.2). On the other hand, subsequent increases in long-term interest rates were interpreted by some observers

The views represented here are those of the authors and not those of the Bank of Canada or its staff. We would like to thank Jagjit Chadha, Jean-Marie Dufour, Jean Helwege, Michael King, Gregor Smith, Demosthenes Tambakis and seminar participants at the Bank for International Settlements, European Central Bank, Bank of England, Northern Finance Association 2009 Annual Meetings, Canadian Economic Association 2010 Annual Meetings, CIMF and MMF Cambridge 2010 conference, and the 2010 Econometric Society World Congress for useful comments, and Amberly Jane Coates and Firas Abu-Sneneh for excellent research assistance.

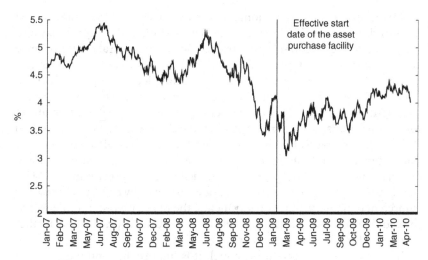

Figure 7.1 UK ten-year government bond yields

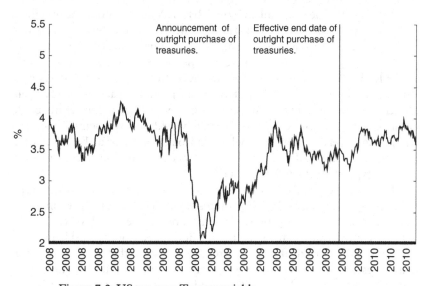

Figure 7.2 US ten-year Treasury yields

as evidence that quantitative easing was not particularly effective. Clearly, a more rigorous analysis is needed, one that accounts for other factors that may influence yields, including inflation expectations, the supply of government debt, future expected short-term rates, investors' views on risk premia and the overall state of the macroeconomy.

The impact of unconventional monetary policy, however, may not be solely related to specific interventions per se – rather, the impact may also be related to the overall size and composition of the central bank's balance sheet. That is, the impact of central bank interventions could extend beyond the assets being purchased. For example, the impact of central bank purchases of mortgage-backed securities can affect MBS yields through two channels. First, investors' risk aversion in the aftermath of the Lehman crisis, combined with increased uncertainty with respect to US housing markets, meant that the MBS market was affected by severe illiquidity at the time of the announcement. Consequently, Federal Reserve purchases would have reduced illiquidity directly in the MBS market and thus led to lower interest rates. Second, by providing a new net source of demand for these instruments, the purchase programme would provide a source of generalised upward pressure on prices (and further downward pressure on interest rates).

In considering the second channel, it is important to note that in the absence of market segmentation, the introduction of a new net large-scale purchaser of a subset of assets could put upward pressure on asset prices more generally. The mechanism by which broader effects could be obtained relies on a portfolio reallocation channel, which assumes that markets are not segmented. In particular, central banks' purchases of Treasuries or MBS would put upward pressure on the prices of these assets, which could lead other investors to substitute away from the targeted assets and into others. To account for the potential for a portfolio reallocation channel, this chapter focuses on the link between the overall size of the central bank balance sheet and interest rates. Ultimately, with less segmented markets, the portfolio reallocation channel should be stronger and the effect of a change in the size of the central bank balance sheet on the interest rate on any one type of asset will be smaller.[1]

The objective of this chapter is to examine the effectiveness of large-scale asset purchases at lowering interest rates. This is done by estimating the historical relationship between central bank assets and forward rates for the United States and a sample of developed countries. Using pre-crisis data, the empirical analysis provides evidence that large-scale asset purchases should be effective at lowering nominal interest rates. The analysis draws on Laubach (2009) and importantly controls for inflation

---

[1] Central bank balance sheets have expanded considerably since autumn 2008 in numerous countries, not just those undertaking quantitative easing. Moreover, both the asset and the liability sides of the balance sheet have evolved; central banks have taken on riskier assets and, depending on the degree of sterilisation and the status of the banking system, government deposits and/or excess bank reserves have increased.

expectations, projected deficits/debt, expected real economic activity and other variables. Consistent with Laubach, increases in government borrowing are associated with higher neutral interest rates.[2] Also, as expected, neutral interest rates rise with expected inflation and projected growth. The important contribution of this chapter is the finding that an increase in central bank assets is associated with a significant decline in long-term forward rates. This result is found to be robust to alternative estimation approaches and holds not only for the United States but also over a panel of developed countries. The predictions of the effects on US interest rates of the unconventional policies enacted by the Federal Reserve during the latest crisis are similar to the estimates obtained by Gagnon et al. (2010) for the crisis period.

This analysis can also provide insights into several important policy questions. First, as central banks assess the impact of exit from the unconventional policies, they will be interested in understanding the implications of their actions on interest rates. For instance, how would a gradual sale of assets purchased outright affect interest rates? Just as announcements of asset purchases resulted in lower interest rates, announcements of asset sales could lead to increases in interest rates.

Second, as central banks contemplate exit from their accommodative stance during the crisis period, they will want to know what the neutral rate is. The analysis in this study can help to assess the implications of developments in sovereign indebtedness, the outlook for growth and changes in central bank asset holdings for the neutral interest rate.

Third, the recent experience may provide insights into the design of the monetary policy framework and decisions about the ultimate goals of monetary policy. Recently, it has been suggested by Blanchard et al. (2010) and others that inflation targets should be raised to 4 per cent. Their argument is that relative to the more typical inflation goal, which is closer to 2 per cent, a higher inflation target would provide an additional cushion for monetary policy to ease in times of severe economic distress. However, if unconventional measures such as asset purchase programmes can reliably provide additional monetary ease once the short-term nominal policy rate hits its effective lower bound, then there is less need to raise inflation targets.

Section 2 reviews the actions taken by central banks in the latest crisis, the implications of these actions for the central bank balance sheet and the evidence of their effectiveness. The empirical model used to examine the impact of changes in the size of the central bank balance sheet for long-term forward rates is presented in Section 3. Section 4 describes the data

[2] In this context, the terms neutral and equilibrium are used to refer to the level to which interest rates will return after the effects of cyclical shocks dissipate.

and Section 5 presents the results. Section 6 provides a review of the implications of the results for monetary policy and offers avenues for future research.

2   Unconventional monetary policy in 2007–10

The recent crisis forced authorities to take dramatic and often unconventional policy actions. While central bank initiatives differed across countries in their content, implementation and ultimately effect, they can be placed into two broad groups: liquidity facilities designed to improve functioning of interbank markets and credit facilities and asset-purchase programmes designed to improve market function in impaired parts of the money and capital markets and, when unsterilised, to provide additional monetary easing.[3] These unconventional actions were, by definition, unusual in both size and scope, producing more than the usual degree of uncertainty about their potential impact. Ex post, there is general agreement that many of these policies were effective. Anecdotal evidence and a number of recent studies suggest that the following broad conclusions can be drawn.

2.1   Liquidity facilities

In reaction to the freezing up of interbank markets, central banks undertook numerous initiatives to ease funding conditions for banks and, in some cases, dealers. Open market operations and *existing* liquidity facilities appear to have been effective in reducing liquidity strains in interbank markets, provided that the access came at a low cost and a wide range of collateral was accepted. However, by themselves, these measures were seldom sufficient.

Newly introduced liquidity facilities appear to have helped address funding needs and contributed to lower Libor–OIS (overnight indexed swap) spreads. For the United States, McAndrews et al. (2008) found that Term Auction Facility announcements and their implementation led to a cumulative reduction of more than 50bp in the Libor–OIS spread.[4] However, there is less evidence to suggest that the Primary Dealer Credit Facility (PDCF) and Term Securities Lending Facility (TSLF) improved liquidity (Wu, 2008). For the United Kingdom, analysis also suggests that the Bank

---

[3] At the same time, fiscal authorities began to inject capital into the banking system, placed guarantees on deposits and bank debt and instituted substantive fiscal stimulus.

[4] Taylor and Williams (2008), however, do not find that the TAF was successful, and In et al. (2008) find mixed evidence.

of England's Special Liquidity Scheme (SLS) led to a fall in sterling Libor–OIS and an increase in the supply of gilt collateral. US dollar swap lines between central banks were also seen as highly effective and significantly alleviated US dollar funding pressures (CGFS, 2010). Although some swap lines were never drawn, this coordinated action among central banks nevertheless contributed to market liquidity through positive signalling.

The use of liquidity facilities had varying effects on the size of central bank balance sheets. In most cases, central banks neutralised the effects on the size of their balance sheets of the operations associated with their liquidity facilities. For instance, as shown in Figure 7.4 on p. 184, the Federal Reserve initially managed the impact on its balance sheet by redeeming and selling securities in the System Open Market Account portfolio. However, in some cases, particularly with the intensification of the financial crisis after the failure of Lehman Brothers, central bank balance sheets increased with expanded use of liquidity facilities as well as with use of credit facilities and asset purchases.[5]

2.2 Credit facilities and asset purchases

Central banks intervened in a targeted manner to improve conditions in credit markets, in order to avoid further economic disruption, through purchases of commercial paper (e.g. the Commercial Paper Funding Facility (CPFF) in the United States), asset-backed commercial paper, corporate and covered bonds, and facilities to support money market mutual funds. Measures targeting the commercial paper market in the United States (Bernanke, 2009) appear to have been effective, reducing spreads and increasing issuance.

Central banks in the United States and the United Kingdom began purchasing government-issued securities in order to further ease overall financing conditions. These purchases increased the size of central bank balance sheets.[6] The Asset Purchase Facility of the Bank of England was set up to purchase UK government securities (gilts) in the secondary market and high-quality private-sector assets, including commercial paper and corporate bonds. In the United States, large-scale asset purchases by the Federal Reserve included purchases of Treasury debt, agency debt and agency MBS (given the effective nationalisation of Freddie Mac and Fannie Mae).

---

[5] Initially, the post-Lehman rapid expansion of liquidity was being sterilised with Treasury deposits in a Treasury Supplementary Financing Account.

[6] For this reason, some analysts refer to such purchases as 'quantitative easing'. However, there is no single accepted definition of quantitative easing. Generally, quantitative easing is used to refer to the unsterilised outright purchase of assets, but the authors acknowledge that the Fed does not refer to its Treasury purchase programme as quantitative easing.

The Fed's purchases of government-sponsored enterprise direct obligations appear to have been effective: GSE credit spreads tightened and mortgage rates fell significantly, supporting refinancing activity. Purchases of MBS also appear to have been effective (Bernanke, 2009). Finally, purchases of government securities appear to have had an impact on asset prices and interest rates, helping to spur economic activity (Dale, 2010; Gagnon et al., 2010; Joyce et al., 2010; Neely, 2010). Clearly, though, additional analysis is needed.

2.3   Caveats

While preliminary assessments are positive, assessing the effectiveness of the various central bank measures encounters several hurdles. First, the primary objectives of the various initiatives differed greatly. Liquidity facilities were typically aimed at resolving a specific market failure, while asset purchases were often motivated by a desire to lower interest rates and thereby stimulate real economic activity. In addition, many of the initiatives had benefits beyond their primary objectives. Consequently, the metrics of success are hard to determine. Even if the metrics of success can be agreed upon, gauging the effectiveness of individual measures is complicated by numerous identification issues, including the following:

- Contemporaneous measures and effects: in some cases, several liquidity measures were announced within the same period, making it difficult to isolate their respective effects. Bank guarantees and capital injections were also concurrently implemented, further complicating identification. The impact of asset purchases on longer-term interest rates may also be difficult to gauge owing to contemporaneous macro-policy initiatives and macroeconomic developments.
- Ongoing nature of the crisis: while many central banks have begun to exit from unconventional policies, the effects of the crisis are still being felt and some unconventional policies are still in place. Thus, it may be too early to fully evaluate the effects of unconventional policies.
- Selection bias: the countries that undertook the most dramatic actions were often those that were the most severely affected by the crisis. The positive effects of the measures may therefore be obscured by the impaired state of their financial systems and the absence of any counterfactual data with which to judge what might have happened were it not for the measures.
- Spillovers: there may be positive spillovers across countries and across markets (e.g. policies aimed at reducing the Libor–OIS spread may also affect other spreads).

- Policy lags: certain measures might have affected markets with a long lag, due to uncertainty about the features of the measure, scepticism regarding its implementation and the nature of the transmission mechanism.
- Fiscal policy: unconventional monetary policies and extraordinarily low interest rates may have amplified the effects of fiscal policy. Failure to control for this may produce misleading estimates of the effects of unconventional monetary policy on macroeconomic outcomes.
- Prices versus quantities: while central bank facilities may have affected spreads, turnover in markets may have remained weak, thus providing a mixed picture of the actual impact of the measures taken.

These measurement and identification issues suggest that understanding the effects of the various central bank measures will require ongoing research.

The contribution of this chapter is to provide additional analysis to evaluate the effectiveness of asset purchase programmes to influence long-term interest rates, controlling for inflation expectations, projected deficits/debt, expected real economic activity and other variables. The analysis provides predictions of the likely size of the effect of the latest asset purchase programmes on interest rates that can be compared to studies of the latest crisis (Gagnon et al., 2010; Meyer and Bomfim, 2010) and to less formal evaluations. In the next section, the empirical model that will be employed is described.

3   Empirical framework

There are numerous factors, in addition to central bank purchases of assets, that could affect long-term interest rates, including the government's fiscal position, inflation expectations, the rate of future economic growth and other factors. For example, while increases in central bank holdings of government debt, all else being equal, will decrease the supply of government securities available to the market and may consequently lead to higher bond prices and lower yields, increases in the supply of government debt (due to deficit stimulus spending, for example) would attenuate these effects. In addition, interest rates incorporate a component to compensate for expected inflation and inflation risk. Thus, while higher debt/deficits may raise concerns about monetisation and future increases in inflation, and thus higher long-term interest rates, reductions in the size of the central bank balance sheet could counteract monetisation concerns. To account for these factors, the empirical analysis of this chapter extends Laubach (2009) to allow forward rates to vary with the size of the central bank balance sheet in addition to controlling for other economic variables. The following regression is estimated:

$$E_t f_{t+k} = \beta_0 + \beta_1 E_t \pi_{t+k} + \beta_2 E_t d_{t+k} + \beta_3 x_t + \beta_4 cb_t + \varepsilon_t \qquad (1)$$

where the dependent variable is the time t expectation of a k-year-ahead forward rate, $E_t \pi_{t+k}$ is a measure of expected inflation, $E_t d_{t+k}$ is a measure of expected future debt (or deficit), cb_t is a measure of the size of the central bank balance sheet, and x_t are other possible regressors, such as expected future growth rates or measures of risk tolerance, that influence long-term forward rates.

The use of long-horizon forward rates and long-horizon expectations of fiscal variables has a key advantage, as it removes a potential source of endogeneity. Specifically, contemporaneous data on interest rates and the fiscal variables are likely to both contain strong cyclical components: in the case of interest rates, countercyclical monetary policy would lead to countercyclical policy rates and expectations of a path of short-term interest rates that should gradually return to a neutral, or equilibrium, level. Similar arguments apply to the fiscal variable where automatic stabilisers would generally induce cyclicality in f_t. For both variables, at a sufficiently long forecast horizon, i.e. a sufficiently large k, it is reasonable to expect that interest rates should return to neutral and that the purely cyclical effects on f_t should dissipate.

The estimated coefficients are expected to be as follows. The coefficient on expected inflation, β_1, should be close to one: higher expected inflation should be compensated by higher nominal interest rates. Increases in the fiscal variable indicate greater levels of sovereign debt and are expected to raise the neutral interest rate – this is owing to the effects of a relative increase in the supply of government securities as described above, or to an increase in the risk premium related to a possible increase in the probability of a sovereign debt default. Therefore, β_2 should be positive. Economic theory suggests that the coefficient on long-horizon expected future growth will be positive if this variable proxies well for the equilibrium growth rate of technological progress that drives per capita consumption growth.[7] An increase in the size of the central bank balance sheet should lead to lower long-term forward rates and a negative estimate of β_4, due to the direct effect of central bank purchases on asset prices, and any indirect effects if market segmentation is less than complete. While an expansion of the balance sheet that is deemed to be excessive in the context of the overall price objective of monetary policy could be expected to lead to higher

---

[7] Economic theory implies that in steady state, $r = \sigma g + \theta$ where r is the steady state real rate, σ is the inverse of the intertemporal elasticity of substitution, g is the growth rate of per capita consumption and θ is the household's rate of time preference.

forward rates by raising expected inflation, inclusion of long-term inflation expectations in the regression should control for this effect.

An additional benefit of the analysis is that it can provide an assessment of the implications of fiscal policy and monetary policy as summarised by the size of the central bank balance sheet, for neutral, or equilibrium, interest rates.[8] By using forward rates implicit in yields, the measure of neutral corresponds to a market view. However, it is important to note that forward rates also contain a component reflecting term premia and thus they provide a biased estimate of the level of the neutral rate. But, as argued by Laubach (2009), an increase in term premia affects real allocations similarly to an increase in expected future short-term interest rates. Thus, it is not essential to distinguish between the effects on these two components when examining the implications of changes in the size of central bank balance sheets for interest rates.

Lastly, it is important to note that to the extent that the empirical results capture effects on neutral interest rates, in an environment with policy rates at their effective lower bound, the effect on yields would be expected to be smaller. This is because yields incorporate an expectation of the path of short-term interest rates over the maturity horizon of the security. With the policy path expected to remain at the effective lower bound in the near term, balance sheet effects cannot lower the path further. Moreover, term premia are very small at such short horizons, also limiting the implications of balance sheet developments for relatively short-term yields.

4   Data and descriptive statistics

This section describes the data used to estimate (1) for the US and a panel of developed countries. For the US, the approach and data choices of Laubach (2009) are followed closely. The dependent variables considered are the five-year-ahead ten-year forward rate, the five-year-ahead five-year forward rate and the ten-year constant maturity government bond yield. Inflation expectations are proxied using long-horizon inflation expectations by market participants and professional forecasters for the US from 1981–2009.[9]

---

[8] The analysis of this chapter is best thought of as outside the scope of a typical DSGE modelling environment. In particular, the neutral interest rate here is most closely aligned with a stability condition of the model and the 'steady state' concept around which the model equations would be log-linearised.

[9] Following Laubach (2009), the inflation expectations series is based on the Hoey survey of bond market participants from 1981:Q2 to 1991:Q1 (expectation of CPI inflation over the second five years of a ten-year horizon) and the Survey of Professional Forecasters conducted quarterly by the Federal Reserve Bank of Philadelphia (expectation of the average CPI inflation rate over the next ten years) from 1991:Q3 to 2009:Q2.

Expected future debt and deficit to GDP ratios are five-year-ahead projected debt and deficit to GDP ratios based on data from the Congressional Budget Office (CBO), which is available at an annual frequency from 1980 to 1984, and at a semi-annual frequency from 1985 until August 2009. Regressions also include a proxy for expected trend consumption growth (CBO's five-year-ahead projections of the growth rate of real GNP or GDP) and a proxy for risk (the dividend yield, which is defined as the dividend component of national income divided by the market value of corporate equity held (directly or indirectly) by households as reported in the Federal Reserve Board's Flow of Funds data).[10]

Total central bank (CB) assets are used to capture the effect of central bank balance sheets.[11,12] Central bank assets are expressed as a ratio to potential nominal GDP. Data are available from 1980 to 2009, monthly. Potential nominal GDP as estimated by the CBO is used rather than nominal GDP, so that variation in the latter is not the source of cyclicality in the scaled central bank balance sheet variable.[13] Over time, the ratio of central bank assets to GDP has been slowly increasing, with some cyclicality (Figure 7.3). The graph also clearly shows that the massive expansion of the Fed's balance sheet during the recent global financial crisis is unprecedented in history, both in absolute terms and relative to GDP. Central bank assets tripled from around $800 billion pre-crisis to more than $2.3 trillion in March 2009 (Figure 7.4).

To capture the historical relationship between long-term forward rates and central bank variables, the sample is restricted to the pre-crisis period (1980H1–2007H2).[14] This allows examination of the implications of the current expansion of balance sheets from a historical perspective, without distorting the regression results by including the large outliers in the data

[10] Note that several variables should be, theoretically, $I(0)$, including the debt and deficit variables, as well as central bank variables. However, given the small sample size, the test for stationarity has low power. Moreover, Laubach (2009) argues that in the context of this regression framework, unit roots in data series do not pose serious problems. Nevertheless, as non-stationarity may be an issue, sensitivity analysis is conducted accordingly.

[11] Data are from the IMF *International Financial Statistics*. Central bank assets are calculated as series 11+12a+12e+12s. 12s is not available pre-2001, but can be calculated by adding 12g, b, c and d. Claims on the central government are given by line 12a.

[12] Preliminary analysis also used central bank claims on the central government as a measure of the size of the central bank balance sheet. Over history, these two measures moved together. However, over the crisis period in the United States, with initial efforts to sterilise the effects of liquidity facilities, they diverged.

[13] However, dividing central bank variables by actual GDP versus potential GDP does not significantly change the series and only marginally changes the regression results.

[14] Including observations until 2009H1 results in somewhat weaker coefficients, which remain statistically significant.

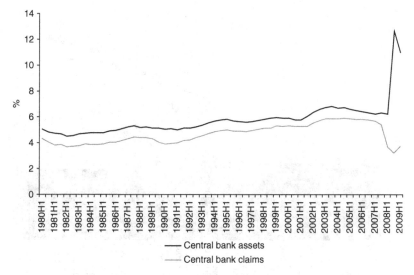

Figure 7.3 US central bank assets and claims to potential GDP

from 2008 onwards. That is, the chapter aims to establish whether there is a relationship between the central bank balance sheet and long-term forward interest rates in 'normal' times, in order to understand the impact of expansion of the balance sheet during the crisis.

4.1   Data for panel regression

Panel regressions include data for six developed countries (Australia, Canada, Switzerland, Japan, the UK and the US).[15] Unfortunately, the data are much more limited and in practice only current interest rates and contemporaneous fiscal variables are used. Ten-year constant maturity government bond yields, available at a monthly frequency, are used for the dependent variable. Inflation expectations are measured using the semi-annual Economic Consensus 5–10 Year Forecast from 1990–2009. Central bank assets are obtained from the IMF IFS, at monthly frequency

---

[15] The sample is expanded to European countries, including Germany, Spain, France, Italy, the Netherlands, Norway and Sweden. However, data on central bank assets for the eurozone countries are sometimes inconclusive (break in series at time of euro adoption) or incomplete for others. Including these countries in the panel yields similarly signed coefficients – however, few are statistically significant.

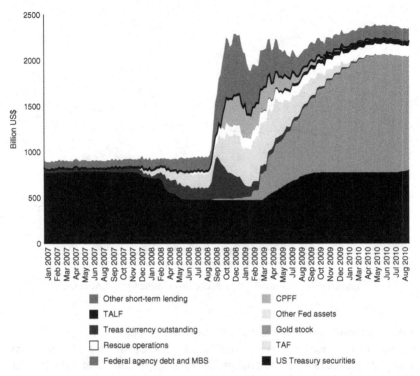

Figure 7.4 Federal Reserve balance sheet assets

(see footnote 11), scaled by potential GDP. For the fiscal variables, we use actual deficit data, available at a quarterly frequency for Australia, Canada, Japan, the UK and the US (and interpolated from annual data for Switzerland), and actual debt available at quarterly frequency for Australia, Canada, Japan and the US (and interpolated from annual data for Switzerland and the UK). Instead of GDP growth forecasts, actual quarterly GDP growth rates are used.

5   Regression results

5.1   US regression results

Table 7.1, columns 1–3 report OLS results (GMM (generalised method of moments) results appear in columns 4–6) of regressing the five-year forward ten-year rate on central bank assets, controlling for other macro variables and deficits and debts, respectively. The coefficients on expected

Table 7.1 *Baseline results for US regressions*

Variable	OLS (1)	OLS (2)	OLS (3)	GMM (4)	GMM (5)	GMM (6)
Inflation expectations	1.237***	0.962***	1.014***	1.125***	0.869***	1.048***
	(0.161)	(0.232)	(0.228)	(0.226)	(0.280)	(0.279)
Projected deficit	0.096*	0.152*		0.147**	0.203**	
	(0.057)	(0.066)		(0.068)	(0.077)	
Projected debt			0.020			0.020
			(0.012)			(0.014)
Projected growth		0.740*	0.771		0.705**	0.703
		(0.403)	(0.499)		(0.399)	(0.511)
Dividend yield	−0.117	−0.209*	−0.129	−0.131	−0.223	−0.118
	(0.153)	(0.142)	(0.151)	(0.157)	(0.146)	(0.164)
Central bank assets	−0.742***	−1.234***	−1.154***	−0.839***	−1.278***	−1.058***
	(0.301)	(0.440)	(0.457)	(0.358)	(0.480)	(0.488)
R2	0.907	0.916	0.909	0.891	0.902	0.889
Hansen-J				0.344	0.193	0.213
N	51	51	51	49	49	49

This table presents results of OLS and IV GMM regressions of forward interest rates on central bank assets. The data is semi-annual from 1980 to 2007. The dependent variable is the five-year forward ten-year interest rate. Inflation expectations are 5–10 years ahead inflation expectations. Projected deficit is the five-year-ahead CBO forecast of the deficit-to-GDP and the projected debt is the five-year-ahead CBO forecast of the debt-to-GDP. Projected growth is the five-year-ahead projection of the growth rate of real GDP. Central bank assets are the ratio of central bank assets to potential GDP. The dividend yield is defined as the dividend component of national income divided by the market value of corporate equity held (directly or indirectly) by households as reported in the Federal Reserve Board's Flow of Funds data. Bootstrapped (1000 reps) standard errors are in parentheses. For the IV GMM specification, lagged assets are used as instruments. *, ** and *** indicate statistical significance at the 10%, 5% and 1% levels.

inflation are positive and insignificantly different from unity in all regressions.[16] In theory, and abstracting from business cycle effects, higher debt and deficit levels should be associated with higher long-term interest rates. The coefficients on projected deficits are positive and statistically

[16] A coefficient on expected inflation larger than 1 is consistent with the view that investors demand higher risk premia on nominal assets when inflation expectations rise to compensate for greater uncertainty about future inflation (see, e.g., Okun, 1971 and Ball and

significant, but somewhat weaker than in Laubach (2009) (10–20 bp per percentage point of the ratio). Coefficient estimates on projected debt are also weaker than in Laubach (2009) and are not statistically significant. The trend growth rate enters with the expected sign predicted by the neoclassical growth model and is statistically significant in the specifications that include projected deficits. Lastly, the dividend yield, as a proxy for risk aversion, is negative, but generally not significant for most of the regressions.[17] Estimation by GMM does not change the results.

The coefficients for central bank assets range from −0.74 to −1.28 and are statistically significant in all regressions.[18] This suggests that higher central bank assets (and more government bonds held by the central bank) imply lower long-term forward interest rates. That is, there appears to be a historical relationship between the size of the central bank's balance sheet and long-term interest rates that perhaps goes beyond that which would be associated with the implementation of monetary policy through the targeting of a short-term policy rate. Moreover, if one assumes that the long-term forward interest rate used in this analysis is a reasonable proxy for the 'neutral' interest rate, the results suggest that variation in the size of the central bank balance sheet can actually affect the neutral rate. While this would seem to be at odds with the notion that the neutral rate should be determined by the deep structural parameters in the economy, such as preferences and technology, the evidence presented here would imply that central bank actions may at least have persistent effects (as opposed to permanent effects) on neutral interest rates.

5.1.1 Robustness One concern is that by focusing on the five-year forward ten-year yield, the analysis is limiting itself to assessing the impact of unconventional policies on a single interest rate, which for institutional or other reasons (e.g. preferred habitat on the part of investors for the assets affected) may be particularly sensitive to central bank interventions. To check the robustness of the results, alternative specifications are considered which use current ten-year Treasury yields and five-year-ahead

---

Cecchetti, 1990). In addition, Feldstein (1976) points out that, because taxes are levied on nominal returns, nominal interest rates have to increase more than one-for-one with expected inflation.

[17] Laubach (2009) argues that higher dividend yield may be interpreted as a sign of elevated risk aversion, as investors' demand for higher than usual compensation for bearing risk may coincide with greater demand for safe Treasury securities, reducing their (current and expected) yields.

[18] The regressions are repeated for central bank claims on the government, with similar results (not shown).

Table 7.2 *Alternative specifications for US regressions (1)*

Variable	Ten-year yield (1)	Five-year forward five-year yield (2)	Ten-year yield (3)	Five-year forward five-year yield (4)
Inflation expectations	1.191***	1.148***	1.251***	1.197***
	(0.162)	(0.150)	(0.204)	(−0.159)
Deficit	−0.297***	0.005		
	(0.074)	(0.077)		
Projected deficit			−0.060	0.074
			(0.073)	(0.059)
Dividend yield	0.494***	−0.000	0.061	−0.108
	(0.188)	(0.201)	(0.165)	(0.150)
Central bank assets	−1.130***	−0.983***	−1.119***	−0.909***
	(0.243)	(0.316)	(0.238)	(0.301)
R2	0.931	0.903	0.905	0.906
N	51	51	51	51

This table presents results of IV GMM regressions of forward interest rates on central bank assets. The data are semi-annual from 1980 to 2007. The dependent variables are the ten-year government yield and the five-year forward five-year interest rate. Inflation expectations are 5–10 years ahead. Projected deficit is the five-year-ahead CBO forecast of the deficit-to-GDP or the current deficit-to-GDP. Projected growth is the five-year ahead projection of the growth rate of real GDP. Central bank assets are the ratio of central bank assets to potential GDP. The dividend yield is defined as the dividend component of national income divided by the market value of corporate equity held (directly or indirectly) by households as reported in the Federal Reserve Board's Flow of Funds data. Bootstrapped standard errors are in parentheses. Lagged claims are used as instruments. *, ** and *** indicate statistical significance at the 10%, 5% and 1% levels.

five-year forward rates as the dependent variables and current fiscal variables and projected fiscal variables, respectively. Following Laubach (2009), CBO projections for the current fiscal year are used instead of the latest realised deficit/GDP ratio, which is available only at annual (fiscal-year) frequency (current-year fiscal projections are fairly close to actual outcomes). As shown in Table 7.2, regardless of which combination of dependent variable and fiscal variable is used – the coefficients for central bank assets remain negative and statistically significant, and are relatively robust to alternative specifications. However, current deficit variables are often no longer significant and change signs, presumably reflecting the endogeneity problem due to cyclical responses of fiscal variables and interest rates (see Laubach, 2009). Inflation expectations are again robust to alternative specifications, entering with a positive and statistically signifi-cant coefficient.[19]

Another concern stems from the fact that an expansion of the central bank's balance sheet could lead to higher inflation expectations and in turn higher interest rates, thus biasing the results. In fact, in the current context, it has been argued that the expansion of the Fed's balance sheet has led to a rise in inflation expectations. If this is true, the positive correlation of central bank assets and long-term interest rates could be primarily a result of higher inflation expectations. To account for this concern, *real long-term rates* are regressed on central bank assets. Specifically, the five-year-ahead ten-year forward rate minus long-term inflation expectations is regressed on central bank assets. The results are as before, with an increase in central bank assets being associated with lower long-term interest rates (Table 7.3). Using the 'real' five-year ahead five-year forward rate and the 'real' ten-year Treasury yield as dependent variables yields similar results.[20]

The regression framework used in this chapter relies on the assumption that the impact of the short-run cyclicality of monetary policy should not affect sufficiently long-horizon forward interest rates. However, if this is not true, estimating the impact of central bank balance sheets on long-term interest rates could lead to biased results. To check the robustness of the results, the model is re-estimated including the twelve-month Fed futures rate as a right-hand side variable to capture the short-run expected path of monetary policy (Table 7.3 column 4). The coefficient of the Fed futures is positive, but not significant: importantly, the coefficient on central bank assets remains negative and significant.[21]

---

[19] Also, one might argue that some of the negative correlation between CB variables and long-term forward rates might be driven by the positive trend in the former and the negative trend in the latter variable over the sample period. For robustness, the regressions are also estimated using detrended data. Results suggest that coefficients are robust to detrending. However, some of the coefficients on CB variables are no longer statistically significant.

[20] Some observers note that the use of the dividend yield may not be the best proxy for risk. To better account for risk, the Chicago Board Options Exchange index of volatility (VIX) is introduced as a right-hand side variable while the coefficient is still negative, it is not statistically significant. However, the VIX is not available for the whole sample and so the sample size was reduced considerably.

[21] Another interesting question is how foreign demand for US Treasuries has impacted long-term forward rates. Data from the Treasury International Capital (TIC) System on net purchases of US Treasuries for the largest holders of US Treasury securities (China, Japan, the UK, oil exporters, Russia and Brazil) are used. Net holdings refer to net purchases of US long-term Treasuries (purchases by foreigners minus sales by foreigners). Ideally, the regression would include the stock, i.e. holdings of US Treasuries. However, the data are not a smooth series because they are constructed by adding up purchases and get updated once a year using surveys. Increased demand from China appears to be associated with a fall in long-term forward rates, but purchases of the group do not yield significant results.

Table 7.3 *Alternative specifications for US regressions (2)*

	Real five-year forward ten-year rate GMM (1)	Real five-year forward five-year rate GMM (2)	Real ten-year rate GMM (3)	Five-year forward ten-year rate GMM (4)
Inflation expectations				0.648**
				(0.082)
Projected deficit	0.188**	0.164**		0.224**
	(0.063)	(0.063)		(0.082)
Deficit			−0.280***	
			(0.081)	
Projected growth	0.602*	0.501*	0.147	0.839**
	(0.293)	(0.298)	(0.316)	(0.409)
Fed futures				0.116
				(0.118)
Dividend yield	−0.246*	−0.233	0.552***	−0.164
	(0.146)	(0.147)	(0.205)	(0.157)
Central bank assets	−1.106**	−1.193***	−1.326**	−1.269**
	(0.243)	(0.239)	(0.208)	(0.496)
R^2	0.585	0.582	0.678	0.906
N	49	49	49	49

This table presents results of IV GMM regressions of forward real interest rates and real interest rates on central bank assets. The data are semi-annual from 1980 to 2007. The dependent variables are the real ten-year government yield, the five-year forward ten-year real rate, and the five-year forward five-year real interest rate. Projected deficit is the five-year ahead CBO forecast of the deficit-to-GDP. Projected growth is the five-year ahead projection of the growth rate of real GDP. Fed futures refer to the twelve-month Fed futures rate. Central bank assets are the ratio of central bank assets to potential GDP. The dividend yield is defined as the dividend component of national income divided by the market value of corporate equity held (directly or indirectly) by households as reported in the Federal Reserve Board's Flow of Funds data. Bootstrapped standard errors in parentheses. Lagged claims are used as instruments. *, ** and *** indicate statistical significance at the 10%, 5% and 1% levels.

5.1.2   Interpreting the results   The estimated coefficients for central bank assets (between −0.7 and −1.3) appear large. It is therefore important to note that the estimated historical relationship between central bank balance sheets and long-term forward rates is mostly related to changes in the holdings of Treasuries, as they relate to hitting the central bank's operational target. The recent initiatives undertaken to address liquidity issues (such as the TAF) that led to much of the increase in central bank balance sheets were inherently short-term and did not represent a permanent (or even cyclical shift) in the central bank's balance sheet. Consequently, any inference on the impact of current expansion of central bank balance sheets on long-term forward rates using estimated coefficients should be seen as an upper bound. That said, to get a better sense of the quantitative impact of the change in the size of the central bank's balance sheet, consider the following. The Federal Reserve's purchase of Treasuries in 2009Q2 represented an increase in central bank assets of 1.2 per cent of potential GDP. Given an estimated coefficient of about −0.9, this would suggest that the recent increase in Treasury holdings was associated with a 1.08 percentage point decrease in long-term forward rates. This is about twice the size of the initial impact of the announcement of Treasury purchases on ten-year Treasury yields, but of the same order of magnitude as estimated by Gagnon et al. (2010).

Given this sizeable historical relationship, it is in fact surprising that the Fed's purchase programme of Treasuries and its other facilities that led to a rapid expansion of its balance sheet did not result in a larger drop in long-term interest rates. However, it is important to keep in mind the context and factors that are likely to have simultaneously impacted long-term interest rates. For example, the supply of debt has increased massively as the US is financing two large fiscal stimulus programmes. The increased supply of debt should, in theory, lead to a rise in yields. Second, inflation expectations started to increase in the second half of 2009 as concerns about the inflationary impact of the Fed's sizeable balance sheet emerged. Third, the economic outlook started to improve in 2009, contributing to the rise in long-term interest rates.

A strong historical relationship suggests that an exit from sizeable balance sheets is likely to positively impact long-term rates. Although markets initially expected Treasury yields to increase by about 0.5 percentage points as the Fed's purchase programme of mortgage-related securities ended in March 2010, this outcome did not materialise, suggesting that it is the stock of assets held by the central bank rather than the flow of purchases/sales that is more relevant for the level of interest rates. If long-term rates respond immediately to announcements of future asset sales, then transparency of the exit strategy could be compromised as there may be an incentive to hold back details on asset sales until the Federal Reserve believes that economic conditions justify an increase in long-term interest rates.

5.2   Panel regression results

The regression results for the US suggest that an expansion of the central bank's balance sheet leads to lower long-term interest rates. However, is

Table 7.4 *Panel regressions*

	Central bank claims	Central bank claims	Central bank assets	Central bank assets
Inflation	2.356***	1.819***	1.841***	1.712***
expectations	(0.027)	(0.095)	(0.104)	(0.096)
Debt	0.042***		.005***	
	(0.004)		(0.005)	
Deficit		0.094***		0.039*
		(0.025)		(0.021)
Growth	0.022	0.088**	0.011	0.038**
	(0.034)	(0.035)	(0.038)	(0.042)
Claims	−0.336***	−0.120***		
	(0.027)	(0.020)		
CB assets			−0.073**	−0.074***
			(0.009)	(0.010)

Instrumented: claims or CB assets
Instruments: inflation, debt (or deficit)
GDP, lagged claims or CB assets, inflation

This table presents results of IV GMM regressions on a panel of six developed countries, comprising Australia, Canada, Switzerland, Japan, the UK and the US. The data are quarterly from 1996 to 2007. The dependent variable is the ten-year government bond yield. Inflation expectations are 5–10 years ahead. Deficit and debt are in per cent of GDP. Growth is the annual growth rate of real GDP. Central bank assets are the ratio of central bank assets to GDP. Central bank claims are the ratio of central bank holdings of government securities to GDP. Standard errors in parentheses. *, ** and *** indicate statistical significance at the 10%, 5% and 1% levels.

the US representative of the experience of other countries? (That is, do US long-term interest rates behave differentially, perhaps due to the status of the US dollar as an international reserve currency?) In order to provide further evidence of the link between central balance sheets and long-term rates, the analysis is extended to a set of developed countries. Table 7.4 reports regression results for panel regressions that include Australia, Canada, Switzerland, the UK, the US and Japan, using a GMM instrumental variables estimator. Again, expected inflation is a positive and statistically significant determinant of long-term interest rates in all regressions. Debt and deficit enter with a positive coefficient, consistent with expectations, and the coefficients are statistically significant in all four cases. The first two columns use central bank claims on the central government (i.e. holdings of government debt) as an explanatory variable, and as expected, the variable enters with a negative coefficient, which is statistically significant in all cases. The third and fourth columns repeat the regression for central bank assets and find similar results: the coefficient on central bank assets has the expected sign and is statistically significant in both regressions. The results confirm that central bank assets are an important determinant for long-term interest rates, not only for those countries engaging in large-scale asset purchases.

For robustness, alternative regression techniques are also employed (not shown). Using either fixed or random effects panel OLS, both central bank assets and claims carry a negative sign – central bank assets are statistically significant, but not claims. All other variables keep their signs and are significant. Using GLS, similar results are obtained, and the coefficients on central bank assets are statistically significant (but not claims). Last, when the dynamic panel estimator proposed by Arellano and Bond (1991) is used, results are somewhat weaker – when central bank assets are specified as predetermined or endogenous, the coefficient is negative and smaller than in previous regressions, but not statistically significant. Overall, the results are relatively robust to various regression methods.

6   Concerns, policy implications and avenues for future research

The regression results presented above suggest that there is a link between the size of the central bank's balance sheet and long-term forward interest rates. But one major concern of the empirical framework is that the innovations in the balance sheet are simply proxies for the short-term policy rate, and as such, the effect of changes in the central bank sheet are overstated. However, if one assumes that forward rates, being sufficiently in the future, are immune to changes in short-term policy rates associated with the business cycle, then this concern is mitigated.

The policy implications from these results would suggest that the recent expansion of central bank balance sheets could have sizeable effects on long-term forward interest rates, all else being equal. However, it is important to note that the estimated historical relationship between central bank balance sheets and long-term forward rates is mostly related to changes in the holdings of Treasuries. Many of the recent initiatives undertaken to address liquidity issues (such as the TAF) were inherently short-term and did not represent a permanent (or even cyclical shift) in the central bank's balance sheet. Consequently, any inference on the impact of current expansion of central bank balance sheets on long-term forward rates using estimated coefficients should be seen as an upper bound. That said, the results appear to be broadly consistent with those found in the literature.

The results suggest that central banks, through the use of their balance sheets, retain considerable flexibility with respect to their ability to deliver monetary easing when policy rates are at the effective lower bound. However, it remains to be seen whether lower interest rates resulting from central bank intervention in the form of balance sheet expansion provided support to economic activity during the latest crisis or whether the transmission mechanism was somehow impaired. In addition, there are concerns that low interest rates may lead to poor resource allocation (BIS, 2010). Nevertheless, in times of crisis, such actions may also provide necessary support to confidence and fight the fear of deflation.

Going forward, it might be insightful to complement the analysis with case studies, examining the US, the UK and Japanese experience of large-scale asset purchases in greater detail. Further, it would be interesting to assess the impact of unconventional policies on broader measures of financial market functioning and economic variables. For instance, future research could aim to measure the impact of central bank assets on spreads, such as credit spreads and other financial variables, and try to estimate the ultimate impact on real variables.

References

Arellano, M. and Bond, S. (1991) Some tests of specification for panel data: Monte Carlo evidence and an application to employment equations, *The Review of Economic Studies*, 58(2), 277–97.

Ball, L. and Cecchetti, S. G. (1990) Inflation and uncertainty at long and short horizons, Brookings Papers on Economic Activity, 1, 215–45.

Bank for International Settlements (BIS) (2010) Low interest rates: do the risks outweigh the rewards?, BIS Annual Report.

Bernanke, B. (2009) The Federal Reserve's balance sheet: an update, Speech at the Federal Reserve Board Conference on Key Developments in Monetary Policy, Washington, D.C., 8 October.

Blanchard, O., Dell'Ariccia, G. and Mauro, P. (2010) Rethinking macroeconomic Policy, IMF Staff Position Note, SPN/10/03.

Borio, C. and Disyatat, P. (2009) Unconventional monetary policies: an appraisal, BIS Working Papers, No. 292.

Committee on the Global Financial System (CGFS) (2010) The functioning and resilience of cross-border funding markets, CGFS Publication, No. 37.

Dale, S. (2010) QE – one year on, Remarks at the CIMF and MMF Conference, Cambridge, 12 March.

Feldstein, M. S. (1976) Inflation, income taxes and the rate of interest: a theoretical analysis, *American Economic Review*, 66, 809–20.

Gagnon, J., Raskin, M., Remache, J. and Sack, B. (2010) Large-scale asset purchases by the Federal Reserve: did they work? FRB of New York Staff Report, No. 441.

In, F. H., Cui, J. and Mahraj, A. (2008) The impact of a newterm auction facility on LIBOR-OIS spreads and volatility transmission between money and mortgage markets, Abstract.

Joyce, M., Lasaosa, A., Stevens, I. and Tong, M. (2010) The financial market impact of quantitative easing, Bank of England Working Paper, No. 393.

Laubach, T. (2009) New evidence on the interest rate effects of budget deficits and debt, *Journal of the European Economic Association*, 7(4), June, 858–85.

McAndrews, J., Sarkar, A. and Wang, Z. (2008) The effect of the term auction facility on the London Inter-Bank Offered Rate, Federal Research Board of New York Staff Report No. 335.

Meyer, L. H. and Bomfim, A. N. (2010) Quantifying the effects of Fed asset purchases on Treasury yields, Monetary Policy Insights: Fixed Income Focus, Macroeconomic Advisers, LLC.

Neely, C. (2010) The large-scale asset purchases had large international effects, FRB of St. Louis Working Paper 2010-018A.

Okun, A. (1971) The mirage of steady inflation, Brookings Papers on Economic Activity, 2, 485–98.

Taylor, J. and Willams, J. (2008) A black swan in the money market, Federal Reserve Bank of San Francisco Working Paper 2008–4.

Wu, T. (2008) On the effectiveness of the Federal Reserve's new liquidity facilities, Federal Reserve Bank of Dallas Working Paper No. 2008-08.

8   Non-standard monetary policy measures and monetary developments

Domenico Giannone, Michele Lenza, Huw Pill and Lucrezia Reichlin

1   Introduction

Standard accounts of the Great Depression (notably the seminal offering of Friedman and Schwartz, 1963) attribute an important *causal* role to monetary policy errors in accounting for the catastrophic collapse in economic activity observed in the early 1930s. In particular, the Federal Reserve's failure to halt the collapse in the money stock following the banking crisis of 1931 is seen as a crucial mistake (Meltzer, 2007). While views vary on the relative importance of money versus credit contraction in the propagation of this policy error to the wider economy and ultimately price developments (see, e.g., Bernanke, 1983), a broad consensus exists in the economics profession around the view that the collapse in financial intermediation was a crucial intermediary step.

What lessons have monetary policy makers taken from this episode? And how have they informed the conduct of monetary policy by leading central banks in recent times? Using the frameworks developed by Giannone et al. (2010) and Lenza et al. (2010), this chapter sets out to address these questions, in the context of the financial crisis of 2008–9 and with application to the euro area. In doing so, the chapter draws together two strands of literature: one that explores the nature and rationale of non-standard monetary policy measures, understood as those relying on instruments other than changes to short-term official interest rates,[1] and another which investigates the evolution of bank balance sheets, as reflected in monetary and credit developments, and their impact on monetary policy transmission.

We believe that connecting these two literatures is essential when assessing the success of non-standard monetary policy measures during

The views expressed in this chapter are those of the authors and do not necessarily reflect the views of the ECB or the Eurosystem. Material underlying this chapter was presented at the CIMF Cambridge conference on unconventional monetary policy measures in March 2010 and at the Bank of England CCBS research workshop in July 2010.

[1] For a brief summary of measures, see Borio and Disyatat (2009).

195

the recent crisis episode. A growing number of papers evaluate the impact of central bank balance sheet expansion on the slope and level of the yield curve (see, e.g., Kozicki et al., this volume, and the references therein; Gagnon et al., 2010; and Joyce et al., 2010). Yet the first-order objective of the non-standard measures – especially in a bank-centred financial system, like that of the euro area – has been to support ongoing financial intermediation and market functioning – in other words, to avoid the mistakes of the early 1930s. This cannot meaningfully be evaluated by looking at the marginal impact of measures on specific asset markets. A more comprehensive approach is required – one that entails a rich analysis of developments in money and credit aggregates and an evaluation of the effectiveness of monetary policy transmission.

While recognising the practical and methodological challenges entailed, in this chapter we set out to construct counterfactual macroeconomic scenarios that accord a central place to the financial and monetary variables at the heart of recent experience, against which observed outcomes can be compared. To simplify, we focus on a specific phase of the financial crisis, namely the period after the failure of Lehman Brothers (September 2008 through to early 2010).[2]

To anticipate our results, we show that the behaviour of key financial and monetary aggregates – notably M1, short-term bank loans to non-financial corporations and (albeit to a somewhat lesser extent) loans to households – can be explained on the basis of historical regularities estimated in the pre-crisis sample, once developments are conditioned on the *actual* path of economic activity. In other words, one does not need to rely on exceptional or aberrant behaviour in the financial sector to explain developments in money and credit following the failure of Lehman. The ensuing weakness of economic activity suffices to account for what was observed.

To be clear: we do not claim that such exercises demonstrate that financial shocks played no part in the dramatic fall in economic activity observed in the second half of 2008. Nor do we claim that the evolution of loan dynamics in the euro area can be attributed solely to credit demand, rather than credit supply, factors. These are important questions. But answering them requires robust identification of the underlying economic shocks within a fully specified structural model of the euro area economy and financial system, something the analysis employed in this chapter does not provide.

---

[2] That is, before the euro area sovereign debt crisis that emerged in spring 2010 had exerted a strong influence on the time series for monetary and financial variables.

Nonetheless, we believe that our results are informative. In particular, they are consistent with the view that the recent evolution of the euro area economy can be explained as the incidence of a 'big shock', which propagated to economic activity largely through conventional channels, rather than as a fundamental change in the behaviour of the economy (a 'structural break'). Thus, while we necessarily remain agnostic regarding the factors that led to the simultaneous downturn in real activity and financial intermediation in September 2008, we argue that the interactions between financial and monetary flows, on the one hand, and the real economy, on the other, in the subsequent period largely reflect historical regularities, given the introduction of non-standard monetary policy measures by the Eurosystem (and other initiatives by the policy authorities).

We interpret these results as evidence that the non-standard measures introduced by the ECB following Lehman's demise were successful in, at least partially, insulating the liquidity and credit conditions facing households and firms from the breakdown of financial intermediation seen in the interbank money market.[3] By implication, 'propagation via financial collapse' – seen as central to the emergence of the Great Depression in the 1930s – was largely avoided in the recent episode. In this sense, the non-standard monetary policy measures introduced by the ECB in the autumn of 2008 can be viewed as successful.

The remainder of the chapter is organised as follows. As background to the discussion, Section 2 recalls important features of the two financial crisis episodes discussed above. Section 3 then describes how the Eurosystem responded to the financial crisis of 2007–9, emphasising how this response differed from that of other central banks and that of the Federal Reserve in the 1930s. Section 4 presents two model-based exercises to explore the impact of non-standard measures, while Section 5 offers some brief concluding remarks deriving from this analysis.

2   'Textbook' models of broad money supply and some monetary facts

Textbook models of the broad money supply process revolve around the manipulation of a number of accounting identities describing banks' holdings of central bank reserves and private-sector holdings of cash

---

[3] Of course, we recognise that these measures cannot be seen in isolation. Governments also took substantial action in early October 2008, notably by offering guarantees and other fiscal support to the financial system. However, as argued in Section 3 below, we view the malfunctioning of the money market as being a key element of transmission during this episode, and this is where the ECB's actions were most relevant.

and deposits. The standard 'money multiplier' formulation leads to the following expression:

$$M = mH$$
$$= \left(\frac{1+k}{k+r}\right)H$$

where M is broad money, H is high-powered money (i.e. central bank monetary liabilities), k is the ratio of cash holdings to deposit holdings for the non-bank private sector, r is the ratio of central bank reserves to deposits issued by the banking sector and m is the money multiplier.

Figure 8.1 illustrates the significant drop in the money supply in the US during the Great Depression. On the basis of data presented by Rasche (1987), the stock of M1 fell by approximately 20 per cent between 1931 and 1933. The fall in M1 occurred notwithstanding a substantial rise in currency in circulation, which increased by almost half over the same period. Taken together, these developments mechanically imply a substantial fall in the money multiplier.[4]

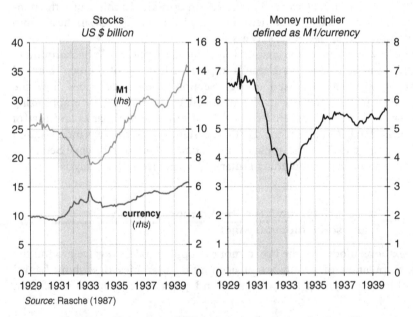

Source: Rasche (1987)

Figure 8.1   Behaviour of US money stocks during the Great Depression, 1929–39

[4] Defined here as the ratio of M1 to currency in circulation.

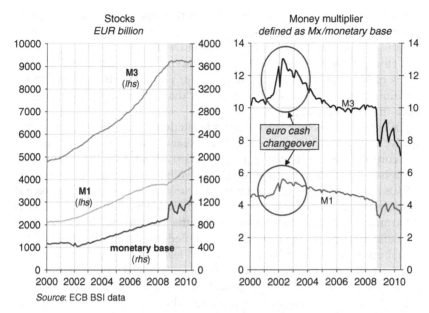

Figure 8.2 Behaviour of euro area money stocks during the financial crisis, 2000–10

It is interesting to compare these developments with those observed during the 2007–9 financial crisis. Figure 8.2 shows data for the euro area. In this chart, we also include the broader monetary aggregate M3, which (inter alia) includes time and savings deposits, in addition to the overnight deposits included in M1. Moreover, we have adopted a more comprehensive definition of the monetary base, including not only currency and central bank reserves held by banks but also recourse made by central bank counterparties to the ECB deposit facility.

In the euro area, money multipliers demonstrate some volatility after the collapse of Lehman in September 2008. This reflects the increased volatility of the monetary base from October 2008, as a variety of non-standard monetary policy measures was introduced by the ECB. That said, notwithstanding this volatility, several features of the data stand out. In particular, the M3 multiplier behaved quite differently to the M1 multiplier: the latter gyrated around its relatively stable, pre-existing downward trend during the two years after Lehman's failure, whereas the M3 multiplier fell significantly, mirroring the fall seen in the US multiplier after 1931.

Prima facie, such similarity gives obvious reason for concern. Yet the drivers of the fall in the euro area M3 multiplier after Lehman were quite different from those seen during the US Great Depression. The broad money stock *remained stable* during the 2008–9 crisis. As a result, the fall in the multiplier owed *exclusively* to the more rapid expansion of the monetary base. In short, unlike during the Great Depression, there was no fall in the stock of broad money, despite the lower money multiplier. And the stock of M1 rose more rapidly than in prior years, with the M1 multiplier continuing on its downward trend rather than collapsing dramatically as seen in the US during the early 1930s.[5]

Of course, this comparison has its limitations. Financial structure has evolved significantly over the past eighty years. This is recognised, in part, by considering a broader aggregate (M3) in addition to M1 in the exercise – but clearly inadequately so. While the events of the early 1930s are explained largely in terms of a run on retail deposits, the recent crisis has been characterised as a run on wholesale bank funding (e.g. what Gorton and Metrick (2009) have labelled the 'run on repo' in a securitised banking system). In the former case, the Federal Reserve is criticised for its failure to act as a traditional 'lender of last resort' by accommodating heightened demand for currency at a time of financial stress.[6] In the latter case (and as discussed further in Section 3 below), the ECB has stepped up its provision of intermediation services through its operational framework for the implementation of monetary policy in order to complement (and, at times, replace) the frozen interbank money market at the centre of wholesale bank funding activity.

The traditional characterisation of the broad money supply process obscures these nuances. For example, one simplistic interpretation of recent events – suggested by the money multiplier identity described above – is that the ECB 'injected' sufficient high-powered money into the financial system so as to offset the contractionary impact of a declining money multiplier on the broad money stock. In other words, the ECB avoided the mistake of the 1930s' Federal Reserve identified by Friedman and Schwartz (1963). But such a view begs new questions: why did the ECB not inject *more* base money, so as to allow M3 to continue to expand at pre-crisis rates? And what was the *cause* of the fall in the money multiplier? Can it really be viewed as exogenous to the ECB's policy decisions, as this treatment suggests?

---

[5] Indeed, it is noticeable that while broad money (M3) continued to expand strongly after the first emergence of money market tensions in August 2007 and stagnated only with the failure of Lehman in September 2008, the pattern of narrow money (M1) developments is quite different: slowing and stagnation after August 2007, followed by a revival of expansion from September 2008 onwards (see Figure 8.2).

[6] More specifically, one might argue that the criticism centres on the Federal Reserve's failure to signal clearly ex ante that it would fulfil such a lender-of-last-resort function. In line with the literature on policy rules, this approach would have altered private expectations and stabilised private behaviour prior to the financial crisis. See, for example, the simulations presented in Christiano et al. (2003).

Answering these questions requires a more structural interpretation of the evolution of various monetary quantities. This, in turn, requires development of a deeper understanding of the intentions and actions of the central bank, the banking sector, and borrowers and depositors in the private sector. As Goodhart (2010) emphasises, the money multiplier framework is an inadequate lens for this purpose.

In the remainder of this chapter, we employ the empirical framework presented in Giannone et al. (2010) to explore these interactions in a data-rich setting. This model has been developed for use in the ECB's regular monetary analysis. It allows us to establish some 'stylised facts' or regularities in the pre-crisis monetary and financial data that can be used as a benchmark against which to compare actual monetary developments (observed in real time) during the financial crisis itself.

3 The ECB's non-standard monetary policy measures after Lehman

This section draws heavily on Lenza et al. (2010), to which readers are referred for more details.

Following the failure of Lehman on 15 September 2008, panic gripped global financial markets. Money market interest rate spreads rose substantially, as interbank liquidity dried up and markets 'froze'. At its peak following Lehman's collapse, the spread between unsecured interbank deposit rates (EURIBOR) and secured repo rates at the three-month maturity exceeded 200 basis points in the euro area (see Figure 8.3) – and the equivalent spreads were even higher in the US and the UK.

On the basis of a structural model of the money market where the existence of informational asymmetries between market participants gives rise to adverse selection among banks, Heider et al. (2009) offer a compelling explanation of these developments. While their model is inevitably highly stylised, it demonstrates how concerns about the solvency of specific banks can lead to the breakdown of interbank trading.

The model distinguishes three regimes: first, a situation of low interest rate spreads and active interbank trading; second, a market exhibiting elevated spreads and adverse selection, with continued but lower trading volumes; and third, a regime where market trading breaks down. What determines the transition from one regime to another in this model is the extent of concerns about counterparty solvency. But when such concerns emerge, the outcome is heightened liquidity risk for *all* banks, not just those which are perceived to face a heightened threat of insolvency as credit risks mount.

Basis points

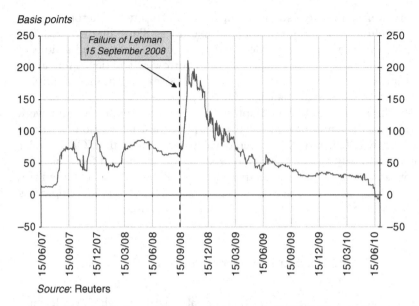

Source: Reuters

Figure 8.3 Spread between three-month EURIBOR and three-month
general collateral (GC) repo rate

At a conceptual level, the various regimes identified in this model can be
associated with the different phases observed during the financial crisis:
the pre-crisis normality; the initial tensions in the euro money market after
August 2007; and the sudden intensification of those tensions after
Lehman failed, leading to a money market 'freeze' in late September
2008. Once it was demonstrated that significant institutions such as
Lehman could default, concerns about counterparty risk mushroomed
to the extent that the interbank money market dried up almost completely.
For a banking sector reliant on the wholesale money market for its marginal funding needs, this posed serious risks to the financial system, to the
flow of credit to the productive sectors and thus to financial, macroeconomic and, ultimately, price stability.

Against this background, the authorities stepped into action. While it
should be recognised that the non-standard measures introduced by the
Eurosystem in this context were part of a broader policy response,[7] they were
nonetheless the crucial element in addressing the immediate liquidity crisis.

---

[7] Involving (inter alia): a substantial easing of monetary policy by conventional means (i.e.
lower key ECB interest rates), fiscal stimulus, and substantial government support to the
financial sector (e.g. in the form of government guarantees to bonds issued by banks or
outright recapitalisation of banks facing solvency problems).

The main objective of the non-standard measures introduced by the Eurosystem was the expansion of central bank intermediation. This was intended to *substitute* for interbank transactions that could no longer take place owing to the malfunctioning private money market. Allowing greater intermediation across the Eurosystem balance sheet prevented a collapse of the financial sector and mitigated the impact of market turmoil on the real economy. In other words, the Eurosystem's actions can be seen as the modern-day equivalent of a 'lender of last resort'. Rather than providing cash to banks so that they could meet retail deposit runs – as the Federal Reserve conspicuously failed to do in the early 1930s – the ECB set out to provide 'intermediation of last resort' as the interbank money market froze, with the goal of preventing a fire sale of marketable assets and the costly premature liquidation of loans, as banks lost access to market sources of liquidity and short-term funding.[8]

How was central bank intermediation expanded? In line with the description of financial intermediation that can be found in any standard banking textbook, the Eurosystem's activities grew along a number of dimensions.

First, *maturity transformation* performed by the Eurosystem increased significantly. By (a) increasing the share of liquidity supplied at its long-term refinancing operations (LTROs) relative to its regular main refinancing operations (MROs) and (b) increasing the maturity structure of its LTROs by offering one-year operations, the Eurosystem substantially increased the average maturity of its outstanding repo operations. And since these operations were 'funded' by the accumulation of excess liquidity at the Eurosystem's (overnight maturity) deposit facility, this resulted in substantial maturity transformation, allowing the banking sector to become less reliant on (very) short-term financing and passing at least part of the maturity mismatch inherent in banking activities to the central bank.

Second, the Eurosystem increased its provision of *liquidity transformation*. In particular, the Eurosystem accepted as collateral in its refinancing operations assets that had become illiquid in financial markets (notably mortgage-backed securities, given the freezing of the private market for securitised instruments). In its operations, the Eurosystem provided cash loans against the security of these assets. The banking sector was therefore able to transform illiquid instruments into cash at relatively low cost, avoiding a need to engage in disorderly fire sales of those assets to raise liquidity. Such fire sales might have led to a self-sustaining downward

---

[8] For the ECB's official description of the specific measures taken as part of its programme of 'enhanced credit support', see Trichet (2009).

spiral in asset markets and collateral values, imposing capital losses and liquidity squeezes on the banks themselves. In short, the systemic threat posed by fire sale externalities was contained by central bank action.

Third, the Eurosystem increased its provision of *transactions services* and its support to the distribution of liquidity within the financial sector. This was facilitated by the very large number of counterparties eligible for Eurosystem operations, which allowed the central bank to establish itself as a central 'hub' in the network of interbank transactions. Participation in Eurosystem operations increased over the course of the crisis as central bank intermediation replaced interbank transactions: at the peak, more than 1,000 different counterparties bid at the operations.

Finally, the Eurosystem contributed to *addressing the information problems* that were widely seen – for example, in the Heider et al. (2009) model – as underlying the financial crisis. In particular, the Eurosystem conducted operations in a manner that protected counterparties' anonymity and thus avoided the danger that operations were 'stigmatised', leading to an exacerbation of adverse selection problems.[9]

The details of the specific operational actions implemented to achieve these objectives have been discussed elsewhere (e.g. by Lenza et al., 2010). Rather than repeat them here, we focus on the key feature of the Eurosystem's approach, namely its adoption of a *fixed rate/full allotment* (FRFA) tender procedure.

Adopting such a procedure in its operations implied that the Eurosystem accommodated banks' demand for liquidity and central bank intermediation *in full*, at price conditions determined by the ECB. In other words, there was no rationing of access to central bank intermediation: at the pre-announced price (i.e. the fixed rate at the MROs), the supply of central bank liquidity and intermediation was perfectly elastic. In line with the prescription offered by Cùrdia and Woodford (2011) on the basis of their theoretical model, banks' demand for central bank liquidity was satiated. In an environment of financial crisis and dysfunctional markets where the demand for central bank intermediation was strong, this led to a significant increase in the volume of outstanding repo operations (on the asset side of the central bank balance sheet) and in the monetary base (on the liabilities side) (see Figure 8.4).

---

[9] Of course, this approach implicitly protected banks from the scrutiny of market discipline in their (very) short-term financing. By implication, the Eurosystem's risk control measures became the key monitoring and disciplining mechanism. The ECB emphasised that the responsible authorities (regulators, supervisors and ultimately the government) would need to address, in a timely way, any underlying solvency and other fundamental problems in the banking sector.

EUR billions

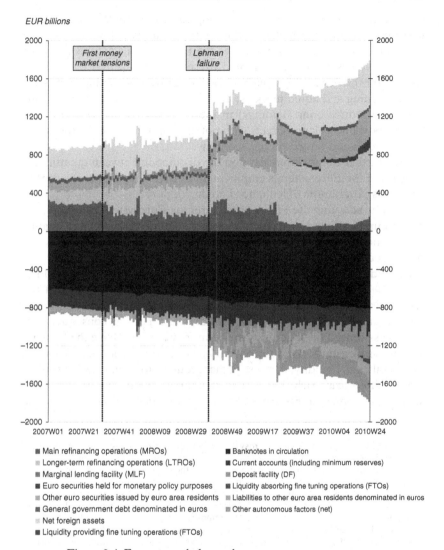

Figure 8.4 Eurosystem balance sheet

What is crucial to see is that the expansion of the Eurosystem balance sheet illustrated in Figure 8.4 should *not* be understood in terms of either (a) an attempt to expand the money supply directly by 'printing money' or (b) an 'injection of liquidity' into the money market by the central bank. Rather, the balance sheet expansion was a *by-product* of a set of non-standard measures aimed at supporting the functioning of crucial segments of the financial market, thereby promoting effective monetary policy transmission and avoiding a financial collapse similar to that of the 1930s.

This characterisation distinguishes the Eurosystem's actions from the quantitative easing policies adopted by some other central banks from spring 2009 onwards.[10,11] Quantitative easing involves purchases of assets in functioning and liquid markets, in an attempt to increase money holdings (and reduce bond holdings) in the private sector so as to prompt further portfolio balance effects with potential implications for the structure of yields and returns in the economy.[12]

Two further observations develop the distinction between quantitative easing and the Eurosystem's employment of FRFA tenders as the central part of its programme of 'enhanced credit support'.

First, by adopting the FRFA procedure, the Eurosystem ceded control over volumes allotted in its operations to its counterparties. Thus quantities on the Eurosystem balance sheet were driven by private choices, not policy decisions.

Second, the 'active' choice made by the counterparties concerned the asset side of the Eurosystem balance sheet (i.e. bidding volumes at the refinancing operations). Recourse to the deposit facility and expansion of the monetary base (as shown in Figure 8.4) was a 'passive' consequence of the excess central bank liquidity in the money market. Since the banking sector's aggregate demand for central bank intermediation led to a stock of central bank liquidity in excess of that required to meet reserve requirements, those 'cash-rich' banks with structurally long liquidity positions simply accumulated reserve holdings at the deposit facility. In the

---

[10] It should be recognised that the Eurosystem's covered bond purchase programme (introduced in June 2009) and securities markets programme (introduced in May 2010) involved outright asset purchases at the initiative of the ECB. However, the overall volume of these measures (reflected in the item 'Euro securities held for monetary policy purposes' in Figure 8.4) was small compared with the overall balance sheet and its expansion. Moreover, these asset purchases took place in dysfunctional markets with the goal of supporting the improvement of market functioning. They were not explicitly intended to expand liquidity (e.g. with the intent to prompt portfolio re-allocation in the private sector). Indeed, the liquidity implications of asset purchases under the Securities Markets Programme (SMP) were offset by special liquidity absorbing fine-tuning operations conducted by the Eurosystem.

[11] As described in Lenza et al. (2010), greater cross-country similarity characterised the central bank response to the emergence of money market tensions in August 2007 and the immediate reaction to Lehman's failure. As in the euro area, in the US and the UK these measures focused on supporting money market functioning, even if the precise means employed varied according to the design of central banks' operational frameworks for monetary policy implementation and the structure of the financial system in the respective jurisdictions.

[12] See Joyce et al. (2010) for a discussion of the various channels envisaged and an empirical evaluation of their efficacy in the UK context.

dysfunctional money market, they were not prepared to lend these hold-ings in the market given concerns about counterparty risk. And even if they bought financial assets and/or made loans when seeking higher returns than available at the deposit facility, such transactions merely transferred the excess liquidity to another bank. Ultimately, the increase in the deposit facility was inevitable – the result of an accounting identity.

In sum, the Eurosystem's non-standard measures should be under-stood as an attempt to accommodate heightened demand for central bank intermediation from the private sector at a time when private markets were dysfunctional. This is reflected (albeit imperfectly[13]) in Figure 8.5, which demonstrates that the decline in interbank credit posi-tions from September 2008 disappears when positions vis-à-vis the Eurosystem are included in the data.

In the money market, this can be characterised as a switch of regimes: from a 'normal' regime, where the Eurosystem supplied sufficient

Intra-MFI (bank) sector credit as a percentage of credit to the non-financial sector

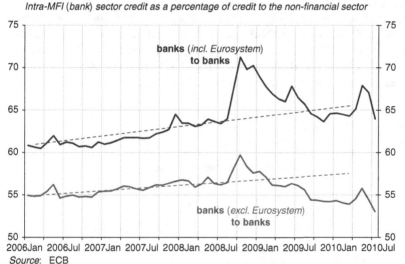

Source: ECB

Note: The term 'banks' is used here to refer to the statistical category 'monetary financial institutions' (MFIs), which include the Eurosystem, credit institutions and money market mutual funds

Figure 8.5 Substitution of central bank intermediation for interbank transactions

---

[13] In particular, the economically relevant nature of this substitution of central bank inter-mediation for interbank activity refers to the *flow* of transactions (many of which have a short maturity) rather than the *stock* of outstanding positions at end-month (illustrated in Figure 8.5). However, transactions data for the money market are sparse.

liquidity to meet the aggregate banking sector's *net* (or consolidated) liquidity needs and relied on the market to distribute that liquidity efficiently across individual banks; to a 'crisis' regime, where tensions implied that the market could no longer be relied upon to distribute liquidity efficiently. In the latter case, the Eurosystem was forced to accommodate the *gross* liquidity needs of individual banks, since the market's netting mechanism no longer worked. Since gross transactions among institutions within the banking sector are much higher than the net liquidity needs of the consolidated banking sector, even a partial switch from normal to crisis regime implied a substantial expansion of the Eurosystem balance sheet – including the monetary base.

These measures were not without their repercussions on market interest rates. The expansion of central bank intermediation allowed banks to bypass money market tensions as necessary. As shown in Figure 8.3, money market spreads at term maturities therefore fell – the underlying adverse selection problem was overcome by relying on the central bank to deal with information problems. Moreover, the presence of excess liquidity in the overnight market and the resulting recourse to the deposit facility implied a fall in the EONIA (i.e. the euro interbank overnight money market rate). More precisely, the spread between the EONIA and the ECB policy rate (i.e. the fixed rate at the MRO) turned negative, as market rates declined towards the deposit facility rate (see Figure 8.6). Through

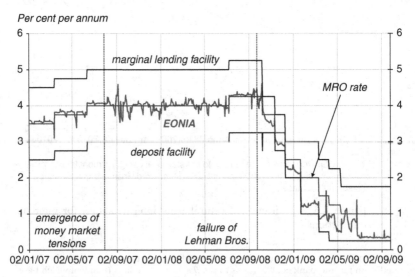

Figure 8.6 Eurosystem interest rate corridor and EONIA

accommodating counterparties' demands in terms of quantities, the Eurosystem was therefore able to influence market prices.

4   Macroeconomic implications of non-standard measures

Having described the intent and content of the Eurosystem's package of non-standard monetary policy measures, we now attempt to evaluate their macroeconomic impact.

Such an assessment is fraught with identification problems. The introduction of non-standard monetary policy measures was triggered by the incidence of very significant and unprecedented financial shocks. Given the necessarily prompt and broad-based response of the policy authorities to the freezing of the money market, the shock and the policy responses to it are inevitably temporally closely aligned. By implication, distinguishing the impact of non-standard monetary policy measures from the impact of the shocks that prompted them or other policy responses is inherently very difficult (a compounding of the problem well understood from the large literature on the identification of (conventional) monetary policy shocks). Furthermore, assessments of the efficacy of the non-standard measures will depend on what is seen as the counterfactual: if the alternative is a repeat of the Great Depression, this will lead to quite different conclusions than an alternative of a return to normality.

In this chapter, we adopt a more limited approach, focusing on a much more specific issue: the transmission of non-standard measures via monetary and financial variables. This is a topic of special interest in the ECB context, given the emphasis that it has traditionally placed on monetary analysis in the formulation of monetary policy decisions (see Fischer et al. (2009) and Papademos and Stark (2010) for discussions). Yet many other central banks and commentators have come to place renewed interest on monetary, credit and balance sheet developments as a consequence of the financial crisis. We thus believe that the analysis is of more general interest.

While recognising that we are creating something of a 'straw man', for expositional purposes it is useful to establish a benchmark for our discussion. This derives from the concerns expressed in some quarters about the effectiveness of the transmission of the ECB's non-standard measures to the economy as a whole. In particular, doubts have surrounded whether the expansion of the monetary base has 'passed through' to stronger broad money and bank credit growth, as the traditional textbook 'money multiplier view of the world' (discussed in Section 2) would imply.

As discussed above, this textbook characterisation relies on the mechanical application of various accounting identities to describe the interactions among central bank measures, bank behaviour, the decisions of borrowers and lenders in the productive sectors, and the evolution of the real economy. Our approach sets out to replace these accounting identities with a richer, behavioural view of how the non-standard measures are transmitted through the financial sector to the real economy, and ultimately to longer-term price developments. It offers a lens to understand this transmission process, taking an empirical view of the behaviour of banks, borrowers and money holders.

Taking this perspective, an entirely different view of the impact of the Eurosystem's non-standard measures emerges. On the basis of the discussion in Section 3, this starts from the recognition that the expansion of the monetary base reflects the ECB's attempt to use central bank intermediation to 'bridge the gap' created by the freezing of the interbank money market and its impact on interbank transactions, rather than a mechanism to expand bank balance sheets mechanically.

Viewed in this light, the Eurosystem's non-standard measures aim at insulating monetary and credit developments from the immediate impact of the financial crisis in the money market. Their success should thus be evaluated on whether they prevented a disorderly deleveraging – associated with a premature calling of outstanding bank loans and asset fire sales – not on whether they induced an immediate renewed expansion of bank credit equi-proportional to the expansion of the monetary base.

To evaluate the Eurosystem's non-standard measures on this basis, we use the analytical machinery developed in Giannone et al. (2010).[14] This paper presents an empirical model of the euro area economy, which – in addition to the normal set of macroeconomic variables – captures the joint cyclical behaviour of a large number of monetary and credit aggregates, as well as interest rate spreads, yields and asset prices. More specifically, the paper constructs a very general multivariate linear model for thirty-nine euro area monthly time series, using a vector autoregressive (VAR) specification with thirteen lags for the (log-) level of these variables. The so-called 'curse of dimensionality' is addressed using Bayesian shrinkage methods, as suggested in Banbura et al. (2010) and De Mol et al. (2008). This model is used to conduct two exercises.

---

[14] For details of the model, readers are naturally referred to the paper itself.

*4.1   Exercise 1: Insulation of money and credit flows
         from the impact of financial crisis*

Using the Giannone et al. machinery, we conduct the following exercise. First, the model is estimated over the pre-crisis sample, from January 1991 to August 2008. This estimation should be understood as establishing the statistical regularities or 'stylised facts' inherent in the 'pre-crisis' euro area economy, with a focus on the monetary and financial aspects. Second, using this model we construct a forecast of monetary and credit variables of interest for the period from January 1999 until March 2010. This forecast is conditional on the actual path of the variables capturing economic activity in the model (i.e. industrial production). Third, we compare these conditional forecasts of monetary and credit variables with the actual observed series. The results of this exercise are shown in Figure 8.7.

As one would expect, the in-sample forecasting performance of the model is good: the forecast path of the variables follows the observed data quite closely from 1999 through to August 2008. The focus of our interest is on the out-of-sample period covering the financial crisis, i.e. from September 2008 onwards.

Our interpretation of the exercise is as follows. The conditional forecast (labelled 'simulated' in Figure 8.7) reflects the anticipated evolution of monetary and credit variables given the observed path of economic activity during the financial crisis, assuming that the historical pre-crisis regularities in the euro area data are maintained. One can conceive of this as a bench-mark capturing 'normal' behaviour of the monetary and credit sector in the context of a marked fall in economic activity.

By its nature, the observed evolution of monetary and credit variables ('actual' in Figure 8.7) is also conditional on the observed path of economic activity. More substantially, it is also conditional on two further factors which differentiate it from the model forecast. First, the actual behaviour of the monetary and financial sector over this period is not (necessarily) 'normal' – indeed, in a context of financial crisis, one might anticipate otherwise. Second, the observed data reflect also the impact of the non-standard monetary policy measures by the Eurosystem, which – again, by their nature – are not part of the 'normal' regime of the pre-crisis regularities captured in the model.

We assume – not unreasonably in our view, given the narrative offered in Section 3 – that the behaviour of the euro area banking system, and thus the evolution of monetary and credit variables, was influenced by the financial crisis. Other things being equal, this would point to a divergence of the actual and simulated paths of these variables shown in Figure 8.7.

Interest Rates, Prices and Liquidity

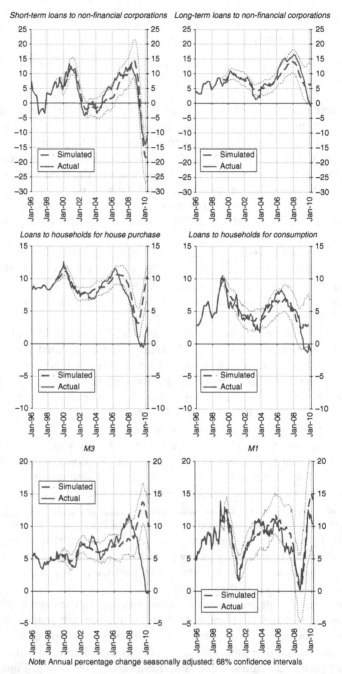

Figure 8.7 Comparison of outturns with conditional forecasts in Giannone et al. (2010) model

But other things are not equal, in particular along one dimension. The actual paths also include the impact of the Eurosystem's non-standard measures. Divergence between the actual and simulated paths can thus be interpreted as a measure of the extent to which the introduction of non-standard measures failed to offset the impact of the financial crisis on the banking sector, resulting in an overall ('reduced form') impact on money and credit growth and their relationship with other macroeconomic variables. And, by the same token, similar actual and simulated paths can be seen as evidence of the success of the non-standard measures in insulating macroeconomic monetary and credit dynamics from the impact of the financial crisis on financial institutions and markets; that is, the extent to which they avoided the failures of the Federal Reserve in the early 1930s identified by Friedman and Schwartz (1963).

Inspection of Figure 8.7 gives rise to the following conclusions. First, the observed behaviour of narrow money (M1) after the collapse of Lehman Brothers is not statistically distinguishable from the model's conditional forecast. This reflects the strong liquidity effect driving the behaviour of M1[15] – the sharp fall in short-term interest rates both observed in the data and predicted by the model (given the contraction of real activity) gives rise to stronger demand for the overnight deposits and currency comprising M1. By implication, conditional on the introduction of non-standard monetary policy measures, the onset of financial crisis does not appear to have weakened the liquidity effect found in the pre-crisis data. The availability of short-term monetary liquidity to the non-financial sector was therefore not impaired by the crisis itself. At a minimum, runs on retail overnight deposits – characteristic of the 1931 financial crisis in the United States, as discussed briefly in Section 2 – were successfully avoided during the recent episode.

Second, in general the behaviour of credit variables has followed a path consistent with the pre-crisis regularities captured by the Giannone et al. (2010) model. In particular, the observed evolution of short-term loans to the non-financial corporate sector – a credit component that is seen as particularly crucial at times of economic distress, given its buffering role in corporate cash flows – also closely mimics that which would have been anticipated by the model in the event of a sharp fall in economic activity.

---

[15] The analysis presented in Giannone et al. (2010) shows that the effect of a monetary policy shock on euro area M1 is large and persistent in normal ('pre-crisis') times, i.e. there is a strong liquidity effect. In the exercise presented in Figure 8.7, the underlying structural shock is not identified. Nonetheless, we find that M1 behaves during the crisis period as expected by the model conditionally on the cycle. This suggests that there was no change in the liquidity effect. This view is supported by the analysis of Lenza et al. (2010) presented below.

This again supports the view that the Eurosystem's non-standard monetary policy measures were effective in supporting financial intermediation and maintaining monetary policy transmission.

Long-term loans to firms appear to be more significantly affected (in both economic and statistical senses) by the financial crisis, especially from the middle of 2009. While prima facie this raises some doubts about the effectiveness of the non-standard measures, one possible explanation is a shift out of longer-term bank borrowing to the issuance of debt securities by large euro area companies. Taking a broader view of the corporate balance sheet rather than focusing solely on bank loans is an important future extension to analysis within this framework. Turning to the household sector, we again see that observed loan growth was weaker (in a statistically significant sense) than the model would have predicted, both for house purchase and for consumption. That said, at least for housing loans, the observed dynamic pattern is similar to that anticipated by the model, with both actual and simulated series showing a recovery from mid-2009 onwards.

Where the biggest deviation between actual and simulated paths emerges is in the evolution of M3 growth. Part of the explanation of this discrepancy comes from the model's failure to explain the observed evolution of the slope of the yield curve during the financial crisis. The slope of the yield curve is an important determinant of M3 behaviour in the Giannone et al. (2010) model. The significant steepening of the yield curve during the financial crisis (as short-term rates were cut aggressively from October 2008 on) is not well captured by the model simulation (which would have foreseen long- and short-term rates falling by more similar amounts). Therefore, the model anticipates less substitution out of monetary assets prompted by higher returns available on longer maturity non-monetary assets. Yet this feature alone cannot fully explain the unanticipated weakness of M3 growth observed during the financial crisis. Developing a better understanding of the behaviour of M3 both in the lead up to and during the financial crisis is an important issue for future study.

This final observation poses a number of interesting and potentially important questions. In seeking behaviour that differs from pre-crisis historical regularities, our analysis focuses attention on the *liability* side of bank balance sheets rather than the asset side. In consequence, one might ask – in contrast with much of the existing literature – whether the propagation of the 2007–10 financial crisis should be seen as via a 'bank funding crunch' rather than as a 'bank credit crunch'. Equally, one might ask whether offering to provide greater central bank intermediation through the introduction of non-standard monetary policy measures has led to a switch from traditional deposit sources of funding to reliance (and potentially dependence) on central bank facilities. More generally, the analysis suggests that, conditional on developments in the real economy, the interaction between the financial and non-financial sectors was in line with historical regularities. In seeking explanations for the financial crisis, one may therefore focus on frictions *within* the financial sector in the manner suggested by Gertler and Karadi (2009) rather than *between* the financial and non-financial sectors.[16]

All these issues entail connections to the narrative discussion of the design and implementation of non-standard monetary policy measures in Section 3. Ideally, we would endeavour to test some of the implications of this narrative discussion in a more structured way. But such an approach requires identification of the structural shocks driving the behaviour of the data, which – as already mentioned – poses significant practical challenges. This is therefore left for further work. Such work would need to start with the development of a model of bank behaviour in the money market, which could provide a theoretical basis for making identifying assumptions. Against this background, the results described above should be characterised as a set of 'stylised facts' for the crisis sample. If it is to be considered an empirically plausible framework to address the underlying substantial questions, any theoretical model should be able to replicate these data regularities.

4.2   Exercise 2: Effect of spreads on monetary and credit variables

To complement the exercise discussed above and relate the results back to the money multiplier discussion in Section 2, we also briefly recall and comment upon the analysis presented in Lenza et al. (2010). Since the details of that exercise are discussed at length in the paper itself, here we simply sketch the main elements of the approach.

The analysis derives from the impact of non-standard measures on money market interest rate spreads, which was described briefly at the end of Section 3. (One aspect of) the effect of non-standard measures is quantified by tracing the implications of changes in these spreads on monetary and financial variables through the Giannone et al. (2010) model.

---

[16] Note that this statement should not be read as suggesting that frictions between the financial and non-financial sectors are negligible or unimportant. On the contrary, the information content of money and credit flows rests on the existence of such frictions. The relevant point here is that such frictions between the financial and non-financial sectors exert influence at all times: in seeking explanations of the crisis, one needs to identify frictions that became more important at the onset of the crisis. In this respect, our analysis suggests that intra-financial sector frictions – and thus heterogeneity within the financial sector – may have a more important role to play.

In other words, the analysis assumes that the financial sector continues to behave more or less in line with pre-crisis regularities captured by the model[17] and evaluates how the impact of non-standard measures on money market spreads influences other macroeconomic variables. Moreover, by construction the exercise explores only one channel of transmission, namely via interest rate spreads. Effects operating through confidence or other channels are neglected and may (substantially) augment the impact of the non-standard measures on the real economy and financial system.

More precisely, two conditional forecasts are constructed on the basis of the model: one based on the observed path of money market spreads (which is labelled the 'policy scenario' (P) since it incorporates the effects of the non-standard measures) $(E_{A(L)}(X_t \ldots _T | X_0 \ldots _{t-1}; P))$ and the other based on the levels of spread observed immediately after the failure of Lehman (which is labelled the 'no policy scenario' (NP) since it is intended to capture the effect of the financial shock coming from Lehman if this had *not* been offset by a policy response) $(E_{A(L)}(X_t \ldots _T | X_0 \ldots _{t-1}; NP))$. The impact of the non-standard measures is then quantified as the difference between these two conditional forecasts, i.e.

$$Impact_{ns} = E_{A(L)}(X_{t\ldots T} | X_{0\ldots t-1}; P) - E_{A(L)}(X_{t\ldots T} | X_{0\ldots t-1}; NP).$$

As described in Lenza et al. (2010), the spread assumptions differ between the two scenarios along three dimensions: (a) the spread between EURIBOR and OIS rates at three-month maturity (see Figure 8.3); (b) the spread between the EONIA and the ECB's MRO rate (see Figure 8.5); and (c) the spread between the one-year and one-month EURIBOR (capturing the slope of the money market yield curve, which was influenced by the conduct of the twelve-month LTROs in the second half of 2009).

Figure 8.8 reproduces the results of this exercise that are relevant for the discussion here. These are based on different paths from the spread starting from October 2008 (i.e. at the Lehman failure) and show the impact of spread effects through to end-2012. Focusing exclusively on these money market spread-related effects allows a number of complementary observations to be made. First, overall the results from this

---

[17] Note we assume that the crisis *did* affect the behaviour of the financial sector, but we also assume that the non-standard measures introduced by the Eurosystem served to offset this impact (at least with regard to the expansion of loans by banks), conditional on developments in real activity. The assumption that the economy behaves in line with pre-crisis regularities is thus consistent with – indeed, draws upon – the previous exercise described in Section 4.1.

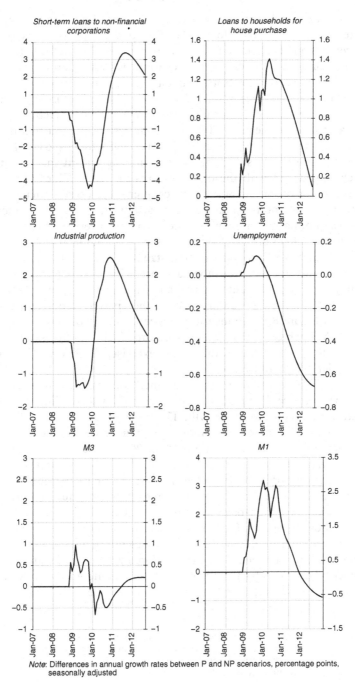

Note: Differences in annual growth rates between P and NP scenarios, percentage points, seasonally adjusted

Figure 8.8 Impact of spread effects of non-standard measures in Lenza et al. (2010)

exercise are consistent with the view that non-standard measures supported the growth of bank loans, even though the impact differed between
households and corporations, and was non-monotonic in the latter case.[18]
At the same time, these results caution against interpreting month-
to-month evolution of sectoral loan data as an indicator of the success of
non-standard measures in real time – given differences in impact across
sectors and over time, a more medium-term perspective is required for the
assessment to be meaningful. Second, the results suggest that the non-
standard measures lent (modest) support to real activity and employment,
even if this was not sufficient to offset the significant macroeconomic
shocks associated with the onset of financial crisis. Third – and most
relevantly for the discussion in this chapter – the exercise demonstrates
that, even while non-standard measures supported loan growth and the
expansion of narrow money M1, they had only a very modest (and non-
monotonic) effect on the evolution of the broad monetary aggregate M3.

Recall that the Eurosystem's non-standard measures were associated
with a strong increase in the monetary base. More precisely, high-powered
money expanded by slightly more than 20 per cent in the months after the
failure of Lehman. By contrast, from the analysis summarised by the
charts in Figure 8.8, the measures appear to have little impact on broad
money M3, which – even at its maximum – increases by only 1 per cent
relative to the baseline in the model exercise. As a result, the money
multiplier falls significantly.

Using Figure 8.8, one can argue that non-standard measures were
supportive of credit and economic activity, notwithstanding the absence
of stronger broad money growth. The richer understanding of the joint
dynamic interactions among monetary and financial variables and the real
economy offered by the Giannone et al. (2010) model demonstrates that
non-standard measures can be successful (at least through the specific
money market spread-related effects analysed in this exercise) even if they
do not lead to an expansion of broad money that is equi-proportional to
the expansion of high-powered money associated with the implementation of those measures. In short, a deeper empirical and behavioural view
of financial intermediation than that reflected in the traditional textbook
money multiplier model helps to develop a better understanding of the
impact of non-standard measures. The Giannone et al. framework for
monetary analysis represents an important advance in that direction.

---

[18] As shown in Figure 8.8, the spread-related impact of non-standard measures on short-
term loans to non-financial corporations and unemployment is negative (and thus
perverse) in the short run, reflecting the lagged responses to monetary policy shocks
reported in Giannone et al. (2010).

5   Concluding remarks

Understanding the macroeconomic impact of non-standard monetary policy measures during the recent financial crisis is a challenging task. Against the background of experiences during the Great Depression analysed in detail by Friedman and Schwartz (1963), we have argued that an important element in quantifying this impact is to explore the interaction of non-standard measures with financial intermediation, especially through the banking sector. This requires development of a framework to relate bank balance sheets (or, equivalently, monetary and credit aggregates) to monetary policy actions (and thus developments on the central bank balance sheet).

Existing textbook models of this relationship in the money multiplier tradition are clearly inadequate. This assertion has been amply illustrated in the narrative presented in this chapter. Yet theoretical modelling has not advanced sufficiently to offer an adequate replacement. In line with the ECB's regular monetary analysis, we have therefore adopted an empirical approach: identifying regularities in the pre-crisis data and using these as a benchmark against which to make a realtime empirical assessment of the evolution of money, credit, bank behaviour and their impact on the macroeconomy during the financial crisis. Such considerations are of special relevance in the euro area, given the bank-centred structure of the financial system.

The results of our analysis are preliminary and multifaceted. It would therefore be misleading to draw definitive or sharp conclusions, especially at this early stage when non-standard measures are still in place and financial tensions persist. Nonetheless, a number of observations about the impact of the Eurosystem's non-standard measures can still be made.

First, we have found evidence that non-standard measures did support financial intermediation, credit expansion and economic activity in the euro area in the face of financial crisis. They were successful in that sense.

Second, we have shown that such support is possible even in an environment where the expansion of the monetary base associated with the implementation of non-standard measures does not lead to an equi-proportional (or indeed any) expansion in broad money. This both illustrates the weakness of the money multiplier model – which would see such an expansion of broad money as key – and points to a need for further work to understand better the behaviour of the banking system and its interaction with the real economy. In particular, we view the impact of heterogeneity within the financial sector as a crucial element in explaining recent developments.

In sum, we interpret our results as offering evidence in support of the view that the introduction of non-standard measures has supported the availability of monetary liquidity to the non-bank private sector and flow of bank loans to households and, especially, corporations – resulting in an outcome that largely mimics what would have been anticipated in the face of the observed sharp fall in economic activity were the financial sector to be functioning normally. Since many concerns surrounding the impact of financial crisis stem from worries about a 'credit crunch' and drying up of bank loan supply, this evidence offers a favourable view of the non-standard measures.

Yet the measures appear less successful in supporting the dynamics of broad money, which is usually seen as having a relationship with macroeconomic stability over longer horizons. Should the impact of the financial crisis be prolonged and broad money exhibit a persistent abnormal weakness, this would be a cause for concern. However, since such persistent weakness is more likely to be symptomatic of structural weaknesses in the financial sector (e.g. underlying solvency problems, governance issues and inefficiencies), the scope for the non-standard monetary policy measures discussed here to manage such concerns may be limited. Thoroughgoing financial reform – involving bank recapitalisations, restructuring of the financial sector and improved regulation and supervision – is the more relevant mechanism to address such underlying weaknesses.

Experience in recent years demonstrates the potentially powerful stabilising effects of non-standard monetary policy measures. But the limits of such measures also need to be recognised and respected.

References

Banbura, M., Giannone, D. and Reichlin, L. (2010) Large Bayesian VARs, *Journal of Applied Econometrics*, 25(1), 71–92.

Bernanke, B. S. (1983) Non-monetary effects of the financial crisis in the propagation of the Great Depression, *American Economic Review*, 73(3), 257–76.

Borio, C. and Disyata, P. (2009) Unconventional monetary polices: an appraisal, BIS Working Paper No. 292.

Christiano, L. J., Motto, R. and Rostagno, M. (2003) The Great Depression and the Friedman–Schwartz hypothesis, *Journal of Money, Credit and Banking*, 35 (6), 1119–98.

Cùrdia, V. and Woodford, M. (2011) The central bank balance sheet as an instrument of monetary policy, *Journal of Monetary Economics*, 58(1), 54–79.

De Mol, C., Giannone, D., and Reichlin, L. (2008) Forecasting using a large number of predictors: is Bayesian regression a valid alternative to principal components? *Journal of Econometrics*, 146(2), 318–28.

Fischer, B., Lenza, M., Pill, H. and Reichlin, L. (2009) Monetary analysis and monetary policy in the euro area, *Journal of International Money and Finance*, 28(7), 1138–64.

Friedman, M. and Schwartz, A. J. (1963) *A Monetary History of the United States*, Princeton University Press.

Gagnon, J., Raskin, M., Remache, J. and Sack, B. (2010) Large-scale asset purchases by the Federal Reserve: did they work? FRB New York Staff Report No. 441.

Gertler, M. and Karadi, P. (2009) A model of unconventional monetary policy, New York University (available at www.econ.nyu.edu/user/gertlerm/gertler-karadiapril2010conference.pdf).

Giannone, D., Lenza, M. and Reichlin, L. (2010) Money, credit, monetary policy and the business cycle in the euro area, ECB (available at www.ecb.int/events/conferences/html/moneymechanism.en.html).

Goodhart, C. A. E. (2010) Money, credit and bank behaviour: need for a new approach, *National Institute Economic Review*, 214, 73–82.

Gorton, G. B. and Metrick, A. (2009) Securitized banking and the run on repo, Yale ICF Working Paper No. 09–14.

Heider, F., Hoerova, M. and Holthausen, C. (2009) Liquidity hoarding and interbank market spreads: the role of counterparty risk, ECB Working Paper No. 1126.

Joyce, M., Lasaosa, A., Stevens, I. and Tong, M. (2010) The financial market impact of quantitative easing, Bank of England Working Paper No. 393.

Lenza, M., Pill, H. and Reichlin, L. (2010) Monetary policy in exceptional times, *Economic Policy*, 62, 295–339.

Meltzer, A. H. (2007) *A History of the Federal Reserve*, Vol. 1, University of Chicago Press.

Papademos, L. and Stark, J. (eds.) (2010) *Enhancing Monetary Analysis*, Frankfurt: European Central Bank.

Rasche, R. H. (1987) M1 velocity and money demand functions: do stable relationships exist? Carnegie–Rochester Conference Series on Public Policy, 17, 9–88.

Trichet, J.-C. (2009) The ECB's enhanced credit support, Address at the University of Munich annual symposium (available at www.ecb.europa.eu/press/key/date/2009/html/sp090713.en.html).

9   QE – one year on

Spencer Dale

1   Introduction

This has been a truly extraordinary year for our economy and for economic policy.

A year ago – almost to this very day – the Monetary Policy Committee conducted its first gilt auction as part of its asset purchase programme, or its policy of quantitative easing as it became known. The need for policy action was clear. The three months to March 2009 are estimated to have seen the sharpest quarterly contraction in GDP since comparable records began in the 1950s. Manufacturing output was contracting at an annualised rate of close to 20 per cent. Claimant count unemployment was rising at the fastest rate on record.

And financial markets remained in a state of shock. By early March 2009, 40 per cent had been wiped off the value of the FTSE companies; corporate bond spreads were at their widest since the 1970s; and banks continued to hoard liquidity, with spreads in the interbank market still around fifteen times higher than their pre-crisis levels.

The financial crisis began in earnest in the summer of 2007, when the burgeoning sub-prime mortgage crisis began to pile pressure on banks. But it intensified dramatically following the failure of Lehman Brothers in September 2008, leading to the most severe banking crisis in living memory. The MPC responded aggressively, cutting Bank Rate from 5 per cent to 0.5 per cent – its lowest ever level – in just five months.

But the need for further monetary stimulus was clear. In principle, it would have been possible to cut Bank Rate a little further, to zero or even to a small negative number. But the structure of many traditional mortgage lenders' balance sheets meant that lowering Bank Rate even further was likely to eat into their profitability and so intensify the credit crunch – exactly

I would like to thank Rohan Churm, Chris Kubelec, James Smith and Jing Yang for their considerable help in preparing these remarks. The views expressed are my own and do not necessarily reflect those of other members of the Monetary Policy Committee.

what the monetary loosening was trying to avoid. Instead, the Bank of England decided to vary the size and composition of its balance sheet to inject money directly into the economy. And so QE was born.

Since then the economy has stabilised, household and business confidence have recovered, and financial market conditions have improved. Taken at face value, the extraordinary policy measures implemented by the Bank, alongside those enacted by the government, appear to have been successful in averting a deeper and more severe recession. And the hope now is that a sustained recovery in demand will follow consistent with the objectives of those policies.

But the contribution of our asset purchases in bringing about this stabilisation is still an open question. One year on, what have we learned about QE? In this chapter I will address three key questions. What is the theoretical foundation for such a policy? What are the key channels of transmission? And what can we say about its impact to date?

These questions are critical for the operation of monetary policy. But they are equally important for the study of monetary policy. The financial crisis posed questions which the models most commonly used to analyse monetary policy were not well suited to answer. There is an emerging literature that responds to these shortcomings. It is important – for both the theory and practice of monetary policy – that this continues.

2   The theoretical foundation for unconventional monetary policy

Let us turn first to the theoretical foundation for quantitative easing.

Over the past fifteen years, the canonical New Keynesian New Classical synthesis model has become the benchmark for economists to study the operation of monetary policy. The attraction of this class of models, as typified, for example, by Walsh (2003) and Woodford (2003), is that its relative simplicity and tractability mean that it can be used to derive clear and precise policy prescriptions. And indeed that is the case when used to analyse monetary policy at the zero bound. The only way policy can gain traction at the lower bound in such a model is through influencing expectations – the most well-known reference here being Eggertsson and Woodford (2003).

This result stems from the fact that the economy behaves as if, in effect, there are only two assets in existence, typically modelled as money and bonds. Agents hold more money up to the point at which the marginal benefit from the liquidity services it confers equals the marginal cost: the nominal interest rate. At the zero bound, both the marginal benefit and marginal cost are effectively zero, and money and bonds become perfect substitutes. It follows that exchanging money for bonds at this point has no impact on activity or inflation. The economy is assumed – by construction – to be in a liquidity trap.

As is well known, the optimal policy within this class of models is for the central bank to commit to low interest rates for an extended period and to a temporary overshoot of the inflation target. Exchange rate depreciations (Svensson, 2001) and interest rate commitments (Krugman, 1998 and Woodford, 2003) are examples of policy recommendations stemming from this result.

The crucial insight emphasised by these models is that expectations matter, and provide a mechanism through which policy makers can seek to influence activity at the zero bound. This is an important channel of monetary transmission and one we will return to.

But the argument that monetary policy can work *only* through expectations management is not a robust result. It rests on very particular assumptions. In this class of models, financial markets are assumed to be complete and frictionless and the representative agent is able to arbitrage across all financial markets. As such, all non-aggregate risk in the economy can be hedged perfectly and asset prices depend only on state-contingent payoffs. Under these assumptions, demand curves for financial assets are perfectly elastic.

But in the real world it seems plausible that demand curves for assets, in addition to money, are downward sloping to some degree, in which case changes in their relative supplies can affect their relative prices. It is this which gives quantitative easing its traction.

Half a century ago Tobin (1958), in pioneering work on portfolio allocation, recognised that a range of assets, in addition to money, are likely to be imperfect substitutes. But Tobin did not articulate fully the frictions that could generate such imperfect substitutability.

More recently, there has been rapid development in micro models of the source of financial frictions which can motivate imperfect substitutability. Recent examples include Brunnermeier and Pedersen (2009) and Vayanos and Weill (2008).[1] These models help to explain when and why investors may face undiversifiable risks when holding specific types of securities, such that they become imperfect substitutes for otherwise similar assets. In Brunnermeier and Pedersen (2009), for example, market makers face uncertainty over the timing of customers' trades. They are unable to hedge perfectly this liquidity risk because of borrowing constraints, so that less liquid securities are imperfect substitutes for more

---

[1] In addition see Duffie et al. (2007).

liquid ones. This liquidity risk leads asset prices to diverge from 'fundamentals' determined by underlying cash flows.

Researchers are also beginning to make a number of important contributions that introduce various forms of financial frictions into otherwise standard macro models. For example, in Kiyotaki and Moore (2008), firms face a 'liquidity constraint' in financing their investment which arises from a combination of borrowing constraints and a difficulty in selling their illiquid assets. This need for liquidity gives rise to an endogenous demand for money. An important feature of this model is that the central bank can offset the effects of liquidity shocks by purchasing illiquid assets with central bank money.[2] Building on Kiyotaki and Moore's (2008) resaleability constraint, Gertler and Kiyotaki (2009) introduce a funding friction for banks, whereby banks need to hold capital in order for depositors to be willing to deposit funds. Such a funding friction affords a role for the authorities to lend directly to firms when capital constraints bite on banks. Andrés et al. (2004) incorporate imperfect substitutability between short- and long-term bonds. Here the lack of a secondary market for long bonds is the source of the friction. In this model, base money expansion by a central bank can relieve portfolio constraints and lead to an increase in demand for long bonds, thereby raising their prices.

Much of this literature is still in its infancy and there is some way to go before it can be combined within an applied, quantitative model that policy makers can use. But the central message we can take from this work is that there are a number of channels through which monetary policy is likely to be able to influence the economy at the zero bound. Unfortunately, the financial crisis meant that we had to put these insights into practice. When doing so at the Bank, we placed weight on three key channels of monetary transmission: the impact of imperfect substitutability and the portfolio rebalancing channel on relative prices, the role of financial market liquidity, and the importance of expectations.

All three channels were important in the design of the MPC's asset purchase programme. Let us take them in turn.

3   Channels of transmission

To date, the Bank has purchased £200 billion of assets financed by the issuance of central bank reserves, the vast majority of which have been relatively long maturity gilts. The central objective underlying those gilts

[2] Del Negro et al. (2009) extend this framework to analyse monetary policy at zero bound.

purchases was to inject a substantial amount of additional money into the economy. The main behavioural assumption underlying this monetary injection was that it would gain traction via a portfolio rebalancing channel.

Most UK government bonds are held by non-bank financial sector companies (OFCs), such as pension funds and insurance companies.[3] As long as these investors do not regard money as a perfect substitute for gilts, they will attempt to reduce the additional money holdings associated with gilt purchases by switching into other assets. This process of portfolio rebalancing will continue until the yields on gilts and on alternative assets, such as corporate bonds and equities, have fallen sufficiently to compensate investors for holding the higher level of money balances. The degree of stimulus associated with the monetary injection will be greater the lower the substitutability between money and gilts, and the higher the substitutability between gilts and other assets.

Trying to estimate the likely size of these effects is very difficult, not least because a policy of this form and scale has never been implemented in the UK. There is a natural limit to what can be learned from past time-series relationships. A standard portfolio model of OFC's money demand, in which money holdings are jointly modelled with movements in asset prices and relative rates of return, would suggest that asset purchases on the scale seen might increase asset prices by the order of 20–30 per cent (see, for example, Thomas, 1997). At first blush, this impact may seem surprisingly large. But it is important to remember that the scale of the asset purchases made over the past year is truly substantial, amounting to 14 per cent of nominal GDP. But there are obviously huge uncertainty bands surrounding this type of estimate and it would not be surprising if it was revised, perhaps significantly, as we learn more about the impact of our current policy.

These higher asset prices should help to stimulate increases in consumption and investment via wealth and cost-of-capital channels. But the transmission of the monetary stimulus through to higher nominal spending may occur only gradually. This suggests that a significant impact from our asset purchases is still to come through.

An important issue when thinking about the likely channels of monetary transmission is the state of the banking system. In normal times, a key channel through which asset purchases might be expected to operate is by increasing banks' stocks of liquid assets, which may encourage them to

---

[3] At the end of 2008, prior to the commencement of the asset purchase programme, almost 60 per cent of outstanding gilts were held by OFCs (of which 40 per cent were held by insurance companies and pension funds) and 35 per cent were held by overseas investors. UK banks and building societies held only 4 per cent of gilts.

extend new loans. But we are not in normal times. Banks are pulling back on their lending as they seek to strengthen their balance sheets and reduce their leverage. For this reason, when making an assessment of the likely impact of asset purchases, the MPC did not factor in a material expansion of bank lending.

Indeed, our asset purchases were designed to facilitate a disintermediation of corporate financing away from banks and towards capital markets. This disintermediation was supported in part by the portfolio rebalancing triggered by our gilt purchases. As investors' demand for alternative assets such as corporate bonds and equities increased, the ability of businesses to raise finance in capital markets improved and the cost fell.

This disintermediation was reinforced by the Bank's operations to improve the functioning of corporate credit markets. The financial market dislocation in the immediate aftermath of the crisis hindered the functioning of the commercial paper and corporate bond markets and led to substantial increases in liquidity premia. In response, the Bank established facilities to make small regular purchases of corporate bonds and commercial paper, with the aim of aiding secondary market liquidity. The significance of these purchases of private-sector debt should not be judged by their scale, which was tiny in comparison to gilt purchases. The purpose of these operations was not to purchase a specific quantity of assets but rather to improve the functioning of those markets. In that respect, the knowledge that the Bank stands ready to purchase assets may be as beneficial as actual purchases.[4]

The importance of expectations also played a central role in the design of our asset purchase programme. It was vital that the MPC was able to introduce a new policy instrument at the point at which Bank Rate reached its effective lower bound. This instrument had to be credible, both in terms of its economic impact and the willingness of the MPC to use the instrument in force. My own view is that the speed with which the asset purchase programme was introduced and the scale of the programme played an important role in reaffirming the MPC's commitment to achieving the inflation target and reinforcing the belief in our ability to do so.

4   Estimating the effects so far

So what impact have our asset purchases had to date?

That's the £200 billion question. Unfortunately, it is hard to provide a definitive answer. To be clear, this is no different from our inability to

---

[4] See Fisher (2010) for a more detailed discussion of these operations.

assess precisely the impact of the reduction in Bank Rate from 5 per cent
to 0.5 per cent. Or indeed of any macroeconomic policy measure.
Without knowing what would have happened in the absence of a policy
action, it is not possible to identify its incremental impact. But what is
different is that this policy instrument is relatively untried and untested, so
the demand to provide some insight into its impact is that much greater.
This demand is quite understandable, but difficult to satisfy.

One possible approach to assessing the impact of our asset purchases
is to consider the growth of broad money. A key principle underlying the
asset purchase programme is the belief in a causal mechanism running
from increased money balances into higher asset prices and nominal
spending. This mechanism can be expressed in terms of a process of
portfolio rebalancing in which yields of different assets adjust in order
for the higher level of money balances to be willingly held. But the same
mechanism could be expressed in terms of a monetarist approach, in
which asset purchases work through measures of money disequilibrium
which in turn spur additional spending. These different frameworks
are sometimes presented as conflicting models of the transmission of
asset purchases. But I view them as essentially two sides of the same coin.
Importantly, they share the same fundamental assumption about why
monetary policy at the zero bound can stimulate nominal spending –
namely, imperfect substitutability between money and other assets.

Over the past year, despite money-financed asset purchases totalling
£200 billion, broad money has increased by just £8 billion.[5] What should
we make of this weakness? In part it speaks to the counterfactual. The falls
in nominal spending and the desire by banks to reduce leverage means
that, absent the monetary injection, broad money almost certainly would
have been far weaker. But it is also symptomatic of the scale of the new
equity and debt raised by UK banks over this period which, together with
retained profits, totals more than £85 billion. Given that the non-bank
private sector is likely to have been the source for much of this funding,
this is likely to have squeezed broad money growth. But the counterpart to
this fall in private-sector deposits is a strengthening in banks' balance
sheets, which in turn should aid the recovery by improving the availability
of bank lending. So the monetary impulse still operates.

One approach to help mitigate the counterfactual problem is to use
event studies which consider the impact of QE announcements on asset

---

[5] This excludes the money holdings of intermediate OFCs. See the box on page 13 of the
May 2009 *Inflation Report* for discussion of the reasons for excluding intermediate OFCs in
measures of broad money.

prices over relatively short windows.[6] Gilt yields may respond to such policy announcements both because of the impact gilt purchases have on the yields at which investors are willing to hold the reduced supply of gilts – the portfolio balance effect – and because of the information the announcement may be perceived to contain about the future stance of monetary policy – one element of the expectations channel.

It is possible to get some indication of the size of the portfolio effect by considering movements in the spread of gilt yields to OIS rates, which should not be affected by changes in the relative supply of gilts. Although precise estimates vary according to the maturity of the gilts and the size of the window, summing movements in gilt–OIS spreads following our announcements suggests that the portfolio balance effect may have reduced gilt yields by around 100 basis points. Again, a pretty sizeable effect.

Similarly, movements in OIS rates following policy announcements may provide a guide to the extent to which the announcements affected expectations about the future stance of monetary policy. OIS rates fell sharply following the initial announcements of QE, particularly at short horizons, suggesting these announcements caused market participants to revise down the expected future path of Bank Rate. However, perhaps not surprisingly, as QE has become better understood, OIS rates have responded less to more recent announcements. This is consistent with market participants increasingly viewing QE as part of the systematic component of monetary policy. To the extent that gilt yields and other asset prices have moved in response to this systematic component, these movements would not be captured by event studies and hence looking only at announcement effects may tend to understate the impact of QE.

Gilts make up a relatively small proportion of total assets held by the private sector. As such, when assessing the overall impact of our asset purchases it is important to consider the increase in other asset prices. Since we started QE, equity prices have increased by more than 50 per cent and corporate bond yields have fallen by more than 400 basis points. These movements have been very beneficial for the economy and, when starting our asset purchases a year ago, I would have been more than willing to have settled for such an outcome.

However, it is difficult to identify the incremental role of QE in driving these improvements. These other asset prices may respond less quickly to asset purchase announcements and so are less easily isolated using event studies. Moreover, these movements coincided with a global rally in financial markets, which further complicates the task of isolating UK-specific

---

[6] This is in a similar spirit to Bernanke et al. (2004).

effects. However, it is important to see this global rally in the context of the similar policy strategies adopted by a number of the world's most important central banks – official interest rates were cut to very low levels and central banks' balance sheets in many parts of the world were greatly expanded. The fact that UK capital markets moved in line with global markets during this period does not suggest that domestic policy had little impact.

Indeed, I have little doubt that our asset purchases contributed substantially to these movements, via the channels discussed here – through a portfolio rebalancing effect, as both retail and institutional investors switched out of gilts into alternative assets, such as corporate bonds and equities, through improvements to market liquidity, aided by our purchases of commercial paper and corporate bonds; and through their impact on expectations, as asset purchases demonstrated our commitment to act, boosted confidence in the economic environment and so reduced the likelihood of further large falls in asset prices.

The ultimate success of QE will depend on whether the monetary injection and increased asset prices stimulate nominal spending and so help achieve the 2 per cent inflation target in the medium term. Much of the impact of our asset purchases to date is still to come through and so it is too early to judge their final impact. However, in that respect, it is perhaps noteworthy that nominal GDP in the UK grew at an annualised rate of around 4 per cent during the third and fourth quarters of 2009. These estimates are still relatively early and so subject to considerable uncertainty. But there are perhaps some tentative signs that nominal spending in our economy is starting to accelerate.

5   Conclusion

It is exactly a year since the MPC started its programme of large-scale asset purchases. The move to quantitative easing met with mixed reactions. Some commentators claimed that it would end in inflationary tears. Many academics questioned whether it would have any impact at all.

From the outside, you may imagine that this was a difficult decision for a committee of nine, conservative central bankers to reach. In fact, from my perspective the decision was relatively straightforward. The inflation target provides a clear, numerical objective for policy. The outlook for inflation suggested further monetary stimulus was necessary to achieve that target. With Bank Rate close to its lower bound, this stimulus had to be implemented via alternative means. And there are clear and convincing economic arguments why – in the real world – injecting money directly into the economy is likely to provide a means of achieving that stimulus.

One year on, there is a range of evidence – some relatively hard, some more circumstantial – that quantitative easing is having its desired effect. Asset prices have increased substantially, companies have made record recourse to debt and equity markets, confidence has recovered and inflation expectations remain firmly anchored. But there is still a long way to go. The bulk of our asset purchases have been made only over the last nine months or so prior to March 2010. Much of their effect on nominal spending and inflation is still to come through. We are likely to learn a lot about the transmission of those purchases and about their ultimate impact over the course of the next year.

At its meetings in February and March 2010, the MPC decided to maintain Bank Rate at 0.5 per cent and to maintain the stock of asset purchases at £200 billion. It is worth emphasising two important considerations underlying these most recent decisions.

First, the portfolio balance channel implies that the primary stimulus from QE stems from the stock of past purchases, not the flow of additional ones. As such, maintaining the stock of asset purchases, together with the low level of Bank Rate, should continue to impart a substantial stimulus to the economy for some time to come.

Second, the MPC stands ready to make further asset purchases should the outlook warrant them. Just as with movements in Bank Rate in more normal times, a pause in monetary loosening does not necessarily mean that loosening has come to an end. It will all depend on how the outlook for inflation evolves.

Looking further ahead, the MPC at some point will need to reduce the current exceptional degree of monetary stimulus. Some commentators have suggested that the MPC has been less forthcoming than other central banks in explaining its exit strategy. But to a large extent this reflects the fact that we have less to communicate. The MPC has two instruments through which it can withdraw the stimulus: raising Bank Rate and selling assets. Unlike some other central banks which need to create new instruments to drain excess reserves or alter the terms of existing facilities, the structure of the Bank's operating framework means these two instruments can be used at any time, in any order. And the strategy guiding its policy decisions will be unchanged – monetary policy will continue to be determined by the outlook for inflation relative to target. The most difficult decision will be the timing of the withdrawal, but that is always the case.

The aftermath of the financial crisis posed many questions for the theory and practice of monetary policy. One year on from reaching the effective lower bound of interest rates and starting a policy of quantitative easing, there is still much for academics and policy makers to learn.

References

Andrés, J., López-Salido, D. J. and Nelson, E. (2004) Tobin's imperfect substitution in optimising general equilibrium, *Journal of Money, Credit and Banking*, 36(5), 665–90.

Bernanke, B. S., Reinhart, V. R. and Sack, B. P. (2004) Monetary policy alternatives at the zero bound: an empirical assessment, Brookings Papers on Economic Activity, 2, 1–78.

Brunnermeier, M. K. and Pedersen, L. H. (2009) Market liquidity and funding liquidity, *Review of Financial Studies*, 22(6), 2201–38.

Del Negro, M., Eggertsson, G., Ferrero, A. and Kiyotaki, N. (2009) The great escape? A quantitative evaluation of the Fed's non-standard policies, Manuscript, Federal Reserve Bank of New York and Princeton University.

Duffie, D., Gârleanu, N. and Pedersen, L. H. (2007) Valuation in over-the-counter markets, *The Review of Financial Studies*, 20(6), 1865–1900.

Eggertsson, G. and Woodford, M. (2003) The zero bound on interest rates and optimal monetary policy, Brookings Papers on Economic Activity 1, 212–19.

Fisher, P. (2010) The corporate sector and the Bank of England's Asset Purchases, Speech to the Association of Corporate Treasurers, 18 February.

Gertler, M. and Kiyotaki, N. (2009) Financial intermediation and credit policy in business cycle analysis, Manuscript, New York University and Princeton University.

Kiyotaki, N. and Moore, J. (2008) Liquidity, business cycles and monetary policy, Manuscript, Princeton University.

Krugman, P. R. (1998) It's baaack: Japan's slump and the return of the liquidity trap, Brookings Papers on Economic Activity, The Brookings Institution, 29(2), 137–206.

Svensson, L. E. O. (2001) The zero bound in an open economy: a foolproof way of escaping from a liquidity trap, *Monetary and Economic Studies*, 19(S–1), 277–312.

Thomas, R. (1997) The demand for M4: a sectoral analysis, part 2 – the corporate sector, Bank of England Working Paper, No. 62.

Tobin, J. (1958) Liquidity preference as behaviour towards risk, *The Review of Economic Studies*, 25(2).

Vayanos, D. and Weill, P.-O. (2008) A search-based theory of the on-the-run phenomenon, *Journal of Finance*, 63, 1361–98.

Walsh, C. (2003) *Monetary Theory and Policy*, Cambridge, MA: The MIT Press.

Woodford, M. (2003) *Interest and Prices*, Princeton University Press.

10 What saved the banks: unconventional monetary or fiscal policy?

Michael Wickens

1 Introduction

Prompted by two keynote papers by Spencer Dale (Chapter 9, this volume) and Richard Harrison (Chapter 5, this volume), both from the Bank of England, this chapter raises the question of whether the most effective instrument in dealing with the financial crisis was unconventional monetary or fiscal policy. Quantitative monetary easing – unconventional monetary policy – is given most of the credit, but a strong case can be made in favour of the recapitalisation of the banks and guarantees to deposit holders which are unconventional fiscal policy as they involve the tax payer's money. The chapter argues that the crisis was a consequence of failing to price risk correctly and that the shortage of liquidity, which prompted quantitative easing, was due to difficulties in pricing default risk. This diagnosis has a major bearing on how to avoid a repetition of the crisis in the future. The chapter concludes with a brief discussion of how the academic literature on macroeconomic modelling has responded to the crisis – unconventional macroeconomic modelling – and how it should amend its models.

2 Unconventional monetary policy

When the Bank of England was made independent in 1997 its role was changed. Since then its prime task has been to control inflation using interest rates and, according to the Bank Act of 1997, only subject to achieving this, to take account of the government's other macroeconomic objectives. Responsibility for supervising banking and finance was transferred from the Bank to a new body, the Financial Services Authority. In effect, the Bank became the main player in macroeconomic policy instead of the Treasury, which focused instead on the microeconomics of budgetary matters. Prior to the financial crisis, the Bank had been extremely successful in achieving its inflation target, as had the US Fed and the ECB, which suggests either a benign environment or good monetary policy.

Either way, confidence in the future and low real interest rates stimulated heavy borrowing by the private sector and a readiness to provide cheap loans by the banking sector.

The financial crisis began with households defaulting on their mortgage payments. Financial innovations over recent years had enabled mutual societies, which are highly regulated, to demutualise and become banks, and had allowed banks to invest on their own account in both financial assets and mortgage lending. Further, due to the Basel II arrangements, the level of capital banks were required to hold in reserve was hugely reduced. When the level of mortgage defaults – initially in the United States – increased dramatically, followed by a sharp decline in the value of mortgage-backed securities, banks around the world were heavily compromised. Not only did they have large exposures on their balance sheets to the mortgage market and to MBSs, many had financed this with short-term borrowing in the interbank market that needed to be rolled over frequently. Consequently, when the crisis erupted, many banks became technically insolvent, having larger book liabilities than assets. These banks included HBOS, Northern Rock and RBS in the UK, Citibank in the US and UBS in Switzerland. Unable to roll over their debt in the interbank market, the banking crisis came to be seen as a liquidity crisis.

Although no longer formally responsible for banking supervision, the Bank of England is still lender of last resort. It therefore provided the banks with the liquidity they required and were unable to obtain from the interbank market, by purchasing gilts from them. £200 billion was assigned for this, which is 15 per cent of GDP. This became known as quantitative easing and was described, somewhat surprisingly as it is in effect just an open market operation, as unconventional monetary policy. Perhaps this name reflects the contrast with what had become conventional monetary policy, namely, interest rate policy.

In normal circumstances open market operations like this, where the consequence is that in effect the Bank is buying government debt instead of the private sector, would cause an increase in inside money through additional bank lending to the corporate and household sectors. Due to the liquidity crisis, banks had sharply curtailed their lending to the private sector. The expectation was that quantitative easing would restore lending. Instead, banks used the money to rebuild their balance sheets and bank lending hardly increased. All that happened was that bank reserves at the Bank of England increased by the amount of the QE causing an increase in outside money, but not in inside money. Apart from alleviating the threat of bank solvency by allowing the banks to liquidate financial assets, despite the popular view to the contrary, quantitative easing therefore did little or nothing to solve the financial crisis affecting the economy as a whole.

Harrison (Chapter 5) makes a different argument about the way QE works. In his view it causes portfolio effects. By buying long-dated securities, mainly from the private sector, the central bank can alter the maturity structure of portfolios and so stimulate economic activity. This argument relies on market segmentation and on long- and short-term debt being imperfect substitutes. He assumes that households have a target ratio of long- to short-term debt and that this allows the central bank to use quantities to affect prices.

Such views are in strong contrast to what is usually assumed about financial markets. The normal view is that the composition of portfolios and the term structure of interest rates are determined by the risk characteristics of assets. Once risk adjusted, investors are assumed to be indifferent between asset classes. The composition of portfolios is determined by attitudes to risk and, in the aggregate, by the supply of assets. Whatever is supplied is held and the price is determined by the risk characteristics of the asset. Hence, in this commonly used framework, quantities do not affect the composition of portfolios. For monetary policy through quantitative easing to work via portfolio effects it is therefore necessary to abandon the usual approach to asset pricing. The empirical evidence does not encourage this.

The Bank did not rely just on QE. Its first action was to cut interest rates to 0.5 per cent, i.e. virtually zero. Normally, by reducing the cost of borrowing, this would increase the demand for loans and hence stimulate economic activity. The problem was that the spread between bank rate and the interbank rate (LIBOR) at which banks could in principle borrow was huge, so cutting interest rates had no effect on the cost of borrowing. Another consequence of QE was that this spread disappeared. Even then the banks were unwilling to lend.

A literature has emerged on monetary policy when interest rates reach zero called the zero lower bound (ZLB). The idea is that interest rates may need to become negative (i.e. banks may be forced to pay interest on their reserves at the Bank, and depositors in banks may need to pay the banks to accept these deposits) in order to generate sufficient monetary stimulus to the economy, but a ZLB prevents this from occurring. While large spreads existed between LIBOR and bank rate, even negative interest rates would be ineffective. This suggests that negative interest rates would need to be accompanied by QE and vice versa.

Since 2006 CPI inflation has usually exceeded its target of 2 per cent above its permitted upper bound of 3 per cent, yet the Bank has not changed its interest rate. Could this be because the Bank, seeking to stimulate the economy and constrained by the ZLB, aims to reduce real interest rates through higher inflation? The danger in such a strategy is that it would threaten to undermine perhaps the most important achievement of the Bank since independence, namely, the anchoring of inflation expectations at 2 per cent.

To summarise, QE provided the banks with the liquidity they needed to roll over their borrowing and rebuild their balance sheets and it virtually eliminated spreads between the rate at which banks lent to each other and the rate at which they can discount bonds at the Bank. It therefore helped to sustain the banking system, but it did not rescue the non-bank sector because the banks were still unwilling to lend to the private sector.

3   Unconventional fiscal policy

The underlying cause of the financial crisis was poor risk assessment. Low real interest rates due to low inflation and low nominal real interest rates and steady economic growth stimulated both mortgage borrowing and housing equity withdrawal in many countries, but notably the US, the UK and, in the eurozone, Ireland and Spain. In addition, the US government positively encouraged the financial sector to expand mortgage lending. The result was a massive increase in lending and a housing boom. The risks in doing this were either ignored or miscalculated. There seems to have been limited scrutiny of the ability of mortgage borrowers to service their debt. Instead, banks were searching for people to whom to lend money with minimal scrutiny. Thus both the banks and households were overlooking the inherent risks in such a large credit expansion.

In order to obtain the finance for these loans, banks securitised their mortgage book rather than relying on taking in additional deposits which would have entailed higher deposit and lending rates. The financial sector – banks and non-banks – bought these securitised assets and financially engineered them, combining high- and low-risk mortgage tranches to produce further derivative assets. In another risk failure, these were given triple-A status in the belief that diversification must reduce risk. The problem here is that diversification reduces risk only if asset returns have a low correlation. In practice, the returns on these assets were highly correlated and so their collapse brought about systemic failure. Encouraged by their low risk rating, these new assets were purchased worldwide. This ensured the contagion that followed the collapse of these financial assets. All of this is the result of a failure to correctly assess the risks involved.

Once the crisis hit, bank balance sheets began to unravel. Some of the world's largest banks, such as RBS and Citibank, were found to be heavily exposed. As no one knew which banks were holding what had become toxic assets, the markets, including other banks, were unwilling to roll over the short-term liabilities used to finance the mortgages and the purchases of the securitised assets. This emerged as a liquidity crisis for banks, but was in reality a risk assessment crisis. Once the risks were known, then liquidity would be restored, but at a price.

Faced with technical insolvency due to having balance sheets with greater liabilities than assets, banks threatened closure. The consequences of the bankruptcy of some of the world's largest banks would have been catastrophic. Not only would all those who held bank liabilities have been affected, including household depositors, but world trade would have become severely compromised.

The solution was for the tax payer to take on the risks of the banks and guarantee their liabilities in return for bank equity and the hope of eventual repayment. This is what many governments undertook on behalf of tax payers. They guaranteed deposits and other bank liabilities, in effect recapitalising the banks. In return they took an equity stake in the banks. In other words, they carried out unconventional fiscal policy.

In the US the Fed injected liquidity into the economy directly by purchasing corporate bonds with good credit ratings. This, too, was on behalf of the tax payer and must be regarded as unconventional fiscal policy.

Having removed the risk of default, banks were then able to borrow once more from financial markets. With the fall in risk, the spread between LIBOR and bank rate virtually disappeared. When eventually banks began to lend to the private sector, the threat of firm defaults declined and corporate spreads also fell.

It is clear that it was the use of unconventional fiscal policy to reduce risk that was the key to resolving the financial crisis. The use of unconventional monetary policy helped by providing short-term liquidity to the banks, which solved their immediate problem of rolling over liabilities. But on its own this was not sufficient, as it did not solve the market's problem of being unwilling to lend while the risks of doing so were unknown but thought to be extremely high.

An interesting question is whether without these interventions the market would have solved the problem on its own. Almost certainly, many banks would have become bankrupt, as would many private-sector firms. The large spreads suggest that the cost of borrowing by banks would have been very high and probably hastened bankruptcy. Even for bankrupt banks, however, there would have been value in some of their assets. Bankruptcy would have resulted in the worthless assets being written off as, in the main, they have been anyway; the other assets would have been redistributed to whoever bought the residual equity of the banks. Nonetheless, provided the bailout is not seen as a licence to repeat the excesses on the grounds of being too big to be allowed to fail, saving the banks was the better solution.

The implication of this analysis for future policy is that banks must better assess risk and must be seen to be doing so. This suggests the need for clear rules about the disclosure of the riskiness of balance sheets. Transparency in this is essential. It entails not allowing banks (or government, for that matter) to put their liabilities off-balance sheet where they are unobserved and so difficult to monitor.

The current debate seems to be taking a different direction, with banks probably being required to hold higher capital-to-loan ratios. While this would reduce the probability of bank default, it would not eliminate the possibility of future crises, nor would it be a cheap solution. Financial crises seem to be endemic to capitalism. To judge from the past, sooner or later a large shock will occur which would precipitate another financial crisis, no matter the size of reserve assets. What is required is an appropriate response mechanism. If crises cannot be entirely eliminated, the cost of holding more capital in reserve must be set against the cost of future crises.

4   Unconventional macroeconomic modelling

There is a widespread perception that the financial crisis was due to flawed macroeconomic and finance theory. Much of this is media criticism, but written by academics. My own view – see Wickens (2010) – is that this is mistaken and that the fault lies more in the failure of banks, and other financial market participants, to use existing theory correctly, especially the theory of risk. Nonetheless, it must be admitted that most modern macroeconomic models do not include a banking sector and much of finance theory takes little or no account of the macroeconomic environment. One consequence is that the financial crisis has stimulated a huge amount of research on how best to model the banking sector in DSGE models. Compared with the previous generation of DSGE models this might be thought of as unconventional macroeconomic modelling. Unfortunately, much of this research is misplaced as it involves introducing arbitrary exogenous restrictions and ignores the key issue.

For example, as already noted, Harrison (Chapter 5) assumes that households have an exogenous target ratio of long- to short-term debt. In a widely cited paper, Kiyotaki and Moore (2008) assume that firms invest with an exogenous probability, that only a fraction of new investments can be funded initially, and only a fraction of a firm's financial capital can be used initially to offset this funding restriction. All of this creates a liquidity constraint. Negative shocks to these frictions, such as those that started the financial crisis, make the constraint more binding and the likelihood of a recession more probable. Not surprisingly, once these constraints are alleviated by, for example, a liquidity infusion by the central bank, the crisis and the recession can be checked.

My criticism of such explanations is that they do not address the real cause of the crisis, namely, default risk. This was largely ignored by the banks when providing new mortgages, by the credit rating companies when evaluating mortgage-backed securities, and by the financial sector when buying these securities. Default risk also lies behind the liquidity crisis as it deterred interbank lending. What is required is the inclusion of a banking sector in these models in which default risk drives a wedge between lending and borrowing rates. The probability of default should be modelled as endogenous rather than exogenous as it depends on the business cycle, being higher in periods of recession than boom.

References

Kiyotaki, N. and Moore, J. (2008) Liquidity, business cycles, and monetary policy, unpublished paper, Princeton, Edinburgh and LSE.

Wickens, M. R. (2010) What's wrong with modern macroeconomics: why its critics have missed the point, CESifo Economic Studies, 56(4), 536–53.

11 Non-conventional monetary policies: QE and the DSGE literature

Evren Caglar, Jagjit S. Chadha, Jack Meaning, James Warren and Alex Waters

1   Introduction

An almost intractable hand was dealt to central bankers in the aftermath of the financial storm of 2007–8, which culminated with the collapse of Lehman Brothers. The scale of the negative demand shock meant that central bankers found themselves bumping up against the zero lower bound for short-term policy rates, as nominal income growth went negative. A parallel debate ensued about the appropriate level of capital and liquidity for financial intermediaries, which has led to the Basel III agreement. Finally, central banks had to deal with the frozen interbank markets and burgeoning levels of bad debt and poorly performing assets. Quantitative easing is a new instrument of monetary policy, which in some degree can be thought of as finessing this triplet, and so in this note we are interested in the extent to which it can substitute for or, indeed, complement the usual instrument, which is the short-term policy rate. This problem is considered here by calibrating and simulating three recently developed DSGE models. These model constructs are used to consider how QE, or more generally balance sheet policies, might achieve their objectives.

Each of the recently developed DSGE models differs from the 'plain vanilla' New Keynesian case by having more than one interest rate. So as well as a New Keynesian core model with forward-looking households and firms, optimising profits and consumption streams – subject to sticky prices and central bank operations conducted with an active interest rate rule – in each model one or more interest rates impact on aggregate demand and have some traction on stabilising the economy. The creation of models with more than one interest rate means that the short-term

This chapter is part of a project to develop aggregate macroeconomic models with financial frictions and banking systems. We thank Francis Breedon, David Cobham, Luisa Corrado, Spencer Dale, John Driffill, Douglas Gale, Richard Harrison, Sharon Kozicki, Marcus Miller, Keisuke Otsu, Huw Pill, Jan Wenzelburger and Mike Wickens for helpful comments and conversations. All remaining errors are our own.

interest rate performs as an approximate control device at all times and an especially problematic one when the zero lower bound (ZLB) acts to constrain the interest rate path.

In the first model, developed by Harrison (Chapter 5, this volume), the consumption Euler equation is tilted by a linear combination of short-(policy) and long-term interest rates.[1] The long-term interest rate deviates from the long-term expectation of the policy rate by a preference term that increases in the relative supply of long to short bonds. The policy maker can offset this premium by buying long-term bonds and reducing the relative supply. And so when policy rates can fall no more, the purchase of long-term bonds will reduce the average economy-wide interest rate and help stabilise output.

The second model, a variant of that developed by Gertler and Karadi (2009), endogenises the commercial bank (financial intermediary) decision on the appropriate level of leverage to match a given loans production objective. The commercial bank choice on leverage impacts directly on the external risk premium paid by firms for lending. A negative shock to aggregate demand can lead to a large increase in the external finance premium and a contraction of leverage, and so a considerable amplification of the initial shock unless the government steps in to provide a bank capital subsidy to allow the premium shock to be attenuated.

In the third model, a variant of Goodfriend and McCallum (2007) developed by Chadha and Corrado (2010), consumers are deposit constrained and banks choose a mix of lending and reserves holding to meet a given level of deposit demand. Banks produce loans using a combination of the value of collateral and monitoring workers and also have preference for liquid reserves. Reserves act as a cushion against hiring and firing of monitoring workers and thus can attenuate movements in the external finance premium, which is essentially the marginal cost of loans supply.

For each model we run a similar exercise and assess two key aspects of monetary policy. In each case, we generate a large negative shock to aggregate demand in the model. This acts to propel the economy into a deep recession. We then explore the stabilising properties of a QE-like policy by examining whether output can still return to its steady state, even in the absence of a (policy) interest rate response. Then we allow policy rates to fall and examine whether the new instrument complements the policy rate over a business cycle. For each model, we assess the extent to which the new instrument of monetary policy is able to generate stability

---

[1] Our version of Harrison (Chapter 5) is not exactly the same as his but captures the key linear equations.

in isolation and a preferable stabilising path when used in conjunction with the policy instrument.

Section 2 outlines the UK experience with QE over 2009–10. We present in simple terms the impact of QE on asset prices and on the broad money numbers. These findings help us to calibrate the models in the following section, in which we outline the impact of new monetary instruments in each model. In Section 3, we outline the impulse response analysis conducted on each model – naturally, the results are highly sensitive to the choice of parameters, but we have tried to present a reasonable result in each case. Section 4 concludes and offers some remarks on future work.

2   QE and the UK

The announcement in March 2009 to develop a bond purchase facility and the eventual purchase of £200 billion of mostly conventional medium-term dated debt has been a far from uncontroversial policy. There have been arguments from both sides of the debate, as some commentators have argued for more comprehensive purchases of more distressed assets and some have been concerned about the inflation consequences of such a large expansion of the central bank balance sheet. Later in this section, we will simply state the monetary balance sheet pre and post the (first) round of QE. But before that we will assess the simple announcement effects on financial prices of QE. This simple analysis allows us to pick appropriate calibrations of the models. Let us first outline the policy carried out. For more details on its intentions read Chapter 1 in this volume.

2.1   Quantitative easing

In the five months immediately following the collapse of Lehman Brothers the Bank of England's Monetary Policy Committee cut Bank Rate aggressively from 5 per cent to just 0.5 per cent by March 2009. Even coupled with a large depreciation of sterling and a fiscal stimulus, conventional interest rate policy seemed to have hit the ZLB and faced the possibility of a liquidity trap as four-quarter growth in nominal GDP fell to −2.4 per cent in the first quarter of 2009. Even before this intensification of the crisis in late 2008, the Bank of England had enacted a number of special measures designed to improve market conditions and liquidity in response to the mortgage, banking and credit crises. The Special Liquidity Scheme was introduced in April 2008, which let banks and building societies exchange high-quality MBS for more liquid UK

Table 11.1 *MPC announcements regarding the asset purchase programme*

Date of MPC meeting	Amount of new, unsterilised asset purchases announced (£bn)	Cumulative total of unsterilised asset purchases (£bn)	Unsterilised asset purchases as a percentage of net debt
5 March 2009	75	75	10.1
7 May 2009	50	125	16.1
6 August 2009	50	175	21.8
5 November 2009	25	200	23.7
4 February 2010	0	200	23.1

Source: Bank of England and ONS

Table 11.2 *Types of asset bought with the creation of new reserves (on a settled basis)*

Type of asset purchased	Quantity (£m)
Gilts	198,275
Commercial paper	80
Corporate bonds	1,384

Source: Bank of England

Treasury bills. This was followed in October 2008 by more permanent liquidity insurance in the form of the Discount Window Facility.

Then, on 5 March 2009, coinciding with the cut of the policy rate to 0.5 per cent, the Bank announced that it would begin a large-scale asset purchase programme to loosen monetary policy even further due to substantial downside risk to the inflation target. These purchases would be funded by issuing new central bank reserves via the Bank of England Asset Purchase Fund Facility and would initially total £75 billion. There have subsequently been announcements of increased purchases after MPC meetings in May, August and November 2009 (Table 11.1) until February 2010 when the programme was held at £200 billion.[2] This figure amounts to 14 per cent of nominal GDP and around 23 per cent of net debt. A full breakdown of the Bank's purchases (Table 11.2) shows the assets bought from the private sector were predominantly government

[2] The Bank of England is keen to communicate that it is prepared to resume purchases should it be considered necessary to do so.

securities (gilts) and there have been relatively small purchases of corporate bonds and commercial paper.[3]

The initial purchase range for gilts was set at 5–25 years maturities, but this was extended to a wider range following the August 2009 MPC meeting.[4] In creating its version of quantitative easing, the Bank of England seems to have mimicked the unsuccessful Japanese idea of the early part of this decade. But it acted quicker in response to reaching the ZLB by beginning asset purchases in the same month as it cut Bank Rate to 0.5 per cent. In so doing it tried to send a strong signal to the economy that the central bank is prepared to take whatever action may be necessary to reach its policy objectives. This is in stark contrast to the Japanese case where a policy rate of 0.5 per cent was set in September 1995 but QE was not introduced until March 2001.

In the Bank of Japan's QE framework up to 2002 the only assets bought were government debt. The Bank of England bought a small amount of corporate assets as well, with the intention of some direct easing of credit conditions. But the most fundamental difference between the two policies is that the Bank of England has purchased assets from the non-banking private sector. The Japanese asset purchase programme bought government debt almost exclusively from banks, which meant the transmission of this increase in the money base to an increase in broad money depended wholly on the banks' decisions on their optimal reserves holdings. What actually happened was that banks held the money as reserves in order to increase their own capital and improve balance sheets.

By buying assets from the non-banking private sector, the Bank of England provides a boost to broad money regardless of whether or not the banks increase lending. This might be important as, following the financial crisis, the banking system is going through a necessary period of deleverage and balance sheet adjustment, so it is likely that any extra reserves would have been used to recapitalise and not necessarily passed on to the wider economy. Of course, the non-banking sector may also decide to use increased money balances to pay off debt and mend balance sheets and banks may still decide to hold reserves holdings or recapitalise. But once broad money holdings have been increased there are a number of channels through which the Bank of England's QE can work, unlike the Japanese concept which relied on the impaired bank-lending channel.[5]

---

[3] Arguably, the purpose of these smaller purchases differed from that of the gilt purchases in that their objective was to ease frozen markets and provide liquidity to firms by bolstering confidence.

[4] Any gilts with a residual maturity greater than three years.

[5] A fuller explanation of the Japanese experience of QE and the problems it faced can be found in Ugai (2006).

The Bank of England's asset purchase programme is somewhat removed from the quantitative easing of the Bank of Japan at the turn of the century. But as the policy involves the temporary swap of central bank money for high-quality government assets, all forms of QE are really just traditional open market operations with a significantly longer maturity and it is the impact of these operations we will try to model.

2.2 The event study

The main problem we face when evaluating the impact of the quantitative easing programme is the difficulty of the counterfactual. How do we try to separate the change in variables caused by asset purchases and changes caused by the myriad of other factors which affect them, particularly in the midst of such a profound financial crisis? How do we know what the economy would have been like in the absence of QE, ceteris paribus? To help isolate just the movements attributable to QE in the UK case, we follow the lead of Bernanke et al. (2004) and Joyce et al. (2010) and try to understand the price movements in a range of variables over the course of policy announcements relating to QE. More specifically, we observe the change over a two-day window for six significant policy announcements made by the MPC. Assuming that much of quantitative easing's impact on prices and yields will not necessarily occur when purchases and auctions physically take place but when the news appears, the key events we focus on therefore are when the monetary policy authority released new information concerning the asset purchase programme (Table 11.3).

Table 11.3 *Announcement dates included in event study*

Event date	Relevent policy announcement
11 February 2009	Publication of the *Inflation Report* and press conference in which it is first suggested the Bank of England is likely to embark on a large-scale asset-purchase programme.
5 March 2009	First announcement of £75 billion of asset purchases by the MPC. Policy rate cut to 0.5%.
7 May 2009	Extension of QE to £125 billion.
6 August 2009	Extension of QE to £175 billion. Extension of initial purchase range to any gilts with a residual maturity of greater than three years.
5 November 2009	Final extension of QE (Phase 1) to £200 billion.
4 February 2010	MPC announces APF will be maintained at £200 billion but will be monitored in case future economic conditions require it to be adjusted.

Source: Bank of England

As with Joyce et al. (2010), a two-day window is chosen and we measure the change in variables from the close of business the day before the announcement to close of business the day after in Table 11.4. Summing across the six policy announcement days gives an estimate for the change that might be attributed to the QE policy. A weakness of this

Table 11.4 *Total impact of QE over event study on key variables*

	Change over six events	Change over five events
Gilt yields		
Level	−104 bp	−29 bp
Slope	−42 bp	−0.7 bp
Curvature	−36 bp	+18 bp
Corporate bond yields		
Investment grade	−69 bp	−39 bp
Non-investment grade	−146 bp	−206 bp
Spreads		
3-month LIBOR	40 bp	−3.8 bp
3-month LIBOR−OIS	27 bp	−5.7 bp
Inflation forwards		
5 years	−40 bp	+23 bp
10 years	−42 bp	−5 bp
20 years	−71 bp	−53 bp
Real forwards		
5 years	−67 bp	−31 bp
10 years	−69 bp	−12 bp
20 years	−59 bp	−3 bp
Nominal forwards		
5 years	−105 bp	−9 bp
10 years	−109 bp	−15 bp
20 years	−136 bp	−54 bp
Exchange rates		
Effective sterling exchange rate	−4%	−3.9%
Eur/£	−3.2%	−2.6%
$/£	−4.7%	−4.1%
Equities		
All Share Index	−3.30% (−93.51 points)	−0.07% (−18.13 points)
Pharmaceuticals	−1.50% (−56.46 points)	−0.13% (−11.83 points)
Mining	−8.95% (−625.11 points)	−6.40% (−521.25 points)
Mobile telecoms	−3.08% (−46.01 points)	0.15% (+11.43 points)
Banks	−7.20% (−58.33 points)	2.04% (+56.78 points)
Oil & gas producers	3.53% (+145.16 points)	3.76% (+154.53 points)
HSBC	1.89%	11.93%
Standard Chartered	−2.50%	−3.27%
RBS	−28.60%	−15.82%
Barclays	−33.97%	−9.06%

methodology is that it fails to capture any lagged or learning effects or may incorporate some misunderstandings about the ultimate magnitude and composition of government purchases. This may lead to some bias in understanding the full impact of QE.

2.2.1 The gilt market We begin with analysis of the sterling gilt market as this is where the vast majority of the APF's direct intervention occurred and where the clearest impact of quantitative easing should be observed. Over the course of the six policy announcements, average gilt yields are estimated to be 104 basis points lower across the initial purchase range. This figure is in line with other studies. The majority of this fall in yields came about in the event window surrounding the 5 March announcement where QE was officially outlined for the first time, suggesting that this is when investors' behaviour, expectations and decisions were most affected by QE. But another reason the March announcement was associated with a larger change is that the introduction of QE was also joint with a cut in Bank Rate of 50 basis points. The latter extensions of the asset purchase programme were widely anticipated so were already built into agents' expectations and decisions to a degree before the announcement, muting their effect.

The yield curve flattened and became less steep in response to asset purchases as the slope fell by 42 basis points and the curvature by 36. This can be viewed as an indicator that the QE announcements helped to reduce term premia across the yield curve and reduce market perceptions of medium- and longer-term risk in the UK economy. Again, the large proportion of this change occurred in response to the introductory March announcement. In the case of the slope variable, there was an initial steepening of the curve following the February *Inflation Report*, attributed by Joyce et al. (2010) to investors erroneously expecting the Bank to buy shorter-term gilts than it eventually did. The March announcement then saw a 41 basis point swing back the other way as investors readjusted their expectations to include the new information from the policy announcement. The movements of slope around the other events were minimal, except in the case of the August announcement, which was accompanied by an extension of the purchase range of gilts the Bank was willing to buy. This caused a 24 basis point fall in the slope of the nominal yield curve.

2.2.2 Corporate bonds We next look at corporate bonds. Investment grade corporate bond yields fell by 69 basis points over the six QE policy announcements, while non-investment grade corporate bond yields fell by 146 basis points. In the case of investment grade bond yields, the change occurred predominantly over the first, second and fourth announcements, hinting, as with the gilt markets, that these were the announcements which contained new information compared with the others which were in general anticipated prior to their official announcement. For non-investment grade bonds, more than three-quarters of the change happened in a single event, but not, as with the other variables so far considered, in the March announcement but following the May announcement. In fact, these results suggest some small widening of the investment grade spread over benchmark Treasuries and a narrowing of the non-investment grade spreads over benchmark Treasuries.

2.2.3   Spreads The LIBOR spread (three-month LIBOR rate less Bank Rate) increased over the course of the QE announcements by 40 basis points and the LIBOR-OIS spread (three-month LIBOR rate less the overnight index swap rate) widened by 27 basis points. We might expect these spreads to narrow if QE helped alleviate liquidity problems in the banking sector. And so this counterintuitive result is explained by closer analysis of the contributions from each interest rate at each announcement date. It is the March policy announcement, that also cut Bank Rate by 50 basis points, that explains the rise in both spreads at 43 and 33 basis points, respectively. If we exclude this anomalous result, our study finds the LIBOR spread narrowing by 4 basis points and the LIBOR–OIS spread by 6 basis points.

Quite simply, as the March announcement not only contained information about QE but was coupled with a cutting of Bank Rate by 50 basis points, and all other things being equal, this would automatically widen the LIBOR spread by 50 basis points. It seems that the LIBOR rate does not respond immediately to changes in Bank Rate and that this delay in its response is what causes us to observe this rise in the spread. We can also assert that the OIS rate reacts quicker to changes in Bank Rate and almost exactly mirrors it.

2.2.4   Interest rate forwards Interest rate forwards fell at longer horizons over the six-day event study by more than 100 basis points. Inflation forwards at the five-, ten- and twenty-year horizons all fell significantly, with the longer maturities responding to a greater extent, but real forwards fell by somewhat more. This implies that the QE announcements impacted significantly on expected real rates as well as inflation forwards.

2.2.5   Exchange rate Using an index of the effective sterling exchange rate where January 2005 equals 100, we see that sterling depreciates by 326 basis points, suggesting that sterling is approximately 3–4 per cent lower thanks to QE announcements than the counterfactual. This result corresponds to a monetary view of the exchange rate where increases in the money supply devalue sterling against other currencies. Of course, the Bank of England was not the only central bank implementing unconventional measures and these would mitigate changes in bilateral exchange rates over the entire time period of QE, but this effect should be largely stripped out as in an events study. We also look at two bilateral exchange rates: sterling against the euro and sterling against the US dollar. The event study finds that sterling fell 3.2 per cent against the euro and 4.7 per cent against the dollar.

2.2.6 Equity markets The event study of all six events shows that equity prices, represented by the FTSE All Share Index, have fallen in response to QE. The index fell by 74.5 over the policy announcements, which equates to a 3.4 per cent decline. The same is true if we take data on the FTSE All Share Total Returns, which fell by 93.5, a very similar 3.3 per cent in percentage terms. However, if we do not include the final February 2010 policy announcement in the event study, the picture changes dramatically. Both All Share measures rise marginally (0.28 per cent and 0.36 per cent, respectively) showing it is just the extreme negative nature of the changes following the final policy announcement which cause the overall event study results to be so skewed. The equity markets do not show any great response to the events studies.

2.2.7 Six- versus five-day announcements There is a considerable difference in the impact when we add up across all six announcements and when we exclude the pivotal March announcement. Figure 11.1 shows first the impact on the term structure of nominal forwards from all six annoucements and also when we exclude the March announcement, at which policy rates were cut by 50 basis points and the first tranche of QE was confirmed. For comparison we also plot the estimated impact on the term structure from a typical 50 basis point cut.[6] There is a 70–80 basis point impact from the March announcement alone that is clearly not well explained by the cut in rates and implies that the announcement of the initial tranche of QE was substantially responsible for the event study results. But it is not clear whether the larger interest rate response from the March announcement results directly from planned purchases of government debt or simply a signal that the 50 basis point cut would be more persistent than normal, or both.

---

[6] The details of this estimation are available on request.

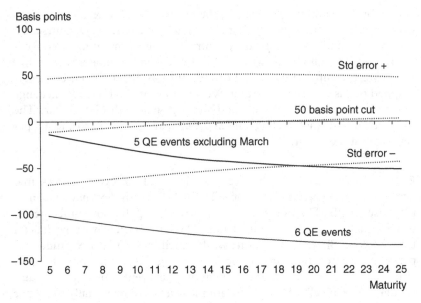

Figure 11.1 Announcement effects

2.3   Bank capital injections

Alongside the Bank of England's asset purchase programme there have been a number of other measures utilised in the attempt to stabilise the UK economy. On 13 October 2008, the UK government announced it would buy £37 billion of shares in banks which had been drastically affected by the financial crisis. The purchases were implemented through the Bank Recapitalisation Fund and comprised a mixture of ordinary and preference shares. The initial announcement was for a capital injection of £20 billion to RBS and £17 billion to the newly merged HBOS/Lloyds Banking Group. This meant that the UK tax payer owned around 58 per cent of RBS and approximately 40 per cent of HBOS/LBG.[7]

In total, data published by the Bank of England show that between 2007 and 2010 the government directly injected around £50 billion of capital into UK banks and building societies,[8] the vast majority of which went to the biggest banks.[9] It should be noted that this capital injection corresponds to 17 per cent of capital held by UK banks pre-crisis.

---

[7] HM Treasury: Financial Services.   [8] Financial Stability Report, June 2010.
[9] 'Big' banks, as defined by the Bank of England, include Barclays, HSBC, Lloyds Banking Group and RBS.

From the public point of view this subsidy may have been necessary to prevent the failure of these institutions. However, it highlights the now apparent problem of an implicit subsidy which has become expected by many of the UK's largest banks, commonly known as 'Too Big To Fail'. This raises the question of how policy makers can best deal with this problem which causes financial institutions which are so large their collapse would cause wider financial instability to experience less downside risk than is socially optimal. This is one of the causes behind the excessive risk taking and high leverage ratios which characterised the pre-crisis banking sector. A fuller discussion of the problems of systematically important financial institutions and a series of policy recommendations can be found in the G20 Financial Stability Board report (2010) released in October 2010.

2.4 Monetary analysis

We turn our attention to the impact of QE on the monetary sector and on the balance sheet of the UK banking sector as this will not only enable us to better understand the monetary transmission mechanism and the destination of the £200 billion but also help to calibrate and evaluate our models. Broad money (deposit) growth over the QE period was weak. Figure 11.2 shows the Bank of England's favoured measure of broad money, M4x (standard M4 less intermediate OFCs) and Figure 11.3 shows the year-on-year growth rate. Immediately following the introduction of QE, the growth rate of M4x continued to fall, reaching just under 1 per cent at the end of 2009. Over 2010 broad money growth remained considerably lower than the Bank's 6–8 per cent target range, but there were some positive signs as it began to rise, reaching 1.6 per cent in August 2010.

This low rate of growth results from a number of factors. First, without QE there might easily have been even weaker growth, if not a significant contraction of broad money. Second, the level of new debt and equity issuance by the UK banking sector, as it aims to recapitalise, may have reduced broad money growth and arguably can be viewed as a destruction of money in much the same way that quantitative easing temporarily creates it. Investors buying newly created debt and equity from banks pay using existing deposits and thus remove them from the system. A measure of the downward pressure on the money supply caused by this recapitalisation of UK banks is captured by net non-deposit liabilities – see Figure 11.4.[10]

---

[10] Non-deposit liabilities (net) consist of capital and other non-deposit liabilities of UK banks less their investments in UK banks and other non-financial assets. In the Bank of England series used (series code LPMVRHV), a negative value indicates an increase in non-deposit liabilities and downward pressure on broad money.

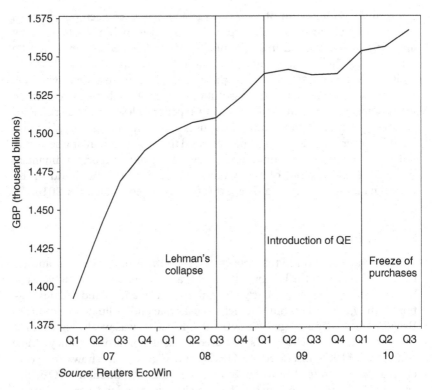

Source: Reuters EcoWin

Figure 11.2 M4x

Over the QE period the cumulative total was approximately £180 billion, suggesting a substantial undermining of the impact the monetary boost might have had on the money supply. Note that the direct effect on the money stock is not the only channel through which QE is designed to work and that the UK banking sector would have had to recapitalise anyway, which without additional quantitative intervention may have led us to a much bleaker counterfactual for money growth.

A sectoral breakdown of M4 money holdings (Figure 11.5) reveals that PNFCs' holdings of M4 have now returned to their pre-crisis levels and show positive year-on-year growth. M4 money holdings of OFCs have jumped, mainly due to a change in reporting practices as of January 2010.[11] So the year-on-year growth rate is perhaps a better example of

---

[11] This adjustment involved off-balance sheet securitised assets being brought onto the balance sheet. The one-off effect was estimated at around £176 billion. For more details see www.bankofengland.co.uk/statistics/ms/articles/art1feb10.pdf.

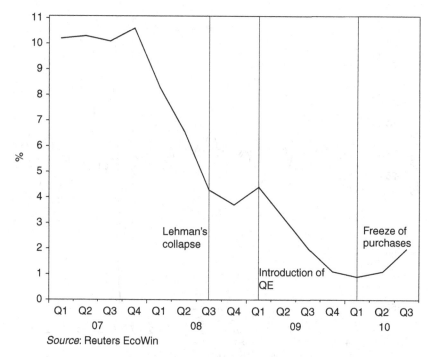

Source: Reuters EcoWin

Figure 11.3 Year-on-year growth of M4x

how OFCs' broad money holdings are evolving (Figure 11.6) and while this remains positive, it has slowed considerably. The growth of households' money holdings slowed through 2008 and 2009 but appeared to be stable around 3 per cent in 2010 (at the time of writing).

On the other side of the balance sheet, claims held by commercial banks against the Bank of England (reserves) rose by £111.5 billion over the course of the asset purchase programme. This is a direct consequence of the creation of new reserves to finance the unsterilised purchases which make up QE (Figure 11.7). Total M4 lending excluding securitisations and loan transfers (M4Lx) fell over the QE period by £197.5 billion, reflecting commercial banks' unwillingness to expose themselves to further risk and lend in the uncertain economic climate post-crisis. A sectoral analysis of year-on-year growth rates of M4Lx (Figure 11.8) shows that there are some signs of improvement, with a return to positive year-on-year growth in lending to households. It reached around 3 per cent at the end of 2009 and continued into 2010, having been contracting in the twelve months following the collapse of Lehman Brothers. Importantly,

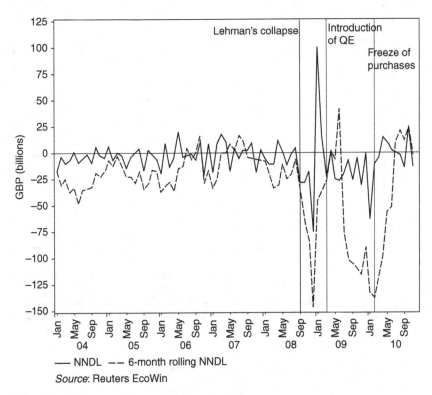

Source: Reuters EcoWin

Figure 11.4 Net non-deposit liabilities

lending to PNFCs also shows signs of recovery. After it hit a year-on-year contraction of 4.2 per cent in May 2010, it managed a fragile but marginally positive growth rate of 0.1 per cent in August.

To summarise, the period concerning the Bank of England's asset purchase programme can be characterised by low but positive growth in deposits counteracted by strong levels of debt and equity issuance by the banking sector. Reserves increased while lending continued to be weak, though with some more recent signs of recovery. While some effects can be seen to be instantaneous, such as that on reserves, our monetary analysis suggests some others may work with a considerable lag and may only just be beginning to be seen. Table 11.5 summarises the composition and size of the consolidated UK banking sector balance sheet immediately before the Lehman bankruptcy, immediately preceding the introduction of QE by the Bank of England, and in March 2010, just after the asset purchases were held at £200 billion, and we can note that the reserves–deposit ratio rose from 2.4 per cent to 9.8 per cent.

Table 11.5 *Balance sheet changes*

	Pre-Lehman bankruptcy	Introduction of QE	Post QE
Deposits (M4x) (£bn)	1500	1539	1554
Non-deposit liabilities (£bn)*	–	–4.06	–243.86
Lending (M4Lx) (£bn)	2614	2810	2594
Reserves (£bn)	36	41	152

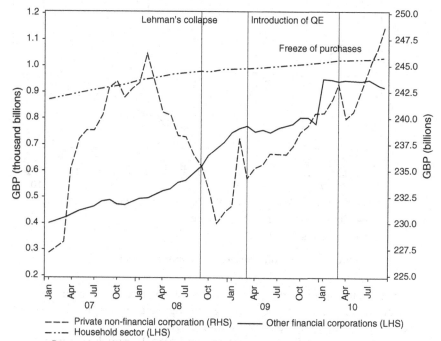

--- Private non-financial corporation (RHS)   —— Other financial corporations (LHS)
--·-- Household sector (LHS)

* Due to a lack of data on the level of non-deposit liabilities we report the cumulative change using the pre-Lehman event date as our point of reference.
Source: Reuters EcoWin

Figure 11.5 Sectoral M4 money holdings

3   The DSGE models

The development of DSGE models with financial frictions represents (at least) two analytical hurdles. First, that the maintained hypothesis of Modigliani–Miller must be put to one side for the macroeconomic models, so that changes in net worth or collateral impact on the optimal split between private-sector debt and equity issuance rather than disappearing

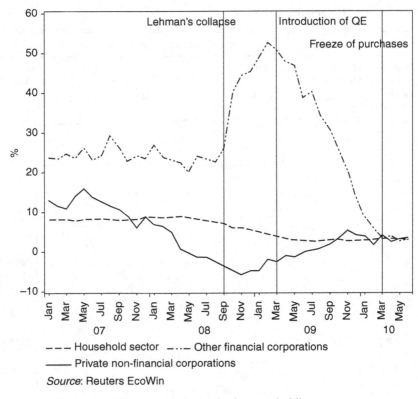

Figure 11.6 Year-on-year growth of money holdings

in aggregate. Second, that the resulting set of interest rates in various credit markets reflects some ongoing heterogeneity, otherwise they would be arbitraged away by our representative agent.

The literature on financial frictions and DSGE models is burgeoning and we do not aim to survey that here.[12] But what we can do is to assess the impact of unconventional policy instruments in three recently developed models. In Harrison (Chapter 5, this volume), the representative agent lives in a standard optimising economy with price stickiness, a New Keynesian Phillips curve and a forward-looking spending equation, albeit one in which there are interest rates of both short- and long-run maturity that tilt expenditures. The long-term rate differs from the expected stream of short-term rates because of a preference for short-term bonds, which

---

[12] See Altug et al. (2003) for a statement of the problem. We leave the technical description of each model to the appendix, as that is not the contribution of this chapter.

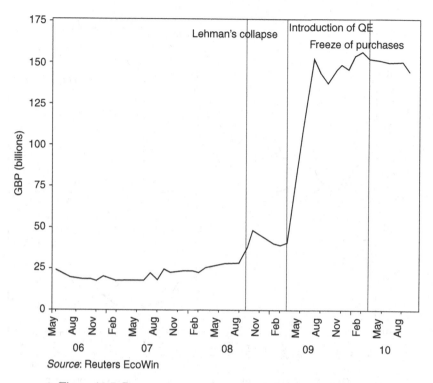

Figure 11.7 Reserves

drives up the liquidity premium on long-term bonds. This implies that even at the ZLB the monetary policy maker has some ability to tilt expenditures by buying long-term bonds and therefore reducing the liquidity premium. And so we consider the impact on long-term bond rates, and hence on consumption, from a monetary authority purchase of 25 per cent of outstanding government bonds.

The Gertler–Karadi (2011) model is a model of unconventional monetary policy with capital and financial intermediation. The flow of funds from savers to borrowers is organised by financial intermediaries. The liability side comprises deposits from households and bank capital, which are matched with loans to firms to finance their investment. The net return from lending minus monitoring costs must always be greater than the cost of funding deposits at the nominal interest rate. There is therefore an equilibrium level of leverage which reduces in monitoring costs and increases in the interest rate spread between lending and deposit rates. Policy rates will act to reduce leverage by reducing the spread and non-conventional policies can directly impact on bank capital by offering state-contingent subsidies or

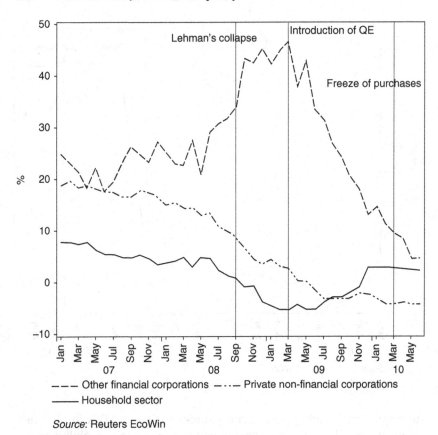

Source: Reuters EcoWin

Figure 11.8 Sectoral year-on-year growth of M4Lx

levies to affect the quantity of loans offered by banks, which are always the product of leverage and bank capital employed.

The Chadha–Corrado model (2010) is an extension of the Goodfriend–McCallum model (2007), in which credit-constrained consumers require loans from a commercial bank in order to effect their planned consumption paths. The bank employs a loans production technology with arguments in the value of collateral and the employment of workers who monitor loans and also has to respect a liquidity constraint in deciding on the optimal levels of the reserve–deposit ratio. The commercial bank's liabilities can thus be funded by a mix of interest rate-paying reserves and external finance premium-paying loans. Chadha and Corrado (2010) find that in this framework, banks can use reserves as a buffer against costly changes in monitoring costs and so can choose to alleviate some of the counter-cyclical variation in the external finance premium. So we examine the implications from increasing the reserve ratio by 7 per cent in this model.

3.1 Results

3.1.1 Simulation scenarios For each model, we use the unconventional policy tool in a manner consistent with the magnitude of unconventional policy measures undertaken in the UK and assess the impact on key economic state variables: output, inflation, finance premia, lending, asset prices and policy rates. Each simulation is undertaken with three scenarios: (i) with the active interest rate rule switched on; (ii) then in conjunction with unconventional policy; and finally (iii) with unconventional policy alone. We can therefore gauge the partial in each general equilibrium policy to the new instrument alone.

PORTFOLIO BALANCE MODEL We simulate the model with a 10 per cent downward shock to real output, which replicates the experience of the UK. We then show three impulse responses (Figure 11.9) to key state

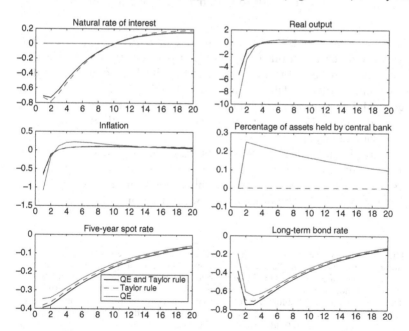

Figure 11.9 Impulse responses of the Harrison model

variables in the portfolio balance model when the monetary policy maker (i) uses a Taylor rule only, (ii) uses a Taylor rule in conjunction with asset purchases and (iii) uses asset purchases only to stabilise the economy.[13] In what might be considered normal times, when the ZLB does not constrain, policy rates fall by around 75bp and output is stabilised in a year or so. When we also allow for asset purchases, these appear to take some of the workload off the nominal interest rate in correcting for the aggregate demand (AD) shock as the policy rate then falls by a little less and allows us to return to equilibrium output at roughly the same time. This suggests a possible but limited role for asset purchases as interest rates become constrained in their movements or if central bankers want to limit the volatility of the policy rate over the business cycle. Asset purchases combined with standard interest rate policy cause the long rate and five-year forward to fall by a little more than would have been the case without QE-style purchases. But clearly asset purchases can bring about a similar fall in long-term interest rates as that implied by a fall in the short rate alone. A long-term interest rate fall of 100bp would seemingly require a much larger purchase of assets than the 25 per cent suggested here, perhaps more in the region of 50–75 per cent. But in any case such purchases will not offset the fall in output as much as a reduction in policy rates because output responds to both the short- and long-term rate.

BANK CAPITAL MODEL   With a model of bank capital, the initial downward shock to output of around 2–3 per cent is stabilised with a cut in policy rates of 50bp and a return to base in about four years and in this scenario inflation falls to around 0.4–0.5 per cent below target (Figure 11.10). If there is no ability to cut interest rates and an injection of bank capital of 17 per cent is employed as the stabilisation device,[14] then output falls by around 2–3 times further and there is a similarly larger downward shock to inflation. While that can lead to some stabilisation in output, if interest rates do not rise once the economy emerges from recession, in around four quarters on this calibration, it seems that there is a significant possibility of an overshoot in both inflation and output.

---

[13] There is no investment or government spending in the baseline version of this model. An interesting extension would be to consider the impact of liquidity premia on the structure of the maturity of private- and public-sector debt, in which we might expect relative over-issuance of short-term compared with long-term debt to reflect the different costs.

[14] Representing the £50 billion direct injection calculated by the Bank of England's Financial Stability Report (June 2010) as a percentage of the £300 billion of sterling capital and other internal funds held by UK banks as of 1 January 2007 (source: Bank of England).

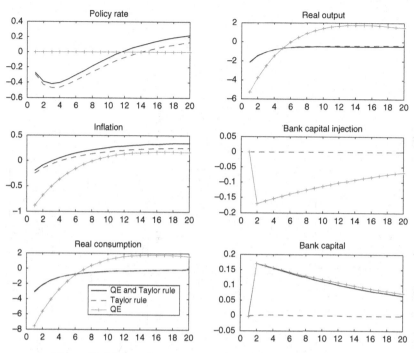

Figure 11.10 Impulse responses of the Gertler–Karadi model

The bank capital model thus suggests that a larger injection of capital than 17 per cent may be required to offset a large negative demand shock and also highlights the need to raise rates once the momentum for recovery is established.

BANK RESERVES MODEL   The fall in output following a negative demand shock is, in this case, shown to be 15 per cent (Figure 11.11). Inflation falls by around 6 per cent, with real wages and employment both falling by something more than 20 per cent, and in this case the increase in monitoring effort by commercial banks puts upward pressure on the external finance premium. The increased issuance of bonds by the government, which tries to stabilise output, also pushes up liquidity premia on bonds. In the two cases where the reserve–deposit ratio is not fixed but chosen endogenously by commercial banks, the contractionary shock leads to an increase in demand for reserves, which are supplied perfectly elastically by the central bank. This increase in reserves acts to limit the increase in the costs of loans supply because banks hold reserves ex ante

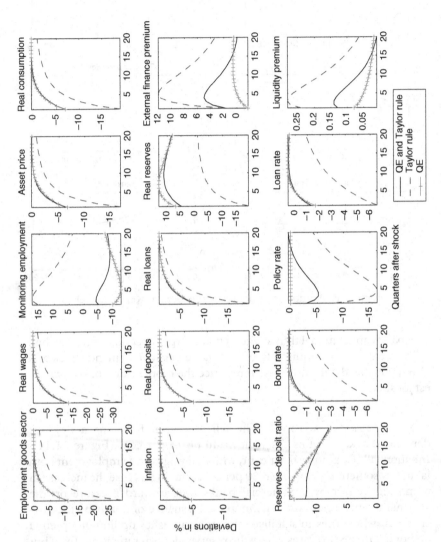

Figure 11.11 Impulse responses of the Chadha–Corrado model

against potential problems with loans. Liquid reserves offset some of the upward shock to interest rate spreads and can mitigate around 30–40 per cent of the shock in this model. In fact, if the non-standard monetary policy increased the reserves–deposit ratio by around 12 per cent, it seems possible to stabilise the economy even if interest rates do not fall at all.

It would appear that some combination of government purchases of bonds, capital and reserves injection can stabilise these DSGE economies following a large contractionary shock. But a number of issues remain. First, the non-conventional policies require careful calibration against an uncertain set of deep parameters and more work is required to understand how to ensure robust results across a wide range of possible parameterisations. Second, the rate of exchange between unconstrained interest rate paths and unconventional policies seems poor, so that not only are we employing policies with an uncertain impact, we seem to have to use them in relatively large amounts to substitute for a standard monetary policy. Third, there seems to be a significant possibility of overshooting when using these policies and there is a difficult choice on how to complement the withdrawal of these policies with appropriately set interest rates. Finally, other than using standard forward-looking models, we have not really been able to understand the importance of signalling and credibility in these models and that may be the most important transmission mechanism for policies when the ZLB matters.

4   Conclusion

The models briefly outlined in this chapter are fully described by their original authors and represent only the tip of a large-scale research agenda recently re-embarked upon by macroeconomists to understand the importance and implications of financial frictions for monetary analysis. It is far too early to provide a clear summary of the results of this research agenda, but a few points are emerging. It does seem possible to modify the canonical DSGE model to incorporate additional conditions for market clearing in credit markets. This modification will ensure that the constellation of interest rates is not strictly proportional to the policy rate. At a stroke this implies that at the very least traditional interest rate policy will have to be supplemented with an analysis of the contributions from other factors on the monetary policy transmission mechanism. The detachment of financial prices, to some degree, from the household and production economy because of the existence of financial intermediaries with incomplete information is likely to endure.

This substantive progress may initially be masked by a need to understand the availability of tools when policy rates approach the ZLB. The models outlined here develop financial market liquidity premium, endogenous capital and reserve allocations for financial market intermediaries. Tentatively, they suggest that governments can substitute for the ZLB and help the theoretical policy maker avoid the liquidity trap. It seems that the scale of interventions required is large by historic standards, not only because the size of the shock that needs to be stabilised is large but also because these interventions operate in model-based financial markets where there is relatively close substitutability across most financial assets and thus require large quantities of net government transactions to lead to a substantive impact on prices.

In reality, though, the main impact of financial intermediation seems to be heavily procyclical – as financial activity seems to heighten and elongate business cycle expansions and exacerbate downturns. The models developed so far allow us to understand somewhat better the mechanisms that drive this impact. But we have yet to turn these essentially qualitative stories outlined here into a fully fledged view on the exact calibration of the macro-prudential tools that may well be required over the business cycle to help staunch the impact of financial intermediation. It seems reasonably clear to us that this research agenda will continue to occupy us.

Appendix

This appendix lays out the systems of log-linearised equations which make up the three models and Tables 11.A1–11.A3b give the parameter values used to simulate each model.

Table 11.A1 *Descriptions and parameter values*

Parameter	Description	Value
σ	Elasticity of intertemporal substitution	6
β	Discount factor	0.9
κ	Slope of the Phillips curve	0.1
ρ	AutoCorr. of real interest rate	0.9
σ_m	Money demand elasticity	6
α_π	Policy response to inflation	1.5
α_x	Policy response to output	0.5
ρ_R	Interest rate smoothing	0.8
ρ_q	Persistence of asset purchases	0.95
$\frac{m}{b}$	Money to bonds in ss	0.001
δ	Ratio of long to short bonds in ss	3
ν	Elasticity of long bonds to portfolio mix	0.1
θ	Feedback parameter in tax rule	0.025

Table 11.A2 *Parameter descriptions and values*

Parameter	Description	Value
$\frac{C}{Y}$	Fraction of output used for consumption	0.7
$\frac{I}{Y}$	Fraction of output used for investment	0.3
α	Cobb–Douglas PF coefficient	0.35
σ	Intertemporal substitution coefficient of consumption	0.97
$1 + \chi$	Elasticity of output to labour hours	4
ϕ	Price elasticity of investment demand	0.5
ε	Price-return pass through	0.95
δ	Depreciation rate of capital	0.025
κ	Slope of the NK Phillips curve	0.1
β	Discount factor	0.9
R_{ss}^K	Steady-state return on capital	0.02
R_{ss}	Steady-state policy/deposit rate	0.01
L_{ss}	Steady-state level of loans	8
D_{ss}	Steady-state level of deposits	7.9
B_{ss}	Steady-state level of bank capital	5.7
θ_1	$\dfrac{L_{ss}\, R_{ss}^K}{B_{ss}\, R_{ss}}$	5.33
θ_2	$\dfrac{D_{ss}}{B_{ss}}$	1.25
γ	Profit elasticity of bank capital	0.3
ρ	Interest rate coefficient of the Taylor rule	0.8
α_π	Inflation coefficient of the Taylor rule	1.5
α_Y	Output coefficient of the Taylor rule	0.5
γ_L	Labour elasticity of marginal cost	1.33
γ_C	Consumption elasticity of marginal cost	$\frac{1}{\sigma}$
ρ_{NR}	Persistence of natural rate shock	0.9
ρ_τ	Persistence of capital injection shock	0.95

Table 11.A3a *Parameter descriptions and values*

Parameter	Description	Value
β	Discount factor	0.9
κ	Coefficient in Phillips curve	0.1
α	Collateral share of loan production	0.65
ϕ	Consumption weight in utility	0.4
η	Capital share of firm production	0.36
δ	Depreciation rate of capital	0.025
γ	Trend growth rate	0.005
rr	Reserve ratio	0.1
ρ	Interest rate smoothing	0.8
ϕ_π	Coefficient on inflation in policy	1.5
ϕ_y	Coefficient on output in policy	0.5
F	Production coefficient of loan	9.14
k	Inferiority coefficient of capital as collateral	0.2
θ	Elasticity of substitution of differentiated goods	11

Table 11.A3b *Steady-state parameter descriptions and values*

Steady state	Description	Value
m	Banking employment	0.0063
n	Labour input	0.3195
R^T	Risk-free rate	0.015
R^{IB}	Interbank rate	0.0021
R^L	Loan rate	0.0066
R^B	Bond rate	0.0052
b/c	Bond-to-consumption ratio	0.56
c	Consumption	0.8409
T/c	Transfers over consumption	0.126
w	Real wage	1.9494
λ	Shadow value of consumption	0.457
v	Velocity	0.31
Ω	Marginal value of collateral	0.237
K	Capital	9.19
r/c	Reserves to consumption	0.58

A: Portfolio balance model

This is our version of Harrison (Chapter 5, this volume). x, π and m are respectively output, inflation and money. The government issues short- and long-term bonds. Long-term bonds (b^L) pay a return (R^L) while short-term bonds pay a return equal to the policy rate (R). There are two further interest rates in this model: the ex post return (R^A) and the real or natural rate of interest (r^*). V is the value of a consol (infinitely lived with no redemption date) and q is the level of assets purchased by the central bank to facilitate quantitative easing.

The Output Gap

$$\hat{x}_t = E_t\hat{x}_{t+1} - \sigma\left[\hat{R}_t^A - E_t\hat{\pi}_{t+1} - \hat{r}_t^*\right] \tag{A1}$$

Money Demand

$$\hat{m}_t = \frac{\sigma_m}{\sigma}\hat{x}_t - \frac{\beta\sigma_m}{1-\beta}\hat{R}_t^A \tag{A2}$$

Ex Post Return

$$\hat{R}_t^A = \frac{1}{1+\delta}\hat{R}_t + \frac{\delta}{1+\delta}E_t\hat{R}_{L,t+1} \tag{A3}$$

Short-Term Bond Return

$$\hat{R}_t = E_t \hat{R}_{L,t+1} + v\left(\hat{b}_t - \hat{b}_{L,t}\right) \tag{A4}$$

Inflation

$$\hat{\pi}_t = \beta E_t \hat{\pi}_{t+1} + \kappa \hat{x}_t \tag{A5}$$

Short-Term Nominal Rate (Taylor Rule)

$$\hat{R}_t = \rho_R \hat{R}_{t-1} + (1 - \rho_R)(\alpha_\pi \hat{\pi}_t + \alpha_x \hat{x}_t) + \varepsilon_t^R \tag{A6}$$

CB Balance Sheet

$$q_t = \rho_q q_{t-1} + \varepsilon_t^q \tag{A7}$$

Government Budget Constraint

$$\hat{b}_t + \frac{m}{b}(\hat{m}_t - \hat{m}_{t-1}) = \delta q_t - \left[\frac{m}{b} + \frac{1+\delta}{\beta}\right]\hat{\pi}_t + \left(\frac{1}{\beta} - \theta\right)\hat{b}_{t-1}$$
$$- \frac{\delta}{\beta} q_{t-1} \tag{A8}$$

Issuance of Long-Term bonds

$$\hat{b}_{L,t} = -q_t + \hat{V}_t \tag{A9}$$

Return on Long-Term Bonds

$$E_t \hat{R}_{L,t+1} = \beta E_t \hat{V}_{t+1} - \hat{V}_t \tag{A10}$$

Real Rate of Interest

$$\hat{r}_t^* = \rho \hat{r}_{t-1}^* + \varepsilon_t \tag{A11}$$

The following two equations are for the two additional impulse responses. The five-year spot is the expected sequence of one-period consol returns $E_t \hat{R}_{t-i}^L$.

Five-Year Spot Rate

$$5ys = \frac{1}{20} \sum_{i=1}^{n} E_t \hat{R}_{t+1}^L \tag{A12}$$

$$R_{L,t} = V_t - V_{t-1} \tag{A13}$$

B: Gertler–Karadi (2011) model

In this model Y, C and I are respectively real output, consumption and investment. Output is a function of total factor productivity (Z), labour hours worked (h) and physical capital (K), which has a price (q). The marginal cost is denoted by X. Commercial banks hold deposits (D) and capital (B) and extend loans (L) to the wider economy. This faces a cost (λ). Policy makers can directly affect banks' capital with a subsidy/levy (τ). The model contains three interest rates: R is the short-term nominal or policy rate, R^n is the natural rate of interest and R^k is the return on physical capital.

The linearised model is:

The Resource Constraint

$$Y_t = \frac{C}{Y}C_t + \frac{I}{Y}I_t \tag{B1}$$

Production Function

$$Y_t = Z_t + \alpha K_{t-1} + (1-\alpha)h_t \tag{B2}$$

Labour Market Equilibrium

$$Y_t = (1+\chi)h_t - X_t + \sigma C_t \tag{B3}$$

Price of Physical Capital

$$q_t = \phi(I_t - K_{t-1}) \tag{B4}$$

Return on Physical Capital

$$R_t^k = (1-\varepsilon)(Y_t - K_t + X_t) + \varepsilon q_t - q_{t-1} \tag{B5}$$

Law of Motion for Physical Capital

$$K_t = \delta I_t + (1-\delta)K_{t-1} \tag{B6}$$

Consumption Euler Equation

$$\sigma C_t = EC_{t+1} + E\pi_{t+1} - R_t + R_t^n \tag{B7}$$

New Keynesian Phillips Curve

$$\pi_t = \beta E\pi_{t+1} + \kappa X_t \tag{B8}$$

No Shirking Condition for Bankers

$$L_t - B_t = \theta_1 R_{t+1}^k - \theta_2 R_t - \lambda_t \tag{B9}$$

Bank Capital Equation

$$B_t = \gamma \left[\theta_2 (R_{ss}^k - R_{ss}) D_{t-1} + R_{ss}^k B_{t-1} + \theta_1 R_{ss} R_t^k - R_{ss} \theta_2 R_{t-1} \right] - \tau \tag{B10}$$

Natural Rate of Interest

$$R_t^n = \rho_{NR} R_{t-1}^n + \varepsilon_{ADt} \tag{B11}$$

Short-Term Nominal Interest Rate (Taylor Rule)

$$R_t = \rho R_{t-1} + (1 - \rho)(\alpha_\pi \pi_t + \alpha_Y Y_t) \tag{B12}$$

Loans

$$L_t = K_t + q_t \tag{B13}$$

Bank Capital Subsidy/Levy

$$\tau_t = \rho_\tau \tau_{t-1} + \varepsilon_{taut} \tag{B14}$$

Balance Sheet Constraint

$$L_t = \frac{Bss}{Lss} B_t + \frac{Dss}{Lss} D_t \tag{B15}$$

Expected Liquidity Premium

$$ER_{t+1}^k - R_t = D_t + \lambda_t \tag{B16}$$

Marginal Cost Equation

$$X_t = \gamma_L h_t + \left(\gamma_C - \frac{C}{Y} \right) C_t - \frac{I}{Y} I_t \tag{B17}$$

as well as identities for the lags.

The coefficient parameters are all chosen using standard values in New Keynesian literature. The steady-state values have required more attention. From Bean et al. (2010), which also uses a version of Gertler–Karadi, we are told that the steady state leverage (L/B) must equal ten and that the steady-state spread between the return on capital and the policy/deposit rate must be 1 per cent. We can use the Bean criteria to calibrate for the

UK economy pre-crisis. For instance, the log value of bank capital before the 2007 crisis was approximately 5.7, so with leverage (L/B) being equal to ten, our steady-state log level of loans was 8. The log level of deposits pre-crisis was approximately 7.9, which gives us our steady-state value. Assuming a quarterly policy rate of 1 per cent is logical, thus in order to set our steady-state spread to 1 per cent our steady-state return on capital is set to 2 per cent. As long as the spread is kept at a constant 1 per cent, however, changes in where we set the levels of these rates seem to have little impact on the model. The shock to bank capital is set to 0.17, as the direct capital injection to UK-owned banks over the crisis period (2007 to present) was approximately 17 per cent of the pre-crisis level of UK-owned banks' capital.

C: Chadha–Corrado reserves (2011) model

In this model households provide labour to the goods production sector (n) or to the banking sector (m) and receive a real wage (w). Agents hold bonds (b) and a price (q) is paid on assets. The aggregate price level in the economy is denoted by P and inflation by π. The model contains five interest rates: R^T is the riskless rate, R^B is the rate paid on bonds, R^L is the rate paid on loans, R^D is the rate paid on deposits and R^{IB} is the short-term nominal/interbank/policy rate.

Supply Labour

$$\frac{n}{(1-n-m)}\hat{n}_t + \frac{m}{(1-n-m)}\hat{m}_t - \hat{\lambda}_t - \hat{w}_t = 0 \qquad (C1)$$

Demand for Labour

$$\hat{m}_t + \hat{w}_t + \frac{(1-\alpha)c}{mw}\left(\hat{c}_t + \frac{\phi}{\lambda}\hat{\lambda}_t\right) = 0 \qquad (C2)$$

Supply of Banking Services[15]

$$\hat{c}_t = \hat{v}_t c + \hat{r}_t c + (1-\alpha)(a2_t + \hat{m}_t) +$$
$$\alpha\left[\frac{bc}{bc+(1+\gamma)kK}(\hat{c}_t + \hat{b}_t) + \frac{kK(1+\gamma)}{bc+(1+\gamma)kK}(a3_t + \hat{q}_t)\right]$$
$$\qquad (C3)$$

---

[15] The relationship is derived by setting $b = \frac{B}{P(1+R^B)c}$ and $b_{t+1} = b_t c_t$.

CIA Constraint

$$\hat{c}_t + \hat{P}_t = \hat{D}_t + \hat{v}_t - \hat{rr}_t \tag{C4}$$

Aggregate Supply

$$\hat{c}_t = (1 - \eta)(1 + \frac{\delta K}{c})(a1_t + \hat{n}_t) - \frac{\delta K}{c}\hat{q}_t \tag{C5}$$

Marginal Cost

$$\hat{mc}_t = \hat{n}_t + \hat{w}_t - \hat{c}_t \tag{C6}$$

Mark-Up

$$\hat{mc}_t = \hat{\xi}_t - \hat{\lambda}_t \tag{C7}$$

Inflation

$$\hat{\pi}_t = \hat{p}_t - \hat{p}_{t-1} \tag{C8}$$

Calvo Pricing

$$\hat{\pi}_t = \kappa \hat{mc}_t + \beta E_t \hat{\pi}_{t+1} + a5_t \tag{C9}$$

Marginal Value of Collateralised Lending

$$\hat{\Omega}_t = \frac{kK}{bc + kK}(\hat{c}_t - \hat{q}_t - a3_t) - \frac{bc}{bc + kK}\hat{b}_t \tag{C10}$$

reported in the main text as:

$$\hat{\Omega}_t = \frac{k_2}{b + k_2}(\hat{c}_t - \hat{q}_t - a3_t) - \frac{b}{b + k_2}\hat{b}_t \tag{C10a}$$

Asset Pricing[16]

$$\hat{q}_t\left[1 - k\Omega(\frac{\phi}{c\lambda} - 1)\right] = \left[\frac{\beta(1 - \delta)}{1 + \gamma} + \frac{\beta \eta mc}{1 + \gamma}(\frac{n}{K})^{1-\eta}\right]\left(E_t\hat{\lambda}_{t+1} - \hat{\lambda}_t\right) + \frac{\beta(1 - \delta)}{1 + \gamma}$$
$$E_t\hat{q}_{t+1} + \frac{k\Omega\phi}{c\lambda}\left(-\hat{c}_t - \hat{\lambda}_t\right) + k\Omega(\frac{\phi}{c\lambda} - 1)\left(\hat{\Omega}_t + a3_t\right) +$$
$$\left(\frac{\beta \eta mc}{1 + \gamma}(\frac{n}{K})^{1-\eta}\right)E_t[\hat{mc}_{t+1} + (1 - \eta)(\hat{n}_{t+1} + a1_{t+1})] \tag{C11}$$

[16] Note that in steady state $\frac{\xi}{\lambda} = mc$ and $\frac{\lambda_{t+1}}{\lambda_t} = \frac{1}{1+\gamma}$.

Government Budget Constraint[17]

$$T\hat{T}_t = \frac{rrc}{v(1+R^{IB})}\left(\hat{re}_t + (1+R^{IB})(\hat{\pi}_t - \hat{re}_{t-1} - \hat{R}^{IB}_{t-1})\right)$$
$$+ b\left(\hat{b}_t + (1+R^B)(\hat{\pi}_t - \hat{b}_{t-1} - \hat{R}^B_t)\right) \tag{C12}$$

Bond Holding

$$\hat{b}_t = a6_t \tag{C13}$$

Riskless Interest Rate

$$\hat{R}^T_t = \hat{\lambda}_t + E_t\hat{\pi}_{t+1} - E_t\hat{\lambda}_{t+1} \tag{C14}$$

Liquidity Service of Bonds[18]

$$\frac{1+R^B}{1+R^T}\left(\hat{R}^B_t - \hat{R}^T_t\right) = \frac{\phi\Omega}{c\lambda}\left(\hat{c}_t + \hat{\lambda}_t\right) - \left(\frac{\phi}{c\lambda} - 1\right)\Omega\hat{\Omega}_t \tag{C15}$$

External Finance Premium

$$E\hat{F}P_t = \hat{v}_t + \hat{w}_t + \hat{m}_t - \hat{c}_t + \hat{rr}_t \tag{C16}$$

Other Interest Rates

$$\hat{R}^{IB}_t = \hat{R}^T_t - E\hat{F}P_t \tag{C17}$$

$$\hat{R}^L_t = \hat{R}^{IB}_t + E\hat{F}P_t \tag{C18}$$

$$\hat{R}^D_t = \hat{R}^{IB}_t - \hat{rr}_t \frac{rr}{(1-rr)} \tag{C19}$$

Policy Feedback Rule

$$\hat{R}^{IB}_t = (1-\rho)\left(\phi_\pi\hat{\pi}_t + \phi_y\hat{mc}_t\right) + \rho\hat{R}^{IB}_{t-1} + a4_t \tag{C20}$$

Velocity

$$\hat{v}_t = a7_t \tag{C21}$$

---

[17] We define the percentage deviation from steady state of flow and stock variables by $\ln x_t - \ln x$, while for interest rates and ratio variables they are $R_t = R + \hat{R}_t$ (rates) and $r_t = r + \hat{r}_t$ (ratio, assuming $r_t = x_t/y_t$), respectively. It can be shown the approximation comes from first-order Taylor expansion: $e^x \approx 1 + x$, while for rate variable: $\hat{R}_t \approx \ln(1+R_t) - \ln(1+R)$ and for ratio: $\hat{r}_t = r_t - r = \ln(x_t/y_t) - \ln(x/y) = \hat{x}_t - \hat{y}_t$.
[18] Log-linearisation of interest rate is defined as difference from steady state: $R_t = R + \hat{R}_t$.

Reserves

$$\hat{r}_t = \frac{1}{rR^T} \left[-\left(\tau + R^{IB} - R^L \right) \hat{R}_t^T + R^{IB} \hat{R}_t^{IB} - R^L \hat{R}_t^L + \tau \hat{\tau}_t \right] \quad (C22)$$

Liquidity

$$\hat{\tau}_t = a8_t \quad (C23)$$

Loans

$$L_t = \frac{1}{1 - rr} D_t - \frac{rr}{1 - rr} r_t \quad (C24)$$

The benchmark model has twenty-two endogenous variables $\{c, n, m, w, q, P, \pi, mc, D, b, \Omega, EFP, R^T, R^B, R^{IB}, R^L, R^D, \lambda, \xi, T, r, re\}$, six lagged variables $\{P_{t-1}, D_{t-1}, c_{t-1}, b_{t-1}, re_{t-1}, R_{t-1}^B\}$ and eight exogenous shocks $\{a1, a2, a3, a4, a5, a6, a7, a8\}$.

References

Altug, S., Chadha, J. S. and Nolan, C. (2003) *Dynamic Macroeconomic Analysis*, Cambridge University Press.

Bean, C., Paustian, M., Penalver, A. and Taylor, T. (2010) Monetary policy after the fall, Federal Reserve Bank of Kansas City, Jackson Hole Conference.

Bernanke, B. S., Gertler, M. and Gilchrist, S. (1999) The financial accelerator in a quantitative business cycles framework, in Taylor, J. and Woodford, M. (eds.) *The Handbook of Macroeconomics*, Vol. 1C, Elsevier Science, Amsterdam: North-Holland.

Bernanke, B. S., Reinhart, V. R. and Sack, B. L. (2004) Monetary policy alternatives at the zero bound: an empirical assessment, Brookings Papers, 2.

Borio, C. and Disyatat, P. (2009) Unconventional monetary policies: an appraisal, BIS Working Paper No. 292.

Chadha, J. S. and Corrado, L. (2011) Macro-prudential policy on liquidity: What does a DSGE model tell us?, *Journal of Economics and Business*, June, unpublished.

Financial Stability Board (2010) Reducing the moral hazard posed by systematically important financial institutions, unpublished.

Gertler, M. and Karadi, P. (2009) A model of unconventional monetary policy, unpublished.

Goodfriend, M. and McCallum, B. T. (2007) Banking and interest rates in monetary policy analysis: a quantitative exploration, *Journal of Monetary Economics*, 54(5), 1480–1507.

Joyce, M., Lasaosa, A., Stevens, I. and Tong, M. (2010) The financial market impact of quantitative easing, Bank of England Working Paper No. 393.

Ugai, H. (2006) Effects of the quantitative easing policy: a survey of empirical analyses, Bank of Japan, Working Paper No. 6/10.

Index

Printed in the United States
By Bookmasters